CULTURAL SEMANTICS

CRITICAL PERSPECTIVES

ON MODERN CULTURE

A series edited by David Gross,

University of Colorado at Boulder

and William M. Johnston, University

of Massachusetts at Amherst

MARTIN JAY

CULTURAL SEMANTICS

✳

Keywords of Our Time

University of Massachusetts Press   Amherst

LC 97-37563
ISBN 1-55849-115-5 (cloth); 116-3 (pbk.)
Designed by Mary Mendell
Set in Quadrat by Keystone Typesetting, Inc.
Printed and bound by Braun-Brumfield, Inc.
Library of Congress Cataloging-in-Publication Data

Jay, Martin, 1944–
Cultural semantics : keywords of our time / Martin Jay.
p.   cm. — (Critical perspectives on modern culture)
Includes bibliographical references and index.
ISBN 1-55849-115-5 (cloth : alk. paper).
ISBN 1-55849-116-3 (pbk. : alk. paper)
1. Semantics.   2. Language and culture.   I. Title.   II. Series.
P325.J34   1998
401'.43—dc21   97-37563CIP
British Library Cataloguing in Publication data
are available.

FOR SHANA AND NED

CONTENTS

ACKNOWLEDGMENTS

In one of its many meanings, "to acknowledge" implies the reluctant disclosure of something that might have been kept secret (acknowledging responsibility, for example, for a long-denied child). If this were the only acceptation of the word, then even the most apparently generous of scholarly acknowledgments would betray a covert aversion to admitting how dependent the author really is on those he thanks. But luckily semantic play is such that "acknowledgment" can also imply a strong and emphatic avowal of a truth worth affirming in public. It is solely in the latter spirit that I want now to disclose for all to see the advice, support, and sustenance of the people and institutions who made this book possible (anyone I've forgotten should take solace in the thought that I may be still too guilt-ridden to fess up to all of my debts).

First, let me express my gratitude to the journals and collections in which many of these essays first appeared: chapter 1 in *Theory and Society;* chapter 4 in *Leviathan* (Athens); *New Formations* and *Rediscovering History: Cultural Politics, and the Psyche,* ed. Michael S. Roth (Stanford: Stanford University Press, 1994); chapter 5 in *Constellations* and *Georges Bataille,* ed. Denis Hollier (Paris, Belin, 1995); chapter 8 in *Tikkun;* chapter 11 in *Auge und Affekt: Wahrnehmung und Interaktion,* ed. Gertrud Koch (Frankfurt: Fischer, 1995) and *The Semblance of Subjectivity: Adorno's Aesthetic Theory,* ed. Tom Huhn and Lambert Zuidervaart (Cambridge, Mass.: MIT Press, 1997); chapter 15 in *Modernism/Modernity;* and chapters 2, 3, 6, 7, 9, 10, 12, 13, 14, and 17 in *Salmagundi.*

As the number of chapters that first appeared as columns in *Salmagundi* indicates, I owe a special debt to its editor, Robert Boyers, for his long-standing and generous support; Peggy Boyers and Mark Woodworth have also made my ten-year association with the magazine a consistently pleasant experience. In a wide variety of ways, I am no less indebted to other friends or colleagues who solicited, criticized, and inspired individual essays: Philip Brady, Susan Buck-Morss, Robert Dietle, Edward Dimendberg, Alexander García Düttmann, Andrew Feenberg, Hal Foster, Jan Gouldner, Denis Hollier, David Hollinger, Bill Honig, Robert Hullot-Kentor, Anton Kaes, Gertrud Koch, Akiba Lerner, Michael Lerner, Laura Marcus, Mark Micale, Lynda Nead, Shierry Weber Nicholsen, Mark Poster, Anson Rabinbach, Paul Rabinow, Lawrence Rainey, Avital Ronnell, Paul Thomas, Joel Whitebook, and Richard Wolin.

The collection as a whole would not have existed without the initiative of David Gross and William Johnston, whose series on Critical Perspectives on Modern Culture I am delighted to join. I am no less happy to thank Clark Dougan and Pam Wilkinson of the University of Massachusetts Press for their expert editorial guidance and Benjamin Lazier for his excellent research assistance and preparation of the index. My children, Shana Gallagher (who became Shana Gallagher Lindsay just as this book went to press) and Rebecca Jay, did the wonderful things they always do to remind me that life can also exist away from a computer screen. Finally, let me acknowledge a debt that is certainly no secret, but which I will always feel guilty about insufficiently repaying. It is to my wife, Catherine Gallagher. She is always the first reader of anything I write and invariably its most insightful critic. There is no semantic play, just the spontaneous overflow of powerful feelings in any acknowledgment I can make to her.

CULTURAL SEMANTICS

"What a glorious book might be written on the life and adventures of a word!" Balzac exclaimed in *Louis Lambert*. "The mere consideration of a word, even if we abstract its functions, its effects, its performance, is sufficient to launch us on a wide expense of meditation."[1] Many authors before and since have taken up Balzac's challenge. producing long and learned philological accounts of the ways words have evolved over the years, acquiring new denotations and connotations and shedding or occluding others. What has been called "the romance of etymology"[2] has produced both "scientific" and "folk" attempts to trace the provenance of words, often with the goal of discovering an ostensible "authentic" first meaning in one of the "ur"-languages out of which our current Babel of tongues emerged. Even at a time when the synchronic workings of a language system as opposed to the diachronic history of one of its components have seemed to many the primary goal of linguistic inquiry, the fascination with semantic evolution has not abated. Indeed, if the success of such amateur practitioners of the craft as William Safire of the *New York Times* is any indication, it has become a popular as well as scholarly pastime.

Philological analysis, however, has never been an entirely innocent enterprise, devoid of ideological functions. As Maurice Olender has recently shown, its nineteenth-century variants, purporting to be purely scientific, were deeply implicated in the production of racist myths whose sinister effects we in the twentieth century have come to know all too well.[3] The supposed language groups called "semitic" and "aryan" could effortlessly be turned into eternal religious or cultural types with invidiously contrastable attributes, whose alleged persistence in the present could produce ominous consequences. Nietzsche's "genealogical" method, derived in part from his philological training, demonstrated, to be sure, a potentially less racist implication, based as it was on a sensitivity to the contingent rather than the teleological status of the narratives of semantic change it traced.[4] But even Nietzsche's account of the origins of the alleged "slave morality" of "good and evil" could be easily abused.

Nearer our own day, Raymond Williams's pioneering efforts in tracing the fortunes of what he calls "keywords" have demonstrated the value of frankly acknowledging the ideological charge on certain pivotal terms, which Williams defines as "significant, binding words in certain activities and their interpretations" and "significant, indicative words in certain forms of thought."[5] His now classic study, Culture and Society,[6] launched a virtual industry of commentary on the vexed term "culture," which is only now beginning to show signs of wearing out its welcome at a time when virtually every humanistic discipline is hastening to transform itself into something called "cultural studies."

Williams's ideologically sensitive etymologies have, to be sure, proven vulnerable to a number of criticisms. As Quentin Skinner pointed out in a review of the original edition of Keywords,[7] the tight relations between words and concepts implied by Williams need to be loosened; it may well be that lacking a precise term for a concept—the term that seems its self-evident equivalent to us now—does not mean that it could not be thought or expressed in a different fashion, perhaps by several other words. Nor is it clear what the criteria are for selecting a "strong" word that can be called "key" over a long period of time; it may be necessary to explore its different functions in the succession of discursive systems in which it is located, systems that may produce subtly altered relations between denotations and connotations. And perhaps most significantly, we need to be aware, as Williams may not have been, that meaning alone is insufficient to exhaust the task of investigating the history of words. We must also be attentive to what words do and perform, as well as what they refer to or signify, to what speech act theorists such as J. L. Austin and John Searle call their "illocutionary" as well as their "locutionary" function. As anyone who follows the recent legal debates over the notion of "fighting words" knows, context determines not only meaning, but also performative force. What might be called a "cultural pragmatics" thus must always accompany a "cultural semantics."

Such an approach must not, however, fail itself to acknowledge the inevitable locutionary openness, perhaps even catachrestic indeterminacy, of the terms whose illocutionary function it hopes to reveal. One of the abiding lessons of deconstruction, whatever one may think of all of its other claims, is that rigorous definition, attempting to still the play in words, is bound to fail. It is even more problematic when applied to the career of a word over time. With this in mind, etymology can avoid an ideologically suspect search for origins and, as Derek Attridge points out,

> be used to unsettle ideology, to uncover opportunities for change, to undermine absolutes and authority—and to do so without setting up an alternative truth-claim. . . . It depends on the way in which words we regularly encounter, and treat as solid, simple wholes (representing solid, simple concepts) can be made to break apart, melt into one another, reveal themselves as divided and lacking in self-identity, with no clear boundaries and no evident center.[8]

Words, moreover, do their work not merely by melting into one another, but by positioning themselves in shifting force fields with other words, creating unexpected constellations of counterconcepts and antonyms, as well as a spectrum of more or less proximate synonyms. Etymology alone can never suffice to reveal how words mean or perform, insofar as the differential relations among them are an intrinsic dimension of their role in linguistic systems that are, of course, far more than mere lexical aggregates. Cultural semantics must, therefore, be sensitive to the ways in which language partakes in and contributes to the larger processes of identity formation through inclusion, exclusion, and even abjection—to highlight one of the terms to be discussed below—in society as a whole.

Among those scholars especially open to these imperatives can be counted those who were trained, as was I, in the discipline of intellectual history.[9] For intellectual historians have traditionally been attuned to the ways in which words crystallize and assume important functions, often different ones depending on the context, and then become stale or overburdened and lose their efficacy. Well before the so-called linguistic turn that has heightened the sensitivity of all historians to these questions,[10] intellectual historians paid close attention to what the practitioners of the old "history of ideas" led by Arthur Lovejoy had dubbed "historical semantics."[11] The recent interest on the part of intellectual historians in the hermeneutics of Heidegger and Gadamer was facilitated by the recognition that one of their most distinguished forebears, Wilhelm Dilthey, had also been a founding father of *Geistesgeschichte*. More recently, German scholars associated with Reinhard Koselleck have systematically pursued *Begriffsgeschichte*, a history of concepts that is often hard to distinguish from a history of the words that bear them. Although some of the earlier work of intellectual historians on linguistic developments may seem naive in the light of recent semiotic, structuralist, poststructuralist, pragmatist, or speech-act theories of language, it nonetheless deserves recognition as an important stimulus to any cultural semantics in our own day.

Certainly in the case of the essays gathered in this volume, that earlier work must be given a significant place. For it was only after the essays were written that it became evident to their author that all were, to one degree or another, motivated by a desire to explore the implications of certain keywords, words that were doing more than their share of cultural work at the present or in the recent past. On reflection, it also became quickly apparent that this concern was not a new one in my research. An earlier project, which sought to trace the history of Western Marxism by following the ways in which its main exponents had evoked the numinous concept of "totality," had, in fact, used the very metaphor of a word's "adventure" in its subtitle, borrowed, to be sure, from Maurice Merleau-Ponty rather than Balzac.[12] I also made shorter forays into the territory occupied by such words as "sovereignty" and "text."[13] Several of the essays in the present collection have come to fruition in the shadow of a more substantial study in which I have been engaged for some time on the vagaries of "experience" in modern European and American thought. So without my always explicitly intending it, it seems clear that a major focus of my work has been a kind of unthematized cultural semantics.

Much of that work has also been informed by an argument advanced by Theodor W. Adorno concerning the special role played by foreign words. In an essay originally composed in the early 1930s, Adorno defended the macaronic use of words from abroad against exponents of a "pure, organic" German, who sought perfect communicable transparency. "Language participates in reification," Adorno insisted. "separation of subject matter and thought. The customary ring of naturalness deceives us about that. It creates the illusion that what is said is immediately equivalent to what is meant. By acknowledging itself as a token, the foreign word reminds us bluntly that all real language has something of the token in it. It makes itself language's scapegoat, the bearer of the dissonance that language has to give form to and not merely prettify."[4] Although most of the words that are brought to the surface in the essays that follow are common English terms, they have been treated as if they were foreign in Adorno's sense. That is, pressure is put on them—sometimes by considering their relation to apparently equivalent words in other languages—to the point that their self-evident naturalness begins to waver. The goal is a kind of semantic defamiliarization in which words that seem commonplace—"theory," "subversion," "experience," "mimesis," "paganism," "the aesthetic," and so on—begin to appear strange, while other words that until recently may have been strange—"abjection," "the uncanny," "psychologism," and so on—are interrogated until they reveal at least a few of their secrets.

Because all of the essays had their own contingent origin and have only latterly come together, it might be useful to provide some specific context for each. What will first strike the reader is the unevenness in tone and disparity in length between those that were intended for a more scholarly audience and those that came into the world as columns for *Salmagundi*. I have been contributing biannual pieces under the rubric "Force Fields" to that journal since 1987, when its editor Robert Boyers generously invited me into its pages. This format has provided me an opportunity to roam more freely over territories that were not fully within my area of putative expertise and to do so in a voice that was more colloquial and personal—at times also more irreverent and flippant—than would be appropriate for an academic journal. The advantage of a column is that it allows writers to shed much of the legitimating apparatus typically cluttering up the bottom half of scholarly pages and trust more in their own intuitions; the disadvantage is that the results may appear to be based on less rigorously sustained arguments and more impressionistic evidence than would be warranted to make the case. I hope, however, that even five finger exercises can stimulate discussion and so I have resisted the temptation to expand these essays, supply full citations, and elevate (or is it tone down?) their prose.

Something useful, in fact, may come from the jarring juxtaposition of the two authorial voices insofar as their disparity brings home the point made in one of the pieces about the performative choices intellectuals must self-consciously make these days in presenting themselves and their ideas, especially those who have some interest in reaching a wider public. The tonal disjunction may also alert the reader to the fact that sometimes what appears to be a keyword may in the end turn out to be nothing more than a "buzzword," which my dictionary describes as "a word or phrase by members of some in-group, having little or imprecise meaning but sounding impressive to outsiders." I will let readers decide for themselves which terms fall in which category (or perhaps which might be both in different contexts).

The initial essay, "For Theory," is itself somewhat of a hybrid, at once scholarly and personal. It was prepared for a conference in February 1995 at the University of California, Davis, to celebrate the coming of age of the journal on whose editorial board I have sat for most of its twenty-one years, *Theory and Society*.[15] Reflecting on the history of the journal and the legacy of its founder, the sociologist Alvin Gouldner, the essay seeks to trace the vicissitudes of one of the most hotly contested keywords of our time, paying special attention to the often contradictory ways in which "theory" has been evoked by exponents or critics of its various usages. "For Theory" was dedicated to the memory of Bill Readings, the gifted literary critic whose death at the age of thirty-seven in a plane crash the year before is still mourned by a very large circle of his friends and admirers. Bill would have doubtless enjoyed the irony that I stubbornly call him a "theorist extraordinaire," even though in a section of his stimulating book on Lyotard explicitly called "against theory," he had protested that "after 1968, theory ought to be recognized as part of the problem, not a potential solution."[16] As in many other matters, he and I would have had a splendid time knocking heads over this contention.

The next essay, originally a *Salmagundi* column of 1992, touches more lightly on the vexed issue of what has come to be called "multiculturalism," which may well be more in the buzzword than keyword category. It strives to rescue the discipline of European intellectual history from the charge that its predominant focus on dead, white, European males means that it is necessarily complicitous with an elitist defense of something called "Western culture." It takes seriously the imperative to link knowledge with "subject positions," including my own, but concludes that ideas need not be reduced entirely to functions of that point of departure. As in an early essay on the critical implications of the apparently conservative notion of hierarchy,[17] it seeks to complicate the ideological and political conclusions that have been hastily drawn from the conventional aura surrounding certain words.

"Songs of Experience: The Debate over *Alltagsgeschichte*" was written for a conference sponsored by the Berkeley German department in the wake of the so-called Historian's Debate over the normalization of the Nazi past. It was then published in 1989 in *Salmagundi*, although with more scholarly apparatus than in a normal column. Focusing on the subsidiary question of the political implications of the so-called history of everyday life, which was decried by some in Germany as a potentially apologetic approach to Nazism, the essay also entered the murky waters surrounding the concept of "experience" (waters in which I am still struggling to stay afloat). It sought to unpack the different, even opposing meanings of the term, especially evident in German usages, in order to complicate the claim that privileging quotidian "experience" in a historical account necessarily means underestimating the structural forces that work behind the backs and against the wills of those doing the experiencing.

The two German terms for experience, *Erfahrung* and *Erlebnis*, have perhaps been nowhere as thematically juxtaposed as in the work of Walter Benjamin, who is the focus of the next essay. Prepared for one of the many conferences called to mark the centenary of his birth in 1992, this one at Birkbeck College in London, it was published first in a Greek translation in *Leviathan*, then in *New Formations* with the conference proceedings, and finally in the *Festschrift* edited by Michael Roth dedicated to the distinguished intellectual historian Carl Schorske.[18] The article was motivated by a desire to find a secular surrogate for the still theological premise of Benjamin's hope for a restoration of that nonsubjective *Erfahrung* whose disappearance in the modern world he so powerfully lamented. Following the lead of Hayden White and Dominick LaCapra, who have imaginatively speculated on the implications of the grammatical "middle voice" and "free indirect style" for larger cultural issues, it locates that surrogate in one place where Benjamin refused to find it: the novel. In so doing, it tries to provide a more plausible account of what "experience without the subject" might mean than the redemptive version that has seemed to many vulnerable to the charge of impotent utopianism.

The next essay, "The Limits of Limit-Experience: Bataille and Foucault," was first presented to a 1993 conference organized by Denis Hollier in Orléans, France, on the theme "Georges Bataille après tout," and then published in its proceedings; it appeared soon after in English in the new journal *Constellations*.[19] Resisting the claim made by poststructuralist critics of unreflective immediacy that "experience" always implies a dubious privileging of phenomenological "authenticity," it explores the ways in which two of the founding fathers of poststructuralist thought themselves relied on complicated notions of "inner experience" or "limit experience" to indicate something that cannot be construed as merely a function of cultural, discursive, or linguistic construction. As in the other essays dealing with "experience," the goal is more than mere historical retrieval; it is also to bring to the surface some variant of the term that might survive the powerful critiques made of its naive usage. How successful such a salvage operation may be must await the larger book on experience that I hope will follow.

If "experience" has once again become one of the most heatedly contested keywords of our day, "soviet," the term that is the focal point of the next essay, originally a *Salmagundi* column of 1991, has clearly lost that status. Its title a mordant reversal of Lenin's famous (and infamously betrayed) slogan, "No Power to the Soviets" reflects not only on the fall of the Soviet Union, but also on the widespread collapse of hopes on the left in the model of the "workers' council" or "soviet" as an alternative to bureaucratic state socialism, trade unionist loyal opposition to capitalism, and parliamentary democracy. Despite a few diehards who continue to equate emancipation with fully autonomous self-management,[20] the council ideal has not really survived into the post-Communist world as a viable solution to the ills of capitalism. Even the recent upsurge of interest in the political theory of Hannah Arendt, who tried to defend the idea of a council freed from its dependence on the workers who might lead it, has not taken much inspiration from the soviet model.[21]

The next essay, "Who's Afraid of Christa Wolf? Thoughts on the Dynamics of Cultural Subversion," was also written in the shadow of the collapse of Communism and published as a column in *Salmagundi* in 1991. Its occasion was the controversy surrounding the East German novelist's autobiographical revelations, but its larger theme was the meaning of the highly charged word "subversion." Although the issue was presented in terms of the German debate, the column also sought to address the fashionable adoption of the rhetoric of subversion in the American academy, where it often functioned as a solace to those remnants of the left whose political impact had grown increasingly indirect and attenuated.

As an uncannily self-confirming postscript to the story told at the beginning of the essay about our friend from Humboldt University, who denied any Stasi ties, it turns out that a year or so later, he revealed (or was forced to acknowledge) that he had done something else that complicated his future: some time in the 1980s, he had acted as a spy for the East German government abroad. Despite all the ambiguities—Is it immoral to serve in the intelligence service of your country, even if it means breaking the laws of another? What happens when that country no longer exists and the one whose law (or allies's law) you broke can now judge you?—his career is in tatters. The Wolf case has itself been complicated by further disclosures about Wolf's earlier involvements with the Stasi, which were unknown when my essay was first composed. Clearly, the stakes are not trivial when it comes to judging what subversion really means and the price one must pay when it fails.

The aftermath of German unification was also the stimulus to the next piece, "Postmodern Fascism? Reflections on the Return of the Repressed," which was originally presented at a symposium organized by Tikkun and the Berkeley Students for Judaism and Social Justice in 1993, led by Akiba Lerner, who was then one of my students. Published along with a response by Elliot Neaman in the November/December 1993 number of his father's journal, it also stimulated a second critique in a later issue, as well as some outraged correspondence.[22] Predictably, any attempt to circumscribe the reach of a term as loaded as "fascism" and confine its historical efficacy to a particular context will seem blind to the possibility that history can repeat itself. Indeed, in one of the essays below dealing with "the uncanny," the issue of precisely such a return of the repressed is broached. Still, nothing has happened in the period since the essay was written that would undermine its tentatively optimistic conclusion that a reunified Germany is not a likely place for this particular repressed to make a successful comeback.

The issue of how one construes subversion returns in another guise in the next essay, "Educating the Educators," which was a *Salmagundi* column in 1994 inspired by the trial and dismissal of California superintendant of schools Bill Honig. Here the emphasis is displaced slightly to the vexed issue of "critique," especially as it might be expanded from a practice of adversarial intellectuals into a more broadly meaningful impulse in popular education. Because mass culture has so successfully co-opted the debunking and unmasking inclinations of critical intellectuals, while turning them in a cynical rather than utopian direction, it is no longer sufficient—if it ever really was—to pit an avant-garde, politically progressive elite against both traditional upholders of high culture and purveyors of conformist kitsch and assume it is somehow the carrier of genuine negation. We are, it seems to me, at an impasse when it comes to knowing how to distinguish real from false critique, having lost a strong sense of what constitutes the horizon of progressive change. One happy footnote to the piece: in December 1996, Honig's sentence was lessened and the charges diminished because of the remarkable community service he had done since his trial.

The following essay, a *Salmagundi* column of 1992 entitled "The Aesthetic Alibi," also grapples with the erosion of a keyword's power to perform one important task it was previously assigned. The term in question is "art" and the issue is how its traditional function as a legitimator of a certain variety of free speech can be maintained when its own privileged status as a special category of human endeavor is no longer self-evident. But rather than allowing that loss of status to countenance the wholesale collapse of "art" into the larger cultural institutions and material conditions that permitted it to emerge and are now threatening it with extinction, the essay struggles to provide a way to salvage its power as a placeholder of some future alternative to the status quo. Without his name being mentioned, the figure of Adorno hovers over this essay.

A more explicit exploration of at least one corner of Adorno's defense of the aesthetic comes in the next essay, which compares his notion of mimesis with that of the French deconstructionist Philippe Lacoue-Labarthe. Prepared for a conference organized by Gertrud Koch at the Kulturwissenschaftlichen Institut in Essen, Germany, in 1994 and first published in its proceedings,[23] it was stimulated by the recent interest in mimesis manifested, inter alia, in the work of the anthropologist Michael Taussig. I had just critically reviewed two of his books for the *Visual Anthropology Review* and came away with a powerful desire to clarify what I thought he had muddied.[24] Lacoue-Labarthe provided an instructive contrapuntal approach to the same question, especially because his positive assessment of mimesis undermined the conventional wisdom that French poststructuralists were uniformly hostile to it as a form of naive realism. By disentangling mimesis from its presumed synonym "imitation" and putting it in a constellation with its putative opposite, "reason," the essay hopes to fend off its reduction to yet another form of a dubious "sympathetic magic."

The issue of mimesis, now in the form of mocking masquerade and self-conscious mimicry, appears as well in the next essay, a *Salmagundi* column of 1993, "The Academic Woman as Performance Artist." "Performativity" has, in fact, become one of the keywords of recent cultural criticism, helping to foreground the illocutionary, rather than the purely locutionary ways in which communication—or its undermining—takes place. Musing on the implications of the challenge presented by certain prominent women scholars to traditional academic etiquette, the essay adopts a cheeky tone to make a serious point: that the unimpeded logic of the better argument is not always the only means by which a putatively rational "culture of critical discourse" operates. But as in the case of the defense of mimesis in the essay on Adorno and Lacoue-Labarthe, the essay stops short of rejecting that culture entirely in the name of a cynical reduction of knowledge to nothing but a tool in the struggle for power. After all, in Habermas's variant of rational discourse as a universal pragmatics, which I have often defended in earlier writings, the performative moment is also taken into account; indeed, the implied promise to be truthful, sincere, contextually appropriate, and so on underlies the communicative act in its nonstrategic mode. In this essay, the proper name "Camille Paglia" is evoked as a warning against understanding performativity solely in narcissistic, power-oriented, strategic terms.

Paglia, we might say, becomes the one academic-performance artist who is abjected in an account that tries to incorporate almost everything else. As the sacrificed scapegoat, she helps to solidify the boundaries of what the

essay accepts as defensible behavior. "Abjection" itself became the subject
of the next essay, originally a *Salmagundi* column in 1994, which reflects on
and partially resists the recent fascination with this term. Here the main
stimulus was the controversial 1992 Whitney Museum exhibition on *Abject
Art*, which produced a vigorous debate in *October* that still rages.[25] Although
I did not want to join the chorus of those cultural policemen who denounced the exhibition as a misuse of public funds, I was disturbed by the
ways in which the loose rhetoric of subversion could combine with what I
had described earlier as "the aesthetic alibi" to produce a problematic
outcome.

One curious footnote to "Abjection Overruled" merits mention. During a
trip I made the following year to Wrocław, the Polish filmmaker Maria
Zmarz-Koczanowicz directed an imaginative television film based on the
column. I was interviewed at length by her husband, the philosopher
Leszek Koczanowicz, against the backdrop of an artists' figure-drawing
class, a voice-over in Polish was provided, and the results were interspersed
with some of the more striking images from the repertoire of abject art.
Nothing makes a talking head look more attractive, I can now attest, than
being juxtaposed to scattered body parts and images of human waste. I
gather the ratings for the show were surprisingly high. In post-Communist
Eastern Europe there may be no power left to the soviets, but there is still a
strong fascination with what might transgress and challenge the pieties of
the bourgeois—or more precisely mass—culture that is now engulfing it.

If "abjection" has been refunctioned as a positive term in the cultural
semantics of our day, the same can be said even more vigorously for the
keyword that served as the basis of the next essay, which was a *Salmagundi*
column of 1995. "The Uncanny Nineties" sought to probe the widespread
invocation of "*das Unheimliche*" (literally, the unhomely) as a master trope
of a widening number of overlapping discourses, psychological, philosophical, aesthetic and political. Not surprisingly, our fin de siècle has
shown itself able to reflect on a metalevel about the ways in which it
recycles the obsessions of its predecessor terminal decades, obsessions
which come back like uninvited ghosts. If, to borrow the title of Hal Foster's recent collection, this has meant "the return of the real," it has been a
real accompanied by the aura of spectral familiarity that has always marked
uncanny repetitions. The essay concludes, however, by cautioning against

the complete conflation of real and metaphoric phenomena, especially that of homelessness, which can too easily legitimate the callous indifference that seems to have numbed many of us in the "uncanny nineties" to literal misery.

The question of cultural repetition is broached as well in the next piece, "Modernism and the Specter of Psychologism," which was prepared for a conference, "The Mind of Modernism," at the Whitney Center for the Humanities at Yale in 1995 and then published in *Modernism/Modernity* the following year.[26] Here the focus is on one of the most powerful terms in a debate that raged a century ago in philosophy and spilled over, the essay seeks to demonstrate, into modernist aesthetics as well. "Psychologism," a notoriously vague epithet that was used to damn any attempt to reduce first logical and mathematical and then ethical and aesthetic truths to the context of their production or reception, seemed to be driven from the field in the early twentieth century. But its ghost has returned to haunt—or inspire—much postmodernist philosophical and aesthetic practice. Whether modernist anti-psychologism is itself a revenant that refuses to die is the question posed, but left unresolved at the end of the essay.

No less of a return of what seemed repressed is evident in the next essay, which ponders the resiliency of the term "pagan" in the modern and postmodern worlds. Prepared as a contribution to a *Festschrift* for the eminent intellectual historian Peter Gay,[27] it pits Gay's defense of the Enlightenment as "the rise of modern paganism" against Jean-François Lyotard's postmodern "lessons in paganism." Contrary to my expectations when conceiving the exercise, it turns out that the similarities between their two evocations of the term outweigh the differences. Acknowledging these parallels can perhaps foster a more nuanced appreciation of the relation between the modern and postmodern than is evident in the thinking of those who either demonize the former as a sinister project in rationalist totalization or excoriate the latter as simply another variant of counter-Enlightenment irrationalism.

The final essay, "The Manacles of Gavrilo Princip," began as a 1995 column for *Salmagundi* and is perhaps the most directly personal piece in the collection. Here the term on which pressure is put is among the most charged of our time: "the Holocaust." The definite article has been used to set apart the Shoah—to use another of the inadequate words we have come to apply to the unspeakable horrors to which they refer—from all other such events in human history. Recounting a visit made to one of the Holocaust's most notorious sites, the concentration camp at Theresienstadt, the essay ponders the inevitable entanglement of "the Holocaust" with other twentieth-century genocidal dramas, most notably that unfolding in the former Yugoslavia during the time of my visit. Its final, sputtering conclusion signals a sense of profound frustration at trying to make sense of a trauma that still shadows our lives a half century after it seemed to end.

If these random exercises in cultural semantics demonstrate anything, it is that what Nietzsche famously called "the prisonhouse of language" allows us inmates a certain amount of leeway in testing the limits of our confinement. Although, to borrow yet another well-known metaphor, we may not be able to let all of the flies out of the flybottles, we can still help a few escape. But in so doing, we must inevitably recognize that there are larger linguistic containers in which they are still confined. It is, we might say, flybottles all the way up.

I

For Theory

✳

In memory of Bill Readings, theorist extraordinaire

For those readers with keen memories, the title of this essay may evoke the parallel title of a collection of essays by *Theory and Society*'s founding editor that appeared in 1973. Alvin W. Gouldner's *For Sociology* was written in the wake of his controversial *The Coming Crisis of Western Sociology* and was designed in part to counter charges that his critique of Talcott Parsons was somehow an abandonment of sociology in favor of political activism, in particular of a Marxist variety. Unlike Louis Althusser, to whose *For Marx* Gouldner's title was itself an oblique response, Gouldner argued for the critical potential of what he called "reflexive sociology." Among other things, this meant a sociology strongly grounded in an interdisciplinary community of committed—although not "partisan"—theorists who would stand apart from actual movements, even if their work might ultimately influence them. "The theorist as theorist," Gouldner argued, "should commit himself to the establishment of *his own* social collectivity, to know intellectually and to create practically the conditions requisite for rational discourse and human liberation, and within whose protection he and his fellows work toward the understanding of the concrete social totality with which they are historically faced."[1]

It is a mark of the distance we have traveled in the scant two decades since this was written that many of Gouldner's assumptions now likely seem highly suspect. Apart from his obviously unselfconscious use of traditional gender language, Gouldner's easy evocation of the goal of knowing "the concrete social totality" betrays his allegiance to a brand of Western Marxism, derived largely from Lukács's neo-Hegelian humanism, which now attracts few adherents. So too his call for a community of theorists, following the rules of rational deliberation or what he would call elsewhere "the culture of critical discourse,"[2] will likely appear to many as grounded in a naive universalism whose self-evident virtue has waned in the wake of multicultural fragmentation; the only community we now seem to inhabit is a virtual one on the internet with faceless and sometimes nameless others. And no less problematic, at least to many in our era of increasing cynicism, is the very project of something grandiosely called "human liberation," especially as a goal to which theorists might usefully contribute.

Indeed, in the years since Gouldner's appeal to found a community of reflexive sociologists, theory itself, after a brief period of apparent triumph,[3] has suffered a series of assaults from many different directions. The time-honored conservative attack on the dangerously utopian pretensions of abstract theory, whose provenance can be traced at least as far back as Edmund Burke's reflections on the French Revolution, was echoed in the late 1970s and early 1980s by an uncannily similar critique from the other side of the political spectrum. Theory became identified as a game of mastery, tainted by its association with the evils of transcendentalism, foundationalism, essentialism, and the vain search for a metalanguage, all of which were seen as unwarranted extrapolations from the privileged position of those who arrogantly pretended to speak for the whole. Once-militant Althusserians were sobered by their leader's confession that he had fallen into the crippling "deviation" he dubbed "theoreticism."[4] Devotees of the Frankfurt School discovered that their version of Critical Theory was vulnerable to the charge of mandarin elitism and feckless utopianism.[5] Advocates of master theories such as semiotics came to recognize the vanity of their quest.[6]

In his 1986 Presidential Address to the MLA, the deconstructionist J. Hillis Miller could still talk confidently of the "triumph of theory," now to be sure using the term to imply something very different from what it meant to those mentioned above.[7] But at virtually the same time, Stanley Fish was proclaiming, with characteristically perverse glee, that "the fading away of theory is signalled not by silence but by more and more talk, more journals, more symposia, and more entries in the contest for the right to sum up theory's story . . . theory's day is dying; the hour is late; and the only thing left for a theorist to do is to say so."[8] And only a short while later, Miller's poststructuralist colleague at U.C., Irvine, David Carroll, would write plaintively that "some would like to blame 'theory' for everything that they consider wrong in the contemporary state of the arts, the humanities, and the social sciences."[9] In Europe as well, a similar mood arose, so that by 1991, the journalist Michael Haller could begin an interview with Habermas by noting, "Today we observe a certain weariness with theory itself, a kind of theoretical exhaustion intoned with resignation, especially from sensitive people."[10]

One effect of this weariness was the emergence of the potent, if at times muddled, category of "culture" as an alternative to general theories that supposedly stand above or beyond cultural heterogeneity. It is now a commonplace to say that the so-called theory wars of the 1970s and early 1980s, the years when Foucauldians, Habermasians, Althusserians, Gadamerians, and the like engaged in mortal combat (or least a struggle for top billing at the MLA), were replaced by—or perhaps incorporated into—the so-called culture wars of the late 1980s and 1990s. The transition is neatly expressed in the appearance of a new, upstart journal a decade or so ago called Theory, Culture and Society, adding, as it were, the mediating term of culture to fill the gap in our own journal's name.

In the humanities as well as the social sciences, theory, while not entirely discredited, went on the defensive. What the literary critic Paul de Man identified shortly before his death as a growing "resistance to theory,"[11] intensified markedly when the scandal over his wartime political journalism broke in 1987. This resistance expressed itself, inter alia, in the rise of a "new historicism," which refused to foreground its theoretical sophistication, and the revival of interest in pragmatism, stimulated by the work of Richard Rorty and Stanley Fish. Two of the leading neopragmatists, Walter Benn Michaels and Steven Knapp, even produced a manifesto provocatively entitled "Against Theory," which triggered a flurry of rebuttals and counterrebuttals.[12]

Here the American provenance of the pragmatist tradition lent a certain plausibility to de Man's lament that a touch of nativist xenophobia may help account for the resistance to theory.[13] In England, where theory had never been as eagerly embraced as in America, the touch, in fact, could easily become a rough kick reminiscent of the one delivered by Dr. Johnson to his famous rock. The enemy in both contexts often came to be characterized not as theory per se, but as something called "French theory" and pronounced as if it were one word, even though such a beast would have been as difficult to find in Paris as that other great Anglo-Saxon creation, French toast.

By the late 1980s, it was even possible to find figures like Foucault, who had once been embraced as one of the high priests of "French theory," defended precisely because they were covertly anti-theoretical. "Any suggestion," wrote one indignant commentator, "that Foucault's work is theoretical—that it could produce more accurate theories, or that it could yield new and improved theories of familiar things and old concepts, or that it could generate theories of newly discovered entities and concepts, or even that it could rehabilitate or revitalize the activity of theorizing itself—facilely overlooks the structural connections and discursive isomorphism between a theoretical approach and modern forms of subjectivity."[14] Presumably knowledge about those forms came from thoroughly nontheoretical investigations into a past—an "analytics" or "genealogy" in Foucault's terms—that revealed its secrets to those who had somehow shed, or at least problematized, their own modern subject positions. "Genealogy's attention to fragmentation, disconnection, difference, diversity, and plurality," wrote the same commentator, "is an intolerable assault on the unity and simplicity that theory requires of itself."[15]

Paradoxically, however, it was precisely the extraordinarily disunified and elastic meaning of the term "theory," which became especially evident when it shed its earlier qualifiers ("literary" or "social" or "political") and set up shop on its own, that may have helped call it into question. Traditional and critical theory, Max Horkheimer had famously argued in 1937, were not to be conflated; whereas the former meant the "sum-total of propositions about a subject, the propositions being so linked with each other that a few are basic and the rest derive from these," the latter was "the unfolding of a single existential judgment" that "it need not be so; man can change reality."[16] When Gouldner in 1973 spoke of "theory," he clearly meant it in the latter sense, as the mainstay of a defiantly value-laden social science. But many other defenders of the term have continued employing it as a synonym for an edifice of increasingly abstract generalizations about the world, which they claim is normatively embodied in natural scientific theorization.

Both uses, however, are a far cry from that employed by a deconstructionist like de Man who claimed that "the resistance to theory is a resistance to the rhetorical or tropological dimension of language, a dimension which is perhaps more explicitly in the foreground in literature (broadly conceived) than in other verbal manifestations or—to be somewhat less vague—which can be revealed in any verbal event when it is read textually."[17] They are even further from the usage of Michaels and Knapp who defined the theory they were so resolutely against as "splitting apart terms that are in fact inseparable,"[18] such as the meaning of a text and the authorial intention allegedly preceding it. The result was that for them theory could be simply defined—and then debunked—as "the name for all the ways people have tried to stand outside practice in order to govern practice from without."[19] With theory meaning all of these things and more, it is no surprise that the 1976 inaugural conference of the U.C., Irvine Critical Theory Institute devoted to the "States of 'Theory,'" had to suspend the word in scare quotes to indicate how problematic it had become.[20]

One complaint against virtually all varieties of theory, however, has been shared by many of its critics: that they are tainted by the same original sin, which could be traced back to the classical Greek meaning of *theoria* as a visually determined contemplation of the world from afar. The hostility to visual distantiation, to that cold, disembodied eye producing the modern subject in what can be called the scopic regime of "Cartesian perspectivalism,"[21] has in fact become a powerful presence in the current antitheoretical climate. It is linked through guilt by association with other terms like specularity, surveillance, and the gaze (often preceded by the adjective "male"), which are also in bad odor at the moment. "Panoptic theory," Michel Serres has typically insisted, must give way in the "age of the message" to new forms of coded information, very different from objects in a visual field.[22]

This is not the place to rehearse the reasons for and implications of the anti-ocularcentric mood, which I have attempted to explore in a recent book,[23] although the irony should at least be acknowledged that many of the arguments against the primacy of theoretical vision have come from the very French thinkers whose work is decried as itself too theoretical. Be that as it may, the critique of theory can be said to be fueled in large measure by a rejection of the alleged God's eye view above the fray supposedly assumed by theorists.

To defend theory, however, may not require a commensurate defense of the visual distantiation of *theoria*, or, even more problematically, the traditional notion of the nobility of sight. Instead, it can be based on the different strategy of examining what normally serve as the counterconcepts to theory and probing their own blindspots. For in revealing the insufficiencies of the alternatives to theory, we may come to understand why some version of it has now become an inevitable element in any attempt to make sense of the world.

Theory, it should first of all be acknowledged, has always been a term that is in a tense relationship with its other, or rather, others, which broadly speaking have taken three forms. The first is the object of that theoretical inquiry, the puzzling obstacle to unmediated and unproblematic belief that requires or at least invites the act of theoretical distantiation itself. Although the earliest notion of theory may have had a participatory moment, even, if Gadamer is right, one of "sacral communion,"[24] it soon came to imply a more strict division between subject and object. Theory, we might say, has generally been solicited by the opacity of the object to sufficient intuitive comprehension, an opacity that the theorist then tries to penetrate through procedures of conceptual mediation and categorical placement. Characteristically, although not exclusively, it does so through an act of subsumption in which a particular is seen to be an instance of—or in the terminology borrowed from legal or medical usage, a case of—a more general category. Theories can be understood as second-order reflections on the first-order conceptual function of language, self-conscious abstractions from the normal linguistic abstractions we call words.

Sometimes, to be sure, theory has come to mean a reflection on the ability of words employed or understood in a certain way to challenge precisely the homogenizing power of conceptuality itself. In the appropriation of the term "theory" by deconstruction, this challenge has been made explicit, as, for example, in Wlad Godzich's opposition of "Writing to the Concept" in his recently published collection *The Culture of Literacy*. According to Godzich, what he labels anti-dialectical "difference-oriented theory"—we might also call it, following Bataille, "heterological theory"—decries the sinister complicity between conceptual sameness and the political suppression of otherness carried out in the name of the "State, Unity, Totality, and Eternal Presence."[25] Here "theory" has come to signify a second-order reflection on the homogenizing tendencies of what normally passes for theory.

In so arguing, to be sure, such a theory may smuggle back in a certain notion of sameness despite itself, which resembles the conceptual thinking it hopes to subvert. Thus, Godzich acknowledges that his version of theory assumes "an equation of operational equivalence between the notion of System in philosophy and that of the State in the social sphere,"[26] without pausing to ask how such equations are not themselves examples of conceptual homogenization. More subtle instances of the deconstructionist use of theory, in fact, recognize the vanity of any hope entirely to escape sameness in the name of pure difference.

Be that as it may, for many defenders of theory, whether pro- or anti-conceptual, homological or heterological, a fruitful balance or productive tension between general and particular, sameness and difference, is an explicit goal. This desire for balance is classically expressed in Kant's celebrated claim that "concepts without empirical intuition (observation) are empty phrases; empirical intuitions (observation) without concepts are blind."[27] His now widely appreciated turn toward reflective as opposed to determinant judgments in the *Critique of Judgment*, judgments based on analogizing from paradigmatic examples rather than general laws, expresses an even greater wariness about the dominating implications of theories that are simple concepts writ large.

But when the procedures of abstraction, subsumption, and even analogizing from paradigmatic examples are understood as threats to dominate and overwhelm the object rather than illuminate its meaning, resistance emerges in the name of the irreducible particularity of objects to the concepts under which they are seen to be being violently subsumed or the examples to which they are analogized. What Theodor W. Adorno liked to call "the preponderance of the object" in his *Negative Dialectics* was precisely a plea for such resistance, which he understood in terms of the nonidentity of a particular thing and a general concept. This plea sometimes inspired Adorno's attempt to outwit language's conceptual powers by privileging its more mimetic capacities, in ways too complicated to spell out now.[28]

Carried to an extreme in the hands of anti-theoretical skeptics—Adorno was never, of course, that—it could lead to what might be called the pathos of ineffability, in which all concepts and a fortiori all theories are seen as violations of their objects. Instead of bemoaning the ability of what we can call the "real" to thwart attempts to render it intelligible through theoretical mastery, such critics identify precisely with that escape, as if theory was another name for the police and its object an innocent victim falsely labeled as something it is not and then brutally forced to submit to that labeling. What is most real is thus sometimes most closely identified with what is inconceivable and untheorizable.[29]

The second "other" of theory has more to do with the ways in which subjects relate to objects than with the objects themselves; here five obvious variants come to mind, which can be called practice, subjective experience, objective (or intersubjective) experience, story-telling (or narrative), and the hermeneutic arts. Perhaps the main counterconcept to a theoretical approach to objects is, of course, a practical one. It would take another essay to untangle the meanings of the word "practice," with it various instrumental, functional, and even moral—think of Kant's second Critique—meanings, but suffice it to say that it generally implies a nonreflective, immediate, and ad hoc relationship to an exigent problem at hand. Whether explicitly instrumental or understood as a kind of accumulated wisdom based on past trials and errors (the Greek notion of phronesis), practice suggests tactile, "hands on," rather than visual knowledge. Unlike theory, which implies the luxury of distance and the willingness to forego or at least delay results, practice entails a more proximate involvement with matters that demand a prompt pay-off. It is at the heart of what the ancients liked to call the vita activa, as opposed to the vita contemplativa, ways of being in the world, which, as Hannah Arendt showed many years ago in The Human Condition, themselves contain more than one modality.[30]

The vexed "relation between theory and practice" is, of course, an age-old conundrum for theoreticians and activists alike.[31] Often they have been seen as mutually supportive, one illuminating and verifying the other, but sometimes, the primacy of practice over theory, along with the superiority

of activists over theoreticians, has been strongly defended. No one who
passed through the politically charged 1960s and early 1970s, when even
the most theoretically self-conscious intellectuals still agonized over how
engagé they were, will forget the incessant questions from the floor after
every lecture demanding to know how such esoteric and abstract ideas,
expressed in the jargon of an intellectual elite, could be translated into
immediate emancipatory practice.[32] At a time when the New Left spawned
battles between groups, their tongues only half in their cheeks, calling
themselves the "Praxis-Axis" and the "Action-Faction," theory could be
denigrated as a mere second-order reflection of practice, rather than its
guide. The first ten "Theses on Feuerbach" could be tacitly forgotten and
the famous eleventh elevated to a status of self-evident primacy.

As one famous philosopher had put it, challenging the traditional picture of the origins of theory,

> What is theoria for the Greeks? It is said that it is pure contemplation,
> which remains bound only to its object in its fullness and in its de-
> mands. The Greeks are invoked to support the claim that this con-
> templative behavior is supposed to occur for its own sake. But this
> claim is incorrect. For, on the one hand, "theory" does not happen for
> its own sake; it happens only as a result of the passion to remain close
> to what is as such and to be beset by it. On the other hand, however,
> the Greeks struggled to understand and carry out this contemplative
> questioning as a—indeed as the—highest mode of man's energeia, of
> man's "being at work." It was not their wish to bring practice into line
> with theory, but the other way around: to understand theory as the
> supreme realization of genuine practice.[33]

Such a redescription of theory as a form of noncontemplative practice, a
passion to be close to and beset by what is as such, could, to be sure,
degenerate into anti-intellectualism, as critics of "mindless activism"
never tired of repeating. It is perhaps indicative of what the problem might
be that the famous philosopher I just cited was not, in fact, a leftist of the
1960s, but Martin Heidegger, whose paean to theory as the realization of
practice came in his notorious rectorial address of 1933, when he defended
the Nazi revolution as a realization of Promethean action and exhorted his
students to join their "knowledge-service" to the labor and military ser-

vices that were to bring about the new order. Be that as it may, "practice" as the superior "other" of theory, indeed as both its source and its telos, still resonates among those impatient with the impotent musings of intellectuals safely ensconced in their proverbial armchairs gazing at their no less proverbial navels, as the recent upsurge of interest in neopragmatism suggests.

Another, not quite as politically fraught version of the "other" of theory invokes the notion of "experience." No less vexed and polysemic a term than "practice," with which it is sometimes conflated,[34] "experience" can itself be divided, roughly speaking, into two salient variants. The first signifies the particular, idiosyncratic, perhaps even incommensurable things that happen to individual or sometimes collective subjects and produce their singular life histories. Such experiences are understood to be unique and so ineffable that any attempt to subsume them under general theoretical categories will destroy their qualitative differences from other equally irreducible experiences. Whether understood as the recalcitrant object of inquiry—as an experience that defies the theorist's attempt at categorical subsumption—or as the subjective source of the theorist's very activity of theorizing—as an experience that produces inevitable bias in the attempt to contemplate from afar—experience can be marshaled to humble theory's pretensions to disinterested universality. In the culture wars of the present, theory has seemed especially vulnerable to the charge of an inevitable ethnocentrism, a failure to acknowledge that its generalizations are always made from the partial vantage point of particular experience.

The second variant of the appeal to experience is less relativistic, but no less anti-theoretical. Here I am speaking of the time-honored notion of empirical evidence, the supposedly "hard" facts that are prior to the attempt to imbue them with larger meaning. Although this notion of experience is objective, or at least intersubjective, rather than subjective or ethnocentric, it too challenges the hegemony of theoretical or conceptual mediation. However widely strong versions of realist, positivist, or empiricist approaches have been discredited, however much even the natural sciences have come to accept the "theory-laden" quality of their observations, it is nonetheless true that, a few French philosophers of science aside, most current thinkers on the subject reject the idea that theory produces its objects solely out of its own activity. To the extent that theories seem to cry out for some sort of testing, whether we understand its goal as verification, falsificaton, or mere modification, experience understood as disinterested openness to the empirical other of pure theory, what we normally call "facts," plays a vital role.

A third nontheoretical mode of relating to objects, which is more evident in the humanities than the social or natural sciences, involves verbs of action that seem specific to the object at hand. In art history, for example, it goes by the name of "looking"; in literary criticism, it is "reading"; and in music, "listening." All of these imply a more intimate and proximate relation to the object, the relation of an educated insider, than theoretical contemplation, which implies the ability to apply generalizations in many different contexts. Theory, we are told, easily travels from genre to genre, from culture to culture, but the acquired skills of looking, reading, or listening—let's call them the hermeneutic arts—are more closely related to the objects they interpret. As Bill Readings once pointed out, building on the remarks of de Man about the alleged foreignness of theory, "it is only by casting theory as foreign that we can suggest that reading is native: a reading that would not be French, would be respectful of, would correspond to, the interiority of texts."[35] Theory, the objection goes, violates that interiority by its illegitimate imposition of entirely external categories that miss the qualitative individuality of the objects they force into their conceptual Procrustean beds.

Another powerful alternative to theory is narrative, understood as the telling of particularized stories whose intelligibility derives from the plausibility of their plots and the lessons they convey to those able to grasp them. Although we are now incessantly told that "grand narratives" are a form of homogenization as nefarious as grand theories, microstories or even the shards of discredited macro ones can still be construed as diachronic antidotes to the synchronic pretensions of explanatory theory. A recent essay on Hannah Arendt goes so far as to identify her work with "the redemptive power of narrative" because of its stress on rescuing the past actions preserved in the stories told about them.[36] The widely remarked resistance of historians to the invasion of theoretical generalizations from outside fields is often carried out in the name of narrative self-sufficiency. The project of recovering the "voices" of those silenced by dominant accounts of the past derives in large measure from a belief in the irreducibility of unique stories to larger patterns, such as those imposed by theoretical generalization.

A final "other" of theory goes in a direction opposite to those we have been discussing, away from the object of inquiry or the mode of relation to the object, and turns instead to the concrete inquirer. We have already noted that one way in which experience is introduced in an anti-theoretical way is to register the subjective bias of the individual theorist. A more ambitious tack is to focus attention on the institutions of theorizing and the community of theorizers as a whole. Here not only is the origin of the word in the Greek verb for gazing, surveying, or contemplating remembered, but so too is its other root in the noun for a collection of representatives who function as the authoritative witnesses for public events and sacred occurrences.[37] Here attention is paid to the groundedness of theory in the power relations of those who practice it. As the case of Gouldner shows, this attention need not always be entirely debunking in intention; he thought the "culture of critical discourse" was more than just an excuse for the domination of those who has mastered its protocols. In the case of other observers, such as Pierre Bourdieu or Stanley Fish, the implications drawn may be more deflationary. For them, theory sometimes seems little more than a tool in the struggle for distinction in cultural fields or power in interpretative communities.

Theory, to summarize our argument so far, must be situated in a semantic network with its multiple others: objects that defy subsumption, practices and experiences that are prereflexive or the posterior test of a theory's validity, hermeneutic arts such as reading, looking, and listening that resist universal generalization, the unique intelligibility of narrative, and the community and institutions of theorists who do the theorizing. With all of these counterconcepts to theory available to challenge its putative primacy, and there are probably more that could be adduced, is it any wonder that theoreticism has become one of the leading deviations of our time, and not only for the dwindling band of Althusser's acolytes? Is it any wonder that a resistance to theory almost automatically emerges along with the claims of theory themselves?

No response to the debunking of theory can ignore the power of its various others, which prevent it from ever complacently assuming its own self-sufficiency, from ever becoming fully transcendent and contemplative.

In whichever of theory's guises, it should be immediately conceded, theory cannot be justified as autotelic or autonomous. In fact, it can only become effective when it acknowledges its inherently parasitic relation to what it distances itself from; there is no theory without an opaque object to be interpreted, a practical implication potentially to be drawn, a prereflexive experience prior to theoretical reflection, modes of representation and understanding irreducible to general theoretical principles, and an institutional context enabling the act of theorizing itself.

And yet, what makes theory necessary, if by itself insufficient, is precisely the no less blatant incompleteness of its others. That is, in the imperfect world we inhabit, indeed in virtually any world constructed by fallible humans, no possibility of self-sufficient immanence exists on the level of practice, experience, hermeneutic interpretation, narrative intelligibility, or empirical facticity. Nor, to look in the other direction, can we reduce theoretical communities to mere stratagems of power, functional only in the acquisition of cultural capital, social distinction, or institutional control. For in so doing, we ignore precisely the reflexivity, the capacity to reflect on their own institutional embeddedness, that necessarily sets such communities apart from others in the world.

What I mean by the lack of self-sufficient immanence would become clearer were we to examine the fractures, tensions, even contradictions in what we call objects, practices, experiences, hermeneutic understanding, empirical facts, narratives, and communities. Each, I think it can be easily shown, is itself a semantically unstable and historically variable term that gains its intelligibility only in relation to the constellation of terms that surround, invade, and oppose it. There is no time to spell this out now in any detail, but I do want to pause for a moment to consider one familiar example, which concerns the central object of theoretical inquiry in the humanities, the so-called work of art.

Arguments against the imposition of allegedly external theoretical notions of the aesthetic on allegedly self-contained works of art are belied as soon as we recognize that the discourse of the aesthetic is at least in part constitutive of the works themselves, which are more than the expression of creative genius. This understanding has, of course, only been self-consciously foregrounded in the wake of avant-garde critiques of the institution of art and assaults on the integrity of the work, critiques that are perhaps best exemplified by a single proper name: Marcel Duchamp. But even before the hypertrophy of theoretical self-consciousness that is signified by that name, art and the discourse about it known since the eighteenth century as "aesthetics" have been inextricably intertwined. No aesthetic theory, that is, can see itself as utterly external to the works it theorizes about simply because such works are always already mediated, to one degree or another, by theoretical considerations of genre, medium, or evaluation.

They are, to be sure, not reducible to merely a function of such considerations, a reduction that even the so-called conceptual art of the 1960s and 1970s ultimately resisted. Duchamp's "readymades," after all, were both effects of the artist's performative statement, "this is a work of art," and the application of that performative to visually present objects open to a formalist or symbolic interpretation in less theoretical terms. It was, in fact, the tension between these two functions that provides much of their power. For, as Daniel Herwitz has recently reminded us in his *Making Theory/Constructing Art*, avant-garde works of art both realize the theories that generate them and exceed those theories.[38] This surplus is evident as well in other "others" of theory, such as experience, practice, facts, and interpretative communities, all of which may be theory-laden, but resist reduction to theory alone.

The larger point I want to make is that what we call "theory" is a moment of reflexive self-distancing, a moment that subverts the self-sufficient immanence of whatever we happen to be talking about. It is precisely such internal distance that, *pace* certain neopragmatists, prevents even beliefs from being so seamlessly undisturbed by what are allegedly outside of them. For the very dichotomy of inside and outside is itself replicated within the seemingly immanent system of belief. As Niklas Luhmann has often argued, every system contains its own blind spots, its own paradoxical assumptions, which prevent the observer from being totally within or completely outside its boundaries. Those who yearn for an entirely immanent position are as deluded as those who think they can find one that is entirely transcendent. Their dreams of undisturbed plenitude are themselves fantasies of mastery, moves in the game of desiring control, that are ultimately as vain as those they attribute to the purveyors of theory.[39] For absolute proximity is as hard to come by as that unbridgeable spectatorial distance supposedly allowing theoretical contemplation from afar.

The same reproach can be made to those who want to privilege ordinary language, the conversational style of quotidian practice and experience, over the specialist's esoteric jargon; for even the most everyday of everyday languages contains conceptual homogenizations, tropic displacements, and rhetorical ambiguities that defy any attempt at finding a mode of expression perfectly adequate to the meaning it is intended to convey. We are all not only speaking prose without knowing it, but also prose that contains its theoretical moment, its moment of reflexive self-distancing, which no amount of nostalgia for a lost language of transparent immediacy can repair. Theoretical discourse is thus not the other of everyday language, but rather its latent self-estrangement made manifest (something that is paradoxically often said about poetic language as well).

It is, however, also for the same reason that "theory" itself as a moment of absolute or pure reflexivity will always be undermined when we acknowledge it as inevitably intertwined with its own other, its own resistance, as de Man would have put it. We are, in fact, rightly uneasy when the abstraction of a general notion of theory per se implies it has somehow risen above that resistance and become itself a fully sovereign activity, a mere specular double of what it purports to understand and explicate.[40] It is this uneasiness that underlies and indeed justifies the reaction against the hypertrophy of theory described earlier in this essay. It is also what renders the at first confusing appropriation of the term "theory" by deconstruction to signify anti-conceptual writing an ultimately felicitous provocation; for it makes clear that "theory" itself cannot contain its own contradictory impulses through a higher-level metatheoretical subsumption. It is, as Fred Botting has recently argued, like a *fort/da* game, which "accedes to a heterogeneity that refuses theoretical mastery even as it stages and repeats the subject's desire to master body, psyche, image, signs, objects and others."[41]

Once it is acknowledged, however, that theory cannot become entirely transcendent or self-sufficient, once the subject of theory is understood as inextricably intertwined in the world it tries to observe from afar, once theory and its resistances are seen as mutually entailing, then the charge that theory is merely an example of a discredited ocularcentrism based on the fantasy of a God's eye view loses much of its force. No longer do we have to fear the threat of a master theory that will somehow subordinate all knowledge to its yoke. After we free ourselves of the need to defend or attack such a false notion of theory, we can then move on to the more interesting and productive task of sorting out and creatively cross-fertilizing the plethora of theories, grand and not so grand, traditional and critical, literary and social, that have emerged into recent prominence, as well as those that are surely still to come. Rather than seeking to construct a grand edifice of theory, solidly grounded on firm foundations, and hierarchically organized in levels of ever more refined abstraction, we can enter the dynamic force field of theories and their others that swirls around and through us. Although the end result may not be the achievement of that "human liberation" Gouldner ambitiously argued was the goal of his community of reflexive sociologists twenty years ago, we are likely to understand a bit more clearly why it will be so hard, if not impossible, to attain and what more modest, but worthwhile tasks still lie before us.

European Intellectual History and the

Specter of Multiculturalism

❋

In 1990, H. Stuart Hughes published his autobiography under the title
Gentleman Rebel.[1] In it, Hughes details his transformation from scion of
a prominent establishment family—his grandfather was Charles Evans
Hughes, Republican candidate for president in 1916 and later Chief Justice
of the Supreme Court—to political radical, who ran a spirited campaign
against Edward Kennedy and George Cabot Lodge for the vacant United
States Senate seat from Massachusetts in 1962. Told with self-deprecating
irony and a great deal of confessional candor, sanctioned by his enthusiastic embrace of psychoanalysis, Hughes's memoir provides a fascinating
account of the ways in which leftist politics often have patrician origins.

It is not, however, this central narrative that most interests me now, but
rather one of the book's subtexts. For Hughes, notwithstanding all his
political activities, was by profession an academic, a historian of European
ideas who had a distinguished career at Stanford, Harvard and the University of California, San Diego. And it was in this capacity that our paths first
crossed, for he directed my doctoral dissertation on the Frankfurt School,
which was completed in 1971. Although *Gentleman Rebel* only summarily
recounts the vicissitudes of his academic career and spends even less time
on the content of his dozen books, it is as the life of a European intellectual historian and not as that of a renegade from the patrician class that
Hughes's autobiography has stimulated the following reflections.

In the current context of culture wars over canons, high culture, and the
primacy of "Western" thought, it might seem as if European intellectual
history would be an inviting target for those who decry the hegemony of

Eurocentrism. What other field, after all, deals so unapologetically with the legacy of dead, white males? What other field so tenaciously resists the populist replacement of elite ideas by cultural meaning in the larger, anthropological sense of the word "culture"? What other field so explicitly requires of its students the kind of broad cultural literacy that would warm the heart of an E. D. Hirsch or Alan Bloom?

And yet, examined more carefully, European intellectual history has functioned and continues to function in a far more complicated way than this caricature suggests. Perhaps inadvertently, its complexity is neatly captured in the title of Hughes's autobiography, *Gentleman Rebel*. That is, on one level, the field appeals to those who want a broad, if perhaps not terribly profound, knowledge of European intellectual traditions, which they assume will provide a veneer of "gentlemanly" culture. As such, it can be called the quintessence of a loosely interdisciplinary, liberal arts education in a traditional humanist mode. Here "great books" of philosophy, literature, and political theory are read with the reverential piety due to "timeless classics" of Western thought.

But on another level, intellectual history attracts those who appreciate the often subversive implications of many of the ideas in those same books, ideas which contested the received wisdom of their original milieux and often have the potential to do so today. It has also proven a magnet for those who identify, explicitly or not, with the embattled outsider status of the figures who generated and elaborated those ideas. For intellectual history—as opposed to the more idealist "history of ideas"—often focuses on the complex interplay of thoughts and lives, texts and contexts, intended production and unintended reception that gives "the life of the mind" so many of its dramatic tensions.

The field's ambiguous function is also evident in the ways in which it can be said to treat "obsolete" ideas that no longer animate the current theoretical debate. From one perspective, the intellectual historian can be accused of contributing to the impotence of such ideas by relegating them to the safety of a no longer relevant past. As such, he or she can be charged with preventing the dead from really speaking to the living and the living from really engaging with the dead. A gentlemen's agreement of sorts is understood to sanction the division of labor between historical and current approaches to ideas.

But looked at differently, intellectual history can be seen as quietly stor-
ing such ideas, preserving their explosive potential until the time when they
will be used by later generations for new and unexpected purposes. While it
has often been virtually impossible, for example, in mainstream departments of psychology to teach Freud or in mainstream departments of
economics to teach Marx, intellectual historians have been allowed to present their ideas with a sympathy that often transcends mere historical
interest. The same might be said, broadly speaking, of the continental
philosophy so long marginalized in Anglo-American philosophy departments. Here too, intellectual history has helped keep alive ideas and approaches that the currently dominant academic paradigm refuses to take
seriously.

Because of its hybrid status, European intellectual history has, moreover,
often attracted scholars who fit somewhat uncomfortably in the traditional
disciplinary rubrics of the academy. Although more widely accepted in
history departments than their counterparts in Europe, where intellectual
history is rarely even an established subfield, they nonetheless are often
ostracized for being too theoretical or abstruse, while their concern for
"high" ideas is decried as elitist. Philosophers, on the other hand, rarely
accept their efforts as contributions to the resolution of current problems.
And literary critics grow impatient with their failure to engage in extended
close readings of texts.

Likewise—and this is really the main point of these remarks—European
intellectual historians have increasingly come to be drawn from hybrid-
ized, ambivalently situated groups in American society. The pioneers of the
history of ideas may largely have been from established Western European
stock, for example, Arthur Lovejoy and his colleagues in the History of
Ideas Club at Johns Hopkins, Crane Brinton at Harvard or Jacques Barzun
at Columbia. But with the influx of emigrés from Europe during the fascist
era, the composition of the field's exponents began to change. German
Jews like George Mosse, Peter Gay, and Georg Iggers were joined by
American-born Jews like Leonard Krieger, Frank Manuel, Harvey Gold-
berg, and Carl Schorske (who had one Jewish parent). In the generation
that followed, roughly speaking that of my own cohorts, the pattern was
intensified as scholars like Andrew Arato, David Biale, Paul Breines, David
James Fisher, Jan Goldstein, Mary Gross, Gerald Izenberg, Russell Jacoby,

Harry Liebersohn, Eugene Lunn, Mark Poster, Anson Rabinbach, Michael Roth, Jerrold Seigel, Debora Silverman, David Sorkin, Richard Wolin, and Lewis Wurgaft began to leave their stamp on the field.

Although there are, of course, many other important European intellectual historians from different backgrounds, the disproportionate number of Jews is striking confirmation of the discipline's hybrid status, at once a vehicle of upward cultural mobility and a means of preserving potentially subversive ideas and covertly identifying with their rebellious proponents. As such, it has functioned as a relatively painless way to negotiate (or even reenact) the "ordeal of civility" that John Murray Cuddihy identified as characteristic of European Jewish intellectuals themselves.[2] For intellectual history has allowed a certain assimilation to mainstream European culture, while preserving some of the critical anger felt by outsiders against their culture's hegemonic functions.

At present, another generational shift appears to be in the works, which may repeat this pattern in somewhat displaced and attenuated form. Although my evidence is anecdotal, and drawn largely from experiences at Berkeley, where ethnic diversity is more advanced than at many other elite universities, there seems to me an unmistakable widening of the constituency for European intellectual history to include groups of many different, non-European backgrounds. There have, to be sure, been distinguished contributors to the field before from these groups—Oliver W. Holmes, Donald M. Lowe, and Harold Mah come immediately to mind—but a new threshold has recently been reached. The number of enrollments in my large lecture classes has remained steady over the past two decades, but the faces staring back no longer look as homogeneous as before. And my graduate seminars are peopled by a broad cross-section of students who often have cultural heritages very different from those of the figures we study.

But what has remained constant is the intense curiosity they feel about those figures and the ideas they generated. Contrary to the widespread fear that politically correct "identity politics" prevents students of minority backgrounds from taking seriously anything from other cultures, they appear far too sophisticated in their appreciation of the internal complexities of the European intellectual tradition, its positive as well as negative legacy, to reject it out of hand. And they seem fully aware that its intellectual resources are too valuable to be ignored merely because of their European provenance. They know full well that when the subaltern (or at least his or her intellectual representative) speaks, the ideas that come out will be at least to some extent in the language of Marx, Freud, Nietzsche, Foucault, Derrida, Irigaray, and so on. They know that in a postmodern, postcolonial world, "travelling theory," as Edward Said calls it, resists reduction to its place of origin and finds new and creative expressions in unexpected contexts. They are supremely aware of the potential of even the most canonical master texts to be read against the grain and provide lessons that transcend those intended by their authors.

This is not to say, to be sure, that the questions they put to the material will be the same as those of their predecessors, or that the answers they provide will ratify conventional wisdom. Nor is it necessarily the case that their ability to identify with the heroic figure in the tradition will be as effortless as it has often seemed for the scholars of my generation, many of whom could find in Marx, Freud, Lukács, Adorno, and so on, exemplary role models. What Dominick LaCapra has called transferential interaction between a scholar and his or her subject will perhaps be more attenuated when the distance between them is greater. The shift from a psychological or social contextualization of ideas, which marked the work of Hughes's generation, to a more impersonal interest in discursive or intertextual patterns, which began with certain historians in my own, is likely to be intensified as a result. The much-debated "linguistic turn" in intellectual history may be given added impetus by the suspicion these new scholars are prone to feel toward the defining power of contextual explanation and the reductive dangers in privileging experience over theory.

Conjecturing about the future of a field is, of course, a risky undertaking, and I don't want to draw too certain a conclusion from what are admittedly impressionistic observations. What does seem clear is that the much discussed face-off between defenders of an embattled "Western culture" and their putative multicultural opponents does not begin to do justice to the evolution of at least this one field. In the American academy, European intellectual history has never been an exclusive club for the preservation and adoration of high culture. It has often maintained an irreverent attitude toward received canons, whose allegedly timeless status its very emphasis on historical contextualization challenges. And it has encouraged the creative appropriation of the ideas it studies in new contexts. The "gentleman rebels" of the past are being replaced by people—often, of course, not gentlemen at all—who may seem, at first glance, unlikely successors, but their energetic arrival can only be welcomed by those who want to get beyond the sterile antinomies so tiresomely repeated in the culture wars of the present day.

3

Songs of Experience: Reflections on the Debate over *Alltagsgeschichte*

✳

There can be few more politically charged and tensely argued scholarly debates than that recently launched by a handful of German historians urging the "normalization" or "historicization" of the Nazi era.[1] By relativizing the horrors of the Holocaust through comparisons with its alleged predecessors—most notably, the Soviet terror after the Revolution—and with its supposed successor—the Russian invasion and occupation of the eastern half of Germany—they have sought to attain for Nazism the cool "perspective" of time granted other regrettable episodes from the distant past. This scholarly version of the attempt by Kohl and Reagan to honor victims and victimizers alike at the military cemetery in Bitburg has not gone unchallenged in Germany and abroad. Philosophers like Jürgen Habermas and historians like Hans-Ulrich Wehler have vigorously contested these calls to "wind up the damages" of a now "decontaminated" past.[2] For them and for most non-German observers, it is still premature to distance ourselves from the deeply disturbing issues raised by a past that remains doggedly "unmastered."[3]

My own sympathies are squarely with those who resist the attempt to "normalize" the Nazi era. But rather than rehearse the reasons for this judgment or go over the ground that other knowledgeable outsiders like Charles Maier and Richard Evans have already effectively covered,[4] I want to take this opportunity to focus on one relatively unremarked aspect of the debate, which has important implications for larger historiographical questions. The issue concerns the role of what in German is called "*Alltagsgeschichte*" or the "history of everyday life."[5] Within the debate over the proper approach to understanding Nazism, it has come to play an unexpectedly important role. The reigning explanation of the German catastrophe, which saw it as an outgrowth of Germany's abnormal road to modernization (its so-called *Sonderweg*), has been associated primarily with the historians of the Bielefeld School. This left-leaning, social science–oriented tradition was inaugurated by Ekhart Kehr during the Weimar era, developed by Hans Rosenberg during his exile in America, and became prominent in the 1960s with the work of Wehler, Jürgen Kocka, and their colleagues at the University of Bielefeld. According to Evans's account of the origins of the *Historikerstreit*, this orthodoxy was "challenged from the left, as younger German historians, many of them outside the academic profession, abandoned the social scientific paradigm, subverted the primacy of political history and the nation-state model, and embarked on a quest to recapture the subjective experience of everyday life in the past at a regional, local or even individual level."[6]

Many comments might be made about the implications of Evans's statement, concerning for example the challenge to professional historians by what has come to be called "barefoot" amateurs or the subversion of the nation-state model, which might be seen as an accomplishment of the Bielefelders themselves in regard to an older "historicist" orthodoxy. For want of space, however, I have chosen to focus on only two aspects of Evans's remarks: first, his claim that the defenders of *Alltagsgeschichte* come from the left, and second, his identification of their challenge with the recapturing of subjective historical experience.

The attribution of a leftist motivation behind the emphasis on everyday life should come as somewhat of a surprise in the light of the linkage that is often perceived by its critics between *Alltagsgeschichte* and the apologetic tendencies of normalizing and even trivializing the Nazi past.[7] Such a connection is not, to be sure, without plausibility. For if the emphasis is on the alleged "normality" of everyday life, then the era may not seem as uniformly aberrant as traditional historians contend. A gap may appear to have existed between the terrible policies of the regime and the cluster of elite groups that supported it, on the one hand, and the quotidian existence of the millions of "little men" (and presumably "little women" as well), who passively suffered the results, on the other. Such a model tacitly calls into question the existence of a fully totalitarian society in which all sectors were, in the notorious Nazi term, *gleichgeschaltet*, or coordinated.

This approach may also provide a subtle defense of the noncomplicity of an ignorant German populace in the events that were foisted on it from above. And it may offer as well ammunition to those who claim that the regime successfully secured a "normal" existence for the majority of its citizens, especially during the years of relative economic prosperity in the mid-1930s. Thus understood, *Alltagsgeschichte* is of a piece with similar apologetic tendencies in popular culture. A salient and widely discussed example is Edgar Reitz's monumental film *Heimat*, with its focus on the daily life of two farmer families over two decades. Kenneth Barkin pungently summarizes this conclusion in the final judgment of his insightful review of the film: "In the new village-centered German history of the 20th century, Nazism and Hitler no longer occupy center stage; that is a conjuring trick that even a village magician would have found difficult to carry off."[8]

It is undeniable that the critics of the apologetic implications of Alltagsgeschichte have a point when they caution against our substitution of a historiography centered on socioeconomic structures, political elites, and the preeminence of the state with one that offers cultural anthropological studies of small town life. Insofar as the point of view of the German "hometowners," to borrow Mack Walker's term,[9] has traditionally been regressive and provincial, it should come as no surprise that a historiography that merely tries to empathize with their experience and make it the central focus of an era may have problematic political implications.

And yet, as Evans has correctly noted, it was originally leftist critics of the Bielefeld orthodoxy who first introduced *Alltagsgeschichte* to the debate. How, we must ask, might it function in politically divergent ways? What is the nonapologetic potential in the history of everyday life? Must a concern for lived experience mean a neglect of the theoretically informed structural explanations favored by critical historians like those of the Bielefeld School? Is it, in short, the "history of everyday life" that is problematic, or only its function in the specifically German debate over the Nazi era?

One way to begin answering these questions is to glance briefly at the non-German discussions of the topic. For it is clear that the history of

everyday life has been more comfortably accepted in other historiographical traditions, for example the Annales School in France and the History
Workshop group in Britain. American scholars, such as Natalie Zemon
Davis, Warren Susman, and Robert Darnton, have also shown the value of a
cultural "history from below." These historians, to be sure, tend to concen-
trate on topics that may have less obvious contemporary relevance than
Nazism, the French for example doing most of their work on medieval or
early modern problems. But they have been able to discern in the everyday
lives they have examined far more than the "normality" which has apparently so preoccupied the German practitioners of *Alltagsgeschichte*. One need
only think of their explorations of the topsy-turvy world of carnival to
realize how abnormal and indeed potentially disruptive the everyday can
be. As a result, they are often taken to task by conservative critics like
Gertrude Himmelfarb, rather than those further to their left.[10]

If we turn as well to more theoretical discussions of the idea of "every-
dayness," such as the late Michel de Certeau's *The Practice of Everyday Life* or
Agnes Heller's *Everyday Life*,[11] it is possible to appreciate the political complexity of the phenomenon itself. For rather than being reducible to quotidian routine, the everyday can also be understood to contain varieties of
resistances to both control from above and internalized conformity from
below. De Certeau, for example, provocatively challenges Michel Foucault's
dark notion of the microphysics of normalizing power in favor of what he
calls "the network of an antidiscipline,"[12] which expresses the creativity of
groups or individuals unmastered by the dominant ideology, hegemonic
culture, or corporeal regime. By rigorously exploring the imaginative devices employed by the consumers of those mechanisms of constraint, he
shows the counternormalizing potential in everyday life, its noncomplicity
with the power of passive integration. And he shows that it exists in the
modern as well as early modern world, contrary to the German historians'
tendency to assign it only to the latter. This potential, of course, may be
only that, but it would be mistaken to assume a priori that the everyday is
nothing but an enclave of depoliticized normality oblivious to the pressures
to colonize it from above.

Secondly, this argument can be turned entirely on its head and rather
than stressing the anti-disciplinary resistance of everyday life, one can
show how deeply permeated it actually was by the same malevolent ide-

ologies and practices that were developed on the level of the regime and the ruling elites. Thus the German historian Detlev J. K Peukert has shown that rather than remaining an innocent enclave of normality during the Third Reich, everyday life shared many of the same attitudes and practices that appeared on the level of the regime's official policy.[13] There was a fatal continuum, he contends, between daily discrimination and racial prejudice, on the one hand, and the final solution, on the other. What we might call, with apologies to Hannah Arendt, the evil of banality undermines the ideology of a radical disjuncture between two incommensurable historical regions. Terror was not, in other words, only initiated from above.

Moreover, Peukert contends that even when the population was able to withdraw into a seemingly depoliticized private existence, which appeared to counter the Nazi call for mass mobilization, it was functionally complicitous with the regime. "The very retreat into privacy," he writes, "crippled possible resistance and weakened people's sense of concern at the excesses of the regime."[14] To pay attention to the apparently private sphere in the Third Reich need not, therefore, entail accepting the Nazi version of what it meant.

Thus, whether we conceptualize everyday life as an arena of anti-discipline and resistance or as one on a sinister continuum with the official policies of the regime, or most plausibly as a complex mixture of both, we need not envisage it as an enclave of benign normalcy untouched by the events outside its borders. Rather than equating *Alltagsgeschichte* with an apologetic historicgraphical tendency *tout court*, we can recognize its critical potential as well. To do so, we need to understand the everyday as a contested terrain with complicated links to the distant currents in the history of the period, not a refuge of innocence unsullied by that larger history. In short, we have to recognize that the connection between an interest in everyday life in a totalitarian era and the apologetic normalization of that era is contingent rather than necessary.

Still another issue that bears stressing is the question of *whose* everyday life is to be examined. In a film like *Heimat*, the focus is on the rural or small town life of a Germany not yet fully modernized. The Nazi *Volksgemeinschaft* ideal also privileged this image of "Germanness." But there is no reason to ignore the everyday life of the urban dweller, a frequent subject of interest, in fact, during the Weimar era in the work of critical thinkers like Siegfried

Kracauer or Walter Benjamin. During the Nazi period, for all the official hostility to the corruption of city life, Germany continued to enjoy what one historian has called "steady and even spectacular urban growth."[15] *Alltagsgeschichte* thus need not mean "barefoot" historians discovering the unbesmirched histories of localities outside of this trend toward urbanization.

Nor must it mean ignoring the histories of groups defined as marginal by the regime, gypsies, homosexuals, Jews, and so on. As Dan Diner has shrewdly noted, the victims of Nazism led anything but "normal" lives.[16] Theirs was an intensifying state of emergency, of growing exceptionalism without the lulling experiences of the majority population before the war. There is no reason that *Alltagsgeschichte* must focus only on the groups favored by the regime rather than those terrorized by it, no compulsion that it must reproduce the Nazis' own sanitized version of the *völkisch* community in its account of daily life. Instead it can probe the experiences of all who lived through the events of those years, victims, victimizers, and those who luckily escaped both fates.

Finally, there is a large group that does not fall neatly into any of these categories, because it cuts across all of them: the women of the Nazi era. In general, *Alltagsgeschichte* has paid far more attention to their history than has the social scientific, structuralist alternative exemplified by the Bielefelders. As the recent work of Claudia Koonz has shown, women in the Third Reich played a complicated role that cannot be understood without probing their daily lives.[17] Here too no easy equation between *Alltagsgeschichte* and apologetic normalization should be assumed. For as feminist historians of many different cultures have demonstrated, the question of gender cannot be adequately treated without transgressing the boundaries of what are traditionally called the public and the private spheres.

If its political implications are therefore uncertain, so too are those that follow from the key concept which underlies the history of everyday life, that of experience. As Anton Kaes has noted in his recent study of postwar German cinema, "*Alltagsgeschichte ist Erfahrungsgeschichte.*"[18] For to repeat the words of Richard Evans cited above, it is a "quest to recapture the subjective experience of everyday life in the past at a regional, local or even individual level."

This emphasis on recapturing subjective experience, with its unmistakable echoes of Wilhelm Dilthey's notion of empathetic *nacherleben* (reexperiencing), has not surprisingly been one of the targets of criticism on the part of social science-oriented antagonists of *Alltagsgeschichte* like Wehler and Kocka.[19] For its smacks too much of a hermeneutically soft approach based on the *Verstehen* (understanding) of past experience rather than on a hard-edged, conceptually rigorous explanation of the historical structures and forces that defy reduction to felt experience. For the Bielefeld School, the analytic concepts necessary in any historical explanation cannot be derived solely from the self-understanding of historical subjects. To a great degree, they are always brought from the outside to the past reality, in order to redescribe it in our own explanatory terms. Thus emphasizing subjective, lived experience and trying through historical "thick descriptions," in the phrase made famous by Clifford Geertz, to recapture it can never provide a sufficiently causal or functional explanation of the totality of historical processes. For history is more than the synthetic recounting of personal stories in the form of a fictionalized metanarrative.

Such a critique will doubtless sound familiar to anyone who knows the perennial argument between advocates of the empathetic reexperiencing of the consciousness of past agents, such as R. G. Collingwood,[20] and the structuralist or functionalist defenders of a history that works, in Marx's famous phrase, "behind the backs and against the wills of men." It was, for example, recently played out in the vigorous debate between the English Marxist historians E. P. Thompson and Perry Anderson over the usefulness of theory (largely Althusser's) to working-class history.[21] It has been no less evident in the running controversy between American feminists, who often seek to recapture a lost women's experience, and their French counterparts, who theoretically question the putative subject of that experience. And it is currently being rehearsed in the spirited debate over the relationship between black literature, the experience of its authors and readers, and a literary theory that is imported from outside, which has set scholars like Joyce A. Joyce and Barbara Christian against Henry Louis Gates, Jr., and Houston Baker.[22] In these and other such controversies, lived experience is pitted against the imposition of a theoretical scheme allegedly alien to it.

It is perhaps impossible to resolve this long-standing dispute, but some comments are in order concerning the concept of experience, which "of all the words in the philosophic vocabulary," to quote Michael Oakeshott, "is the most difficult to manage."[23] Although the term is sometimes employed as a synonym for everything that is particular, concrete, unique, ineffable, and resistant to generalized conceptual reduction, a close look at it will reveal how inadequate such an identification actually is. There is, to be sure, the typically scientific use of experience to signify immediate sentient observation, which is generally prior to any reflection on its meaning. Philosophers sometimes call such experiences "raw feels" or sensations. Although there are of course differences between those who equate these with immediate percepts and those, for example Kantians, who insist on some constitutive role for consciousness, the opposition between experience and concept seems to hold.

But the word can also be used to mean a rectification of a prior understanding of a reality, which philosophers from Hegel to Gadamer have called the "dialectical" notion of experience.[24] In this usage, experience is a negation of a previous misconception; it thus entails a process of discovery over time. The result is captured when we use experience to mean the loss of innocence, as in the idea of sexual experience, or the acquisition of insight or wisdom, which we like to think "only comes with experience." Here experience is understood to be part of a historical rather than an immediate mode of understanding. It is also seen as mediating between abstract concepts and concrete particulars, which is why we can "learn from experience." What we learn is not reducible to either the concepts or the instances, but rather is the interaction of the two. In the Aristotelian vocabulary recently revived by hermeneutics, it can be called *phronesis* or practical wisdom, the type of learning that can't be gained from books, but that must be won by active participation in the world.

As commentators since Dilthey and Benjamin have noted, the two German words for experience, *Erlebnis* and *Erfahrung*, connote different ideas of how this historical process can occur.[25] The former suggests the prereflexively registered influx of stimuli from without or the upsurge of stimuli, either somatic or psychic, from within. In the hands of certain advocates of *Lebensphilosophie*, the philosophy of life, it was accorded a privileged place because of its putative priority over "life-denying" intellect. As such, it later became an honorific word in the Nazi vocabulary. The contrasting term, *Erfahrung*, implies a more complexly mediated, historically integrated, and culturally filtered totalization of those stimuli into a meaningful pattern.

Here "life" and "intellect" are not construed as antagonistic categories. Whereas *Erlebnis* connotes a pragmatic and short-term response to the shocks of external and internal stimuli, *Erfahrung* signifies a more cumulative, often subconscious weaving together of discrete events into a narrative whole with coherence and perhaps even teleological meaning.

It was, of course, Benjamin's contention that in the modern world, the modalities of experience were skewed in favor of *Erlebnis* rather than *Erfahrung*. Faced with an increasingly overwhelming surplus of often threatening stimuli, the individual was forced to rely on the short-term devices of *Erlebnis* to survive and thus lacked the ability to integrate the shocks of daily life into meaningful *Erfahrung*. The result, as the critic Peter Bürger has put it, has been the "shrinkage of experience,"[26] which he ties as well to the overspecialization of subsystems of expertise divorced from the life-world in the differentiation process of modernity.

However one judges these characterizations of modern life and its resulting effects on what we call experience, the crucial point is that the concept is by no means self-evident.[27] Thus, to return to our consideration of *Alltagsgeschichte*, those who are trying to write about the daily experiences of the common citizen as opposed to the workings of the system as a whole need not employ a naive notion of its meaning that smacks of *Lebensphilosophie* at its most anti-reflective. Instead, they can problematize the very category of daily experience. In fact, one way to tell if *Alltagsgeschichte* has the normalizing and apologetic function its detractors claim it has is precisely to ask how the word is used. The normalizers would be those who uncritically assume the existence of a genuinely meaningful *Erfahrung* during the Nazi era, which can then be recovered by the historian willing to empathize with the "little man" beneath the regime's elite. Against this approach the accusations of the structuralist historians would be valid, for not only is such a method suspect because of its reliance on a naive notion of reexperiencing, it is also problematic because of its construction of lived experience in this period in a tendential and ideological manner.

The critical historians of everyday life, however, would avoid this reproach because they reject a simplistic and ahistorical notion of experience. Although it may well have seemed that for the average German real *Erfahrung* was still possible, they would argue that it was largely a simulacrum promulgated by the regime for its own purposes of control. Instead, they would be more open to the likelihood that "subjective experience" in the Third Reich was actually the impoverished, unnarrativized, and untotalized *Erlebnis* characteristic of modern life at its most disorienting. For them "*Alltagsgeschichte ist Erlebnisgeschichte*," not, *pace* Anton Kaes, *Erfahrungsgeschichte*.

Although it would be possible to offer evidence for this version of daily life under the Nazis, my larger point is that whatever the historical era, the simple opposition between a historiography based on empathetic reexperiencing of subjective experiences and one seeking to explain the structural workings of the system as a whole is untenable. For the term "experience" cannot be simply used as the antithesis of conceptual or explanatory theory; like all other placeholders of immediacy, it is inevitably mediated as soon as we try to think it through. *Alltagsgeschichte*, in its critical rather than apologetic mode, is thus not a retrograde antidote to a more theoretically inclined structuralist historiography, but rather its necessary complement. Instead of either merely repeating or resisting Goethe's celebrated remark about the greenness of life and the grayness of theory, we should finally acknowledge that both are far more multihued than a simple-minded opposition would suggest. For to make sense of a phenomenon as radically incomparable as the Third Reich, we surely need all the colors on our historical palette.

4

Experience without a Subject:

Walter Benjamin and the Novel

✳

"However paradoxical it may seem," Hans-Georg Gadamer writes in *Truth and Method*, "the concept of experience seems to me one of the most obscure that we have."[1] "Of all the words in the philosophical vocabulary," Michael Oakeshott agrees in *Experience and Its Modes*, "it is the most difficult to manage."[2] Derived from the Latin *experientia*, which meant trial, proof, and experiment (an acceptation still current in French), it has come to mean a welter of different things. Accordingly, the term has generated enormous controversy. Literary critics like Philip Rahv have denounced the "cult of experience" in American literature, while historians like Joan Scott have bemoaned its privileged role as evidentiary foundation in the work of figures as diverse as R. G. Collingwood and E. P. Thompson.[3] And for all those who resist so-called identity politics, in which legitimation comes from who you are—your "subject position," in the current jargon—and not from the force of what you say, the appeal to something called experience has also become a prime target.

And yet, obscurity and unmanageability notwithstanding, "experience" remains a key term in both everyday language and the lexicons of esoteric philosophies. Indeed, Gadamer, Oakeshott, and a host of other twentieth-century thinkers, from Martin Buber to Georges Bataille from Edmund Husserl to John Dewey, from Ernst Jünger to Jean-François Lyotard, have felt compelled to mull over its multiple meanings and contradictory implications. But perhaps no one has had as profound an effect on our appreciation of its varieties as Walter Benjamin; nor has anyone else made us as sensitive to the crisis of at least one of those varieties. Indeed, experience has rightly been called "Benjamin's great theme . . . the true focal point of his analysis of modernity, philosophy of history, and theory of the artwork."[4]

As a result, a formidable exegetical literature has developed around Benjamin's discussion of the concept, a literature whose central contributors would include, among others, Richard Wolin, Marleen Stoessel, Thorsten Meiffert, Michael Jennings, Miriam Hansen, and Michael Makropolous.[5] It is not my goal to rehearse their complicated arguments, or to provide a way to adjudicate their differences. Instead, I want to suggest that we might find an important confirmation of Benjamin's theory of experience in a place where he himself never thought to find it: in that modern literary genre toward which he felt so ambivalent, the novel. I want to argue that it was in a vital linguistic aspect of the novel, which Benjamin for all his fascination with language failed to explore, that this confirmation can be found.

Before making this case, however, it will be necessary to present in very general terms Benjamin's theory of experience. Most of the attention paid to it has been to his mature reflections, in particular the crucial distinction between *Erlebnis* and *Erfahrung* he developed in such works as *One-Way Street*, "Experience and Poverty," "The Storyteller," and "On Some Motifs in Baudelaire."[6] Benjamin's juxtaposition of these terms was not, to be sure, his own invention. Following the lead of Rousseau and Goethe, Wilhelm Dilthey had contrasted *Erlebnis* (or sometimes *das Erleben*), which he identified with "inner lived experience," to *äussere Erfahrung*, by which he meant "outer sensory experience."[7] Whereas the latter was grounded in the discrete stimuli of mere sensation, the former involved the internal integration of sensations into a meaningful whole available to hermeneutic interpretation. Edmund Husserl had likewise disdained the scientific and neo-Kantian notion of *Erfahrung*, based on conceptual reflection, as inferior to the richer, intuitively meaningful *Erlebnis* of the prereflexive *Lebenswelt*.[8] And Ernst Jünger had celebrated war as the arena of an authentic *Erlebnis* absent from the desiccated *Erfahrung* of bourgeois, civilian existence.[9] In all these cases, *Erlebnis* was an honorific term for subjective, concrete, intuitive responses to the world that were prior to the constructed abstractions of science or the intellect.

What set Benjamin apart from his predecessors was his disdain for both the alleged immediacy and meaningfulness of Erlebnis and the overly rational, disinterested version of Erfahrung defended by the positivists and neo-Kantians. Instead, he favored an alternative closer to what Gadamer has called a dialectical concept of experience, a learning process over time, combining negations through unpleasant episodes with affirmations through positive ones to produce something akin to a wisdom that can be passed down via tradition through the generations.[10] Unlike Dilthey, he did not give the name Erlebnis to such a dialectical process. The immediate, passive, fragmented, isolated, and unintegrated inner experience of Erlebnis was, Benjamin argued, very different from the cumulative, totalizing accretion of transmittable wisdom, of epic truth, which was Erfahrung. Here the echoes of the German word for taking a journey (fahren), a narratable exploration of parts hitherto unknown, could be heard.

Such a historically grounded notion of experience, moreover, was necessarily more than individual, for cumulative wisdom could occur only within a community, which could transmit the tales of the tribe through oral traditions such as storytelling. Thus, it was the Haggadic quality of truth, its ability to be handed down from generation to generation, like the Passover story, through collective memory rather than official historical records, that marked genuine experience. The contrast between the Jewish notion of Zakhor, group memory, and historical science, to which Yosef Yerushalmi has recently drawn attention, was thus implicitly active in Benjamin's antithetical concepts of experience.[11]

Benjamin, as we know, was deeply skeptical about the possibility of restoring genuine Erfahrung in the modern, capitalist world.[12] Although he resisted claiming it had been completely extirpated, he spoke movingly about its "atrophy" (Verkümmerung),[13] in particular after World War One. The continuum of Erfahrung had already been broken by the unassimilable shocks of urban life and the replacement of artisanal production by the dull, noncumulative repetition of the assembly line. Meaningful narrative had been supplanted by haphazard information and raw sensation in the mass media. Only the Revolution, he contended in his more Marxist moods, might create a new community in which the lost "integrity of the contents"[14] of transmitted dialectical truth would be regained.

But even when Benjamin's theory of experience can be called most materialist,[15] his doubts about the restoration of the fabric of genuine Erfahrung remained strong. A primary reason for those doubts was the stubbornly theological dimension of his work, which was never fully disentangled from its Marxist counterpart. For it was here that a powerful component of his theory of experience can also be found, a component Gershom Scholem called his quest for "absolute experience."[15] In one of his first considerations of this theme, his 1917–18 essay "On the Program of the Coming Philosophy," Benjamin explicitly faulted the neo-Kantian concept of experience, exemplified in Hermann Cohen's *Kants Theorie der Erfahrung*, for being too narrowly empirical and scientific, and thus excluding metaphysical and religious experiences.[17] Although unwilling to make the latter the *only* source of genuine experience, which he pluralistically called "the uniform and continuous multiplicity of knowledge."[18] Benjamin clearly thought that without a religious component, experience would remain woefully impoverished. For "there is a unity of experience that can by no means be understood as a sum of experiences, to which the concept of knowledge as theory is *immediately* related in its continuous development. The object and the content of this theory, this concrete totality of experience, is religion."[19]

Religious experience is particularly important, Benjamin suggested, because it transcends the problematic dichotomy of subject and object, which underlay both the scientific notion of empirical *Erfahrung* and the nonrationalist notion of *Erlebnis*. It is a "true experience, in which neither god nor man is object or subject of experience but in which this experience is based on pure knowledge. . . . The task of future epistemology is to find for knowledge the sphere of total neutrality in regard to the concepts of both subject and object, in other words, it is to discover the autonomous, innate sphere of knowledge in which this concept in no way continues to designate the relation between two metaphysical entities."[20] Later, in his more Marxist phase, Benjamin contrasted a collective subjective experience, that of the community to be created after the Revolution, to the isolated individual *Erlebnis* of modern, capitalist life; but here he was arguing for an experience that paradoxically went beyond that of any subject, collective or individual, an experience that might justly be called noumenal or ontological. As such, it was far less a synonym for active human making than his later concept of *Erfahrung* has seemed to Benjamin's commentators.[21]

Rather than musing on the "varieties of religious experience," in the manner of William James, Benjamin focused on only one. The locus of that experience, he argued in "On the Program of the Coming Philosophy," was to be found not in sensation or perception, but rather in language, that region of human endeavor Johann Georg Hamann had been the first to challenge Kant in stressing. "A concept of knowledge gained from reflection on the linguistic nature of knowledge will create a corresponding concept of experience," Benjamin insisted, "which will also encompass regions that Kant failed to integrate into his system. The realm of religion should be mentioned as the foremost of these."[22] Here language reveals itself as more than a mere tool of communication in which the feelings, observations, or thoughts of a subjective interiority reveal themselves to another subject. Here the divine word manifests itself ontologically, prior to the subjective conventionalism of human name-giving.

A religiously inflected notion of language in which the dichotomy of subject and object is transcended and ontological truth revealed—the early Benjamin is clearly invoking a concept of experience unlike any we have previously mentioned. Kantian *Erfahrung* is the empirical experience of the transcendental, scientific, cognitive subject; Diltheyan *Erlebnis* is the inner experience of the contingent subject prior to rational reflection or scientific cognition; even the Haggadic, epic truth transmitted through narrative continuity can be understood as that of a collective subject, a communal metasubject beyond the isolated, damaged subjects of modern life. But religious (or "absolute") experience, as Benjamin describes it, implies a point of indifference between subject and object, an equiprimordiality prior to their differentiation. As Winfried Menninghaus has put it, "his emphatic concept of experience" is "an ultimately messianic category of unrestricted synthesis," which is linked to forms of meaning that might even be called mythical.[23] It was for this reason that even his close friend Theodor Adorno could grow uneasy:

> His target is not an allegedly over-inflated subjectivism but rather the notion of a subjective dimension itself. Between myth and reconciliation, the poles of his philosophy, the subject evaporates. Before his Medusan glance, man turns into the stage on which an objective process unfolds. For this reason Benjamin's philosophy is no less a source of terror than a promise of happiness.[24]

As a consequence, suggestive comparisons might be drawn to a similar notion of ontological experience in the work of Martin Heidegger, who was also skeptical of the overly subjective bias of individual *Erlebnis* and scientific *Erfahrung*, and had no use for collective metasubjects either.[25] Or perhaps the poetry of Hölderlin, important for both Benjamin and Heidegger, might be adduced to demonstrate what they were after.[26] It might also be fruitful to situate Benjamin's search for an experience that transcends the subject/object opposition in the context of many other such attempts by twentieth-century artists. The Surrealists, whose writings Benjamin himself claimed were concerned primarily with experiences, come immediately to mind.[27] And we might focus on the heterodox means, such as hashish, Benjamin explored to provide nonreligious glimpses of absolute experience, those profane illuminations that broke down the barrier between subject and object.

But, rather than follow these well-trodden paths, I want to go down instead the one that Benjamin himself suggested was the locus of nonsubjective experience, that of language. And I want to suggest that even if we jettison the religious and magical underpinnings of Benjamin's own complicated theory of language, with its hope for the recovery of divinely inspired names and nonsensuous, mimetic similarities, we can still discover in the highly secular language of the modern novel unexpected warrant for his argument. We can, I want to claim, identify an intriguing example of experience without a subject that is independent of a redemptive, quasi-mythical notion of metaphysical or religious truth, or a magical notion of analogical correspondences, which are bound to make many of us uncomfortable in this age of cynical reason.

Benjamin's own mixed feelings about the novel are, to be sure, widely appreciated. Following Georg Lukács's lead in *The Theory of the Novel*, he saw it as the genre for an age of "transcendental homelessness" in which the community underpinning the oral transmission of tales was shattered.[28] The printed book undermined the need for collective group memory through public narration; epic meaning survived only in the endangered form of the tale. "The birthplace of the novel," Benjamin charged, "is the solitary individual, who is no longer able to express himself by giving examples of his most important concerns, is himself uncounseled, and cannot counsel others. To write a novel means to carry the incommensurable to extremes in the representation of human life."[29]

Although novels center on "the meaning of life," they never get beyond demonstrating that life in the age of information is inherently meaningless; the experience they depict is thus that of *Erlebnis* at its emptiest. The fate of the characters, indeed their very deaths, can only provide a simulacrum of meaning for readers, whose lives are deprived of it. Novels rely on psychological explanations instead of depicting the inherent meaning of the world of the epic, a meaning which is self-evident and in need of no external explanatory scaffolding. Even when novels like Proust's *À la recherche du temps perdu* attempt to restore coherent retrospective meaning, they can only do so through the subjective gloss of memory rather than through a presentation of objectively intelligible experience.[30] Although "involuntary memory," the technique Proust appropriated from Bergson, was closer than its voluntary counterpart to the anamnestic moment in true *Erfahrung*, it was only artificially generated through the novelist's fiat.

How then, we might ask, can the novel provide any confirmation of Benjamin's belief in the possibility of experience without a subject? How can it serve as the placeholder of an "absolute experience" beyond mere *Erlebnis* or even the lost *Erfahrung* of the storyteller? The answer resides in an aspect of the novel, which Benjamin, to my knowledge, never acknowledged: its frequent adoption of a stylistic mode that was absent from virtually all previous genres, a mode that is known in French as the "*style indirect libre*," in German as "*erlebte Rede*," and in English as "represented speech." It is further connected to the grammatical variant known as "the middle voice," which differs from active and passive voices and has been identified by critics like Roland Barthes as characteristic of "the intransitive" writing of modernism.[31] Although the presence of these linguistic phenomena does not suggest that the novel taken as a coherent, generic whole represents a prefiguration of "absolute experience," it allows us to believe that within certain novels, there exist moments that do. Such moments, to be sure, may not prefigure the fully redemptive version of that experience hoped for by Benjamin at his most utopian, but perhaps they are instances of what he liked to call the "*weak Messianic power*"[32] permitted to us even in the darkest of times.

The "*style indirect libre*" was first singled out for serious analysis by the Swiss linguist and student of Saussure, Charles Bally, in 1912,[33] and then given special significance by Proust in his celebrated essay of 1920 on Flaubert's style.[34] A year later, Étienne Lorck coined the term "*erlebte Rede*" for its German counterpart; and in 1924 Otto Jespersen introduced the less widely adopted "represented speech" for the English variant.[35] In the years since, a host of linguists and literary critics, among them V. N. Vološinov, Stephen Ullmann, Dorrit Cohn, Roy Pascal, Hans Robert Jauss, and Ann Banfield, have explored every aspect of its usage.[36] Even intellectual historians like Dominick LaCapra have evoked it to argue that Flaubert's prose style, rather than his apparently salacious content, led to the trial of *Madame Bovary* in 1857.[37]

Its significance for the issue of experience is suggested, if in somewhat misleading ways, by the fact that the German variant was called "*erlebte Rede*" by Lorck, who was a student of Karl Vossler, the romantic linguist of individualist subjectivism. Vossler, an opponent of Saussure, stressed the psychological content of linguistic performance, psychology understood not in positivist/empiricist terms, but in those of *Lebensphilosophie*.[38] That is, language expressed the internal, subjective state of mind of the speaker, rather than an impersonal sign system, and the linguist studied stylistics and *Sprachseele* (the soul expressed through style) rather than grammar. Accordingly, as one commentator has noted, "the chief reason Lorck invented the term '*erlebte Rede*' was to stress the irrational and rapturous in contrast to the informational function of language. It was thus related to philosophies of 'life' and immediate 'experience.' "[39]

How then can we claim that the indirect free style instantiates Benjamin's notion of "absolute experience" prior to the split between subject and object, if it seems to be an example of *Erlebnis* at its most objectionable? Let us examine more closely its implications for the answer. Lorck contrasted "*erlebte Rede*" to the direct discourse he called "*gesprochene Rede*" (repeated speech) and the indirect discourse he dubbed "*berichtete Rede*" (communicated speech). Direct discourse or repeated speech is uttered by a speaker, say a hero in a play, as his own thoughts—for example, Faust saying "Habe nun, ach! Philosophie, Juristerei." Indirect discourse or communicated speech occurs when a second person cites the speech of a first to a third. "Faust hat gesagt: 'Habe nun, ach! Philosophie, Juristerei.' " But "*erlebte Rede*" takes place when a second person wants to re-create in his own mind Faust's thoughts: "Faust hat nun, ach! Philosophie, Juristerei," or insofar as they are past thoughts, "Faust hatte nun, ach!"

Another, much discussed example comes from *Madame Bovary*, where Emma, looking in a mirror after her first act of adultery, is described in the following way:

> Elle se repétait: J'ai un amant! un amant! se délectant à cette idée comme à celle d'une autre puberté qui lui serait survenue. Elle allait donc enfin posséder ces plaisirs de l'amour, cette fièvre de bonheur dont elle avait désespéré. Elle entrait dans quelque chose de merveilleux, où tout serait passion, extase, délire.

> She repeated: "I have a lover! a lover!" delighting at the idea as if a second puberty had come to her. So at last she was to know those joys of love, that fever of happiness of which she had despaired! She was entering upon a marvelous world where all would be passion, ecstacy, delirium.[40]

What made this passage so scandalous and confusing to Flaubert's critics was their inability to attribute with certainty the shocking sentiments in the last sentence to either the character or the author. Was Flaubert identifying with Emma's fantasy or merely reporting it? His style did not seem to permit a firm answer.[41]

For Lorck, indirect free style was a means of one person reexperiencing the experiences of another (what Dilthey had called *nacher eben*),[42] but not of communicating it to a third. Thus, it is not something actually said in normal conversation, but only exists as a literary convention, only, that is, in written prose. If spoken aloud, it would sound more like a hallucination than a communicative speech act. Lorck thus emphasized its function as an incitement to fantasy, an example of language's ability to transcend the intellect and create anew, as evidence of its status as living *energeia*, to use Humboldt's terms, rather than dead *ergon*.

Subsequent students of free indirect style have agreed with Lorck's claim that intersubjective, public communication is not the goal of language used in this peculiar way. They have further endorsed his belief that it is inherently a written rather than spoken form, showing that language develop-

ment does not always come from innovations in verbal performance. And
they have shared his sense that it provides evidence of a creative capacity in
language that calls into question seemingly watertight distinctions like
direct and indirect discourse.

But they have vigorously challenged Lorck's Vosslerite assumption that
"*erlebte Rede*" is the reexperiencing of an irrational *Erlebnis*. Instead, as Pascal has argued, the subjective function of the style is combined with a
narratorial one, which is "communicated through the vocabulary and
idiom, through the composition of the sentences and the larger passages,
and through the context."[43] That is, there is a subtle distinction preserved
in the style between character and narrator, even if the interiorities of the
two seem to be perfectly conflated. Similarly, Vološinov claims that we hear
a conflict between the evaluative orientation of the character whose speech
is reported, and the narrator whose smooth narration is disrupted by its
representation. "We perceive the author's accents and intonations being
interrupted by these value judgments of another person," he writes. "And
that is the way, as we know, in which quasi-direct discourse differs from
substituted discourse, where no new accents vis-à-vis the surrounding
authorial context appear."[44] The result of all this, as Banfield makes clear,
is that the self whose thoughts are reported in the indirect free style, is not
equivalent to a single, coherent, egocentric subject at all, a subject whose
Erlebnis could be *nacherlebt*. "Represented thought," she thus argues, "is an
attempt to render thought as nonspeech through the medium of language.
Language makes this attempt feasible because it is not synonymous with
speech or communication, because speaker and self are distinct concepts,
both required by linguistic theory and, hence, both posited as part of the
speaker's internalized linguistic knowledge."[45]

In addition to the stylistic expression of this nonpersonalized notion of
experience, there is a grammatical correlate that was most clearly identified
by Emile Benveniste in his 1950 essay "Active and Middle Voice in the
Verb."[46] Not evident in all languages or equally prominent throughout the
history of those where it can be found, the so-called middle voice challenges the alternative between active and passive voices, just as the *style
indirect libre* calls into question the opposition between direct and indirect
discourse. Voice, or to use the technical term, diathesis, indicates the way
the subject of a verb is affected by its action. According to Benveniste,

whereas verbs in the active voice signify a process in which the subject is outside the action that it achieves, the middle voice signifies a subject within that process, even if it entails an object as well. The passive voice was only a late offshoot of the middle voice, produced only when the distinction between agent (subject) and patient (object) came to be regarded as strict. But the middle voice did not entirely die. Familiar examples in French would be "*Je suis né*," I was born, and "*il est mort*," he died. Another from Sanskrit grammar concerns the ritual self-sacrifice of a person, who takes the knife in his own hands and plays the roles of executioner and victim (*yajate* rather than *yajati*, when the priest does the killing).

Benveniste's stress on the importance of the middle voice has had a powerful impact on recent French theory. In his influential 1968 essay, "Différance," Jacques Derrida invoked it to explain the meaning of that crucial deconstructionist neologism. Claiming that différance is an operation that also cannot be conceived as either a passion or an action of a subject, he argued that "the middle voice, a certain nontransitivity, may be what philosophy, at its outset, distributed into an active and a passive voice, thereby constituting itself by means of this repression."[47] Undoing—or at least deconstructing—this repression, he implied, would be an emancipatory gesture, allowing some more primordial operation to reemerge.

Also extrapolating from Benveniste, Roland Barthes contended, in an essay originally written two years before Derrida's, that the middle voice had recovered its central place in modernist writing, writing in which the authorial function was incorporated into the text, which seemed to write itself Such writing could thus be called intransitive rather than transitive in the sense of not having an object exterior to it. Whereas Romantic writing involved a subject anterior to the actions about which it wrote, modernist writing's subject was interior to and simultaneous with the writing itself. According to Barthes, "in the modern verb of middle voice *to write*, the subject is constituted as immediately contemporary with the writing, being effected and affected by it: this is the exemplary case of the Proustian narrator, who exists only by writing, despite the reference to a pseudomemory."[48]

Rather than accepting Benjamin's critique of Proust for providing a retrospective and subjective simulacrum of *Erfahrung* through involuntary memory, Barthes insisted that the writing itself contained what Benjamin was seeking. For here we have an example of a linguistic version of experience without the subject, of *écriture* without an *écrivain*.[49] Although Barthes identified intransitive writing with modernism, where techniques like interior monologue are often employed, it would be possible to see its antecedents in the realistic novel in which the *style indirect libre* also appeared—for example in Flaubert. Thus, both on the level of style and on the level of grammatical voice, there is evidence in the novel of those attributes Benjamin denied to it.

One might also note parenthetically that Benjamin's own vaunted style (or rather several styles, because he did not always write in the same manner) can usefully be described as a form of intransitive writing. Even in his most seemingly autobiographical texts, his own expressive subjectivity was ruthlessly suppressed. Nowhere was Benjamin's yearning to efface his authorial presence more evident than in his celebrated desire to write a work composed entirely of quotations.

Whether or not one reads Benjamin's own writing as an example of how experience without a subject can appear outside the novel, it is significant that several recent theorists have found it in nonliterary phenomena as well. Ann Banfield, for example, has claimed that in certain modern recording instruments, such as the camera, the thermometer, and the tape recorder, non-sensed sensibilia can manifest themselves without an actual subject present when the event occurs.[50] These phenomena she compares to the *style indirect libre* in the novels of Virginia Woolf and the narratives of Maurice Blanchot, and employs them to criticize the claim that sensibilia always need a subject to do the sensing. "The novel," she writes, "contains sentences with deictics which can be said to represent the perspective of no one; not objective, centerless statements, but subjective yet subjectless, they render the appearances of things to no one, akin in this to the light-sensitive plate."[51] Although she does not draw on Benjamin's famous discussion of photography's revelation of an "optical unconscious," her remarks suggest a similar concern for realities that escape subjective apprehension.[52]

In another context, the philosopher Berel Lang and the intellectual historian Hayden White have suggested that intransitive writing in the middle voice may be a helpful way to present the historical narrative of events such as the Holocaust that defy traditional attempts to write about them as an objective story.[53] For White, following Roland Barthes, modernism is "nothing less than an order of experience beyond (or prior to) that expressible in the kind of oppositions we are forced to draw (between agency and patiency, subjectivity and objectivity, literalness and figurativeness, fact and fiction, history and myth and so forth) in any version of realism."[54] This modernist experience, White suggests, is somehow appropriate to that of the Holocaust, "a new form of historical reality, a reality that included, among its supposedly unimaginable, unthinkable and unspeakable aspects, the phenomena of Hitlerism, the Final Solution, total war."[55]

The claims of Lang and White that the unspeakable acts of twentieth-century totalitarianism are best represented in the unsayable sentences we have been calling instances of subjectless experience are, to be sure, controversial; indeed, I have myself vigorously challenged them elsewhere.[56] But they suggest how powerful the appeal of that notion of experience now is. Benjamin's early hope for an "absolute experience," an ontological experience expressed in noncommunicative language prior to the privileging of subjectivity in irrational *Erlebnis* or scientific *Erfahrung*, has found an echo in unexpected quarters, where no explicit residue remains of his theological concerns. Although few commentators have noticed the continuities—Banfield is an exception, as she uses the celebrated lines from "The Task of the Translator," "No poem is intended for the reader, no picture for the beholder, no symphony for the listener" as an epigraph for one of her articles[57]—it is clear that shorn of its religious aura, Benjamin's early theory of experience has shown itself to be remarkably durable.

Can it also be said in conclusion to be persuasive as well? In a recent essay addressing many of the themes we have just been discussing, the literary critic Vincent Pecora has expressed alarm at the way in which Benveniste's work on the middle voice has functioned to short-circuit serious discussions of political agency.[58] Betraying a kind of ethnological nostalgia for an allegedly prior state of undifferentiated unity, its celebrants, he claims, fail to ask the hard questions about how we are to find our way back to such a utopian state. "Like the jargon of phenomenology," Pecora protests, "middle voice only superficially 'dissolves' older logical and ethical dilemmas of subject/object relations."[59] As a result, it may even prove an unwitting handmaiden of an authoritarian politics, as Heidegger's philosophy, itself based on a search for experience without a subject, unfortunately did.

A somewhat less sinister scenario is suggested, however, by a reading of the *style indirect libre* that emphasizes its still contestatory impulses as a "dual style." Vološinov, Pascal, and LaCapra all argue for a dialogical rather than empathetic interpretation of it. That is, they stress the ways in which character and narrator remain in tension rather than smoothly be absorbed one into the other, as the Vosslerite theories of *nacherleben* suggest. Vološinov was a member of Michael Bakhtin's circle in the Soviet Union—in fact, some critics have claimed they were actually the same person[60]—so it is not surprising to find the now familiar idea of carnival associated with that of the *style indirect libre*. According to LaCapra, writing about *Madame Bovary* in particular, "the effect here is a carnivalization of narrative voice and a dissemination of the narrator—at times the author—in the text."[61]

It would not be the first time, moreover, that Bakhtin's notion of carnival has been introduced to flesh out Benjamin's arcane ideas. Terry Eagleton did so in the early 1980s, even suggesting certain similarities between the theological premises of the two positions.[62] The implication of this reading of the *style indirect libre* is perhaps not quite as nostalgic and affirmative as the one Pecora attributes to those who have used the middle voice as a way to overcome subject/object dichotomies. For it suggests a less settled notion of a unity prior to the split into direct and indirect discourse, active and passive voice. Here experience without the subject turns out to be experience with more than one subject inhabiting the same space.

Although Benjamin's early notion of absolute experience might not at first glance appear congenial to this version, it does fit well with one of his most intriguing contentions: that the aura involves an unsublatable interaction of gazes. Jürgen Habermas notes, "The experience released from the ruptured shell of the aura was, however, already contained in the experience of the aura itself: the metamorphosis of the object into a counterpart. Thereby a whole field of surprising correspondences between animate and inanimate nature is opened up, wherein even *things* encounter us in the structures of frail intersubjectivity."[63] Habermas's version of that intersubjectivity is, to be sure, more harmonious and reciprocal than the dialogic heteroglossia of Bakhtin, but he insightfully recognizes the importance of multiple subjectivities (indeed, of objects metamorphosed into subjectivities) in Benjamin's concept of *Erfahrung*. If such a reading of absolute experience is allowed, and admittedly it is highly speculative, it might help

rebut the charge of recent critics like Leo Bersani that Benjamin was hopelessly nostalgic for a putative lost wholeness, which came dangerously
close to the fascist aestheticization of politics he decried.[64]

However one interprets the political implications of absolute experience,
the *style indirect libre* or the middle voice, Benjamin's contention that experience is a multifaceted and internally contested concept has thus been confirmed by the linguistic evidence of novels that Benjamin himself failed to
appreciate. Whether we then conclude that absolute experience has virtually vanished from the world or that its utopian spark remains hidden in
the pages of those novels, waiting somehow to be actualized by their
readers in ways that are impossible to foretell, is a question that no one can
confidently answer.

5

The Limits of Limit-Experience:

Bataille and Foucault

✳

The weakness of Christianity, according to Bataille, is its inability to disengage the non-discursive operations from discourse itself, its confusion of experience with discourse, and thus its reduction to the possibilities of discourse what largely exceeds it. —Julia Kristeva[1]

Perhaps no term has been as heatedly contested in recent Anglo-American cultural debates as "experience." Historians concerned with the issues of agency and structure, epistemologists seeking a ground for reliable knowledge, anthropologists anxious about the sources of ethnographic authority, political theorists wrestling with the implications of identity politics, literary critics grappling with the intricacies of representation and discourse, all have struggled to make sense of a term that Hans-Georg Gadamer has rightly called "one of the most obscure that we have."[2]

Although the results defy easy summary, those theorists who have taken to heart what has become known as "the linguistic turn" and learned from that heterogeneous body of thought categorized, for better or worse, as poststructuralism are far more suspicious of the self-evident value of experience than those who have not. Appeals to the authority of something called experience—or even more emphatically, "lived experience"—they distrust as a naive, indeed ideologically pernicious, residue of earlier epistemologies, which they typically identify with empiricism or phenomenology.

Two recent examples will suffice.[3] In a 1991 essay entitled "The Evidence of Experience," the historian Joan W. Scott critizes R. G. Collingwood, E. P. Thompson, Raymond Williams, and John Toews for assuming a false foundationalist ground for their narratives in prereflective experience.

Whether the privileged term is class, gender, or race, any attempt to unify historical experience around a coherent identity—either that of the historical actors or that of the historian capable of "reexperiencing" their acts—will of necessity, she argues, be ideological. Although conceding that we cannot expunge the word from our vocabularies, Scott nonetheless exhorts us to deconstruct its self-evidential quality by "focussing on processes of identity production, insisting on the discursive nature of 'experience' and on the politics of its construction. Experience is at once always already an interpretation and something that needs to be interpreted."[4]

Even more recently, the feminist theorists Elizabeth J. Bellamy and Artemis Leontis have cautioned against a "politics of experience" based on the claim that the "personal is the political" by drawing on Althusserian and left poststructuralist critiques of ideologically sutured subjectivity, most notably those of Teresa de Lauretis, Ernesto Laclau, and Chantal Mouffe.[5] Providing a modest genealogy of the term, Bellamy and Leontis seek to subvert the tendency to essentialize and reify "experience" as a transhistorical ground of knowledge and politics, an intuitive epistemology, as they put it, "without a method."[6] Acknowledging with Scott that the word cannot, however, be entirely avoided, they propose what they call a distinctly "postmodern' as opposed to "poststructuralist" version of it, in which "experience-as-antagonism would then be defined as the (not readily) locatable intersection of the multiple and conflictual constructions of sexual difference that are constitutive of the category of 'woman.' "[7]

But despite such distinctions, it is clear that these critics of a putatively foundationalist notion of experience, and they are not isolated examples, draw much of their ammunition from the assumed lessons of poststructuralist thought, which they claim fatally undermine the notion of coherent subjectivity subtending any belief in the self-evidence of experience. For such critics, despite the occasional nuance in their formulations, discourse, textuality, language, and structures of power provide the matrix out of which experience emerges, not vice versa. To posit experience as itself a ground is thus a misleading attribution of a constructive capacity to what is itself only a rhetorically or discursively constructed category.

Their reading of poststructuralism's lessons, it should be conceded, is given credence by the critiques of certain versions of experience by a number of leading thinkers forced to huddle under this categorical umbrella in

the Anglo-American reception of their ideas. Thus, for example, Jacques
Derrida does say in *Of Grammatology* that experience "belongs to the history
of metaphysics and we can only use it under erasure [*sous rature*]. 'Experience' has always designated the relationship with a presence, whether that
relationship had the form of consciousness or not."[8] Louis Althusser does
argue in *Lenin and Philosophy* that ideology is identical with "the 'lived' experience of human existence itself."[9] And Jean-François Lyotard does claim in
The Differend that experience "can be described only by means of a phenomenological dialectic," which explains why it is "the word of [Hegel's] *Phenomenology of Mind*, the 'science of the experience of consciousness.' "[10]

   In all of these cases, the target is "experience" construed as unified,
holistic, coherent, and present to itself. More precisely, it is understood to
embody these characteristics in either one of two guises: as a marker for
the immediacy of lived, prereflexive encounters between self and world
privileged by the tradition of *Lebensphilosophie* from Dilthey on under the
rubric of *Erlebnis*, or as a marker for the cumulative wisdom over time
produced by the interaction of self and world that is generally called *Erfahrung*. Although the latter achieves its unity only at the end of a dialectical
process of *Bildung*, what makes both of these concepts problematic for the
critics cited above is the assumption of coherence, intelligibility, and plenitudinous presence at their root. Whereas certain earlier thinkers privileged
one version of experience over another—Martin Buber, for example, gave
priority to *Erlebnis* over *Erfahrung*, while Walter Benjamin did the opposite[11]—from the point of view of the poststructuralists invoked by their
Anglo-American followers, both are equally inadequate. The very quest for
an authentic experience lost in the modern world they damn as yet another
version of the nostalgic yearning for a presence and immediacy that never
has existed and never will.[12]

   But if it is true that poststructuralist scripture can be cited to buttress a
general critique of experience, what is sometimes forgotten in the Anglo-
American eagerness to draw on its authority is that other so-called poststructuralists have been far less hostile. Indeed, as this essay hopes to
show, for at least two of the major thinkers ordinarily given a central place
in the poststructuralist canon, Georges Bataille and Michel Foucault, experience—understood in a specifically nonpsychological manner that was
often lost in translation—was a term far more honorific than pejorative.[13]
By attending to their complicated, if not always fully coherent, usages, we

may be able to go beyond the increasingly sterile debate between those who stubbornly hold on to a naive notion of experience and those who scornfully reject any such notion as necessarily naive. Although, as my title indicates, I think there are limits as well to their ideas of "limit-experiences," which I will discuss in conclusion, Foucault and Bataille nonetheless provide us with possible ways to transcend the either/or alternatives that characterize at least the current Anglo-American debate on the question.[14]

✳

In 1978, the Italian Communist Party journalist Duccio Trombadori interviewed Michel Foucault on his intellectual trajectory. A few years earlier in *The Archaeology of Knowledge*, Foucault had appeared to be retreating from his positive evocation of "experience" in such works as *Madness and Civilization* because, he explained, it had depended on "an anonymous and general subject of history."[15] But now he told his Italian interlocutor instead that all the books that he had written "constitute an experience for me that I'd like to be as rich as possible. An experience is something you come out of changed."[16] Rather than books that seek to capture the truth about the world or demonstrate a theoretical point, his were experiments in self-exploration, which he then invited his readers to share.

Pressed by Trombadori to classify his notion of experience, Foucault responded by distinguishing between the phenomenologist's version and that of another tradition with which he clearly identified:

> The phenomenologist's experience is basically a way of organizing perception (*regard réflexif*) of any aspect of daily, lived experience in its transitory form. Nietzsche, Bataille, and Blanchot, on the contrary, try through experience to reach that point of life which lies as close as possible to the impossibility of living, which lies at the limit or extreme. They attempt to gather the maximum amount of intensity and impossibility at the same time. The work of the phenomenologist, however, essentially consists of unfolding the entire field of possibilities connected to daily experience.[17]

Phenomenology also erred, Foucault continued, in trying

> to grasp the significance of daily experience in order to reaffirm the fundamental character of the subject, of the self, of its transcendental

functions. On the contrary, experience according to Nietzsche, Blanchot and Bataille has rather the task of "tearing" the subject from
itself in such a way that it is no longer the subject as such, or that it is
completely "other" than itself so that it may arrive at its annihilation,
its dissociation.[18]

Such a notion of an experience that undermines the subject, Foucault called
a "limit-experience," because it transgresses the limits of coherent subjectivity as it functions in everyday life, indeed threatens the very possibility of
life—or rather the life of the individual—itself.

Foucault thus provided a vigorous defense of experience, but as he further developed its meaning, it revealed certain paradoxical implications.
For not only did he affirm a proactive notion of experience—the "task of
'tearing' the subject from itself"—but he also endorsed a reactive one:
experience as a post facto reconstruction of that action. Experience, he
explained, "is always a fiction, something constructed, which exists only
after it has been made, not before; it isn't something that is 'true,' but it has
been a reality."[19] While claiming that his works were in large measure
derived from "direct personal experience[s],"[20] earlier encounters with
madness, hospitals, illness, and death, they were nonetheless themselves,
qua intellectual exercises, experience-producing. For experiences did not
simply happen, as perhaps the phenomenologists had thought, but were
written aprés coup, after the fact. Moreover, Foucault further explained, the
writing was not merely for oneself, but also for others. "An experience,"
Foucault claimed, "is, of course, something one has alone; but it cannot
have its full impact unless the individual manages to escape from pure subjectivity in such a way that others can—I won't say re-experience exactly—
but at least cross paths with it or retrace it."[21]

So paradoxical a notion of experience—at once the task of personal,
active self-laceration and the retrospective written fiction that makes it
available for others to appropriate for their own lives—defies easy formulation. Whereas the former usage implies experience without a strong notion
of subjectivity, indeed leading to its subversion, the latter entails some sort
of authorial persona that is powerful enough to represent experience in a
kind of "secondary elaboration"[22] sufficiently coherent to make sense to
those who did not share it from the start. What Foucault seems to mean
by limit-experience, then, is a curiously contradictory mixture of self-

expansion and self-annihilation, immediate, proactive spontaneity and fictional retrospection, personal inwardness and communal interaction.

Not surprisingly, the recent biography—or more precisely, "philosophical life"—of Foucault by James Miller, which makes limit-experience its central organizing principle, has some difficulty in providing a fully satisfactory account of its implications.[23] Miller, who draws on the Trombadori interview as well as on the testimony of Foucault's lover Daniel Defert, builds his reconstruction of Foucault's life around the quest for limit-experiences, in particular those that involved mind-expanding drugs, sadomasochistic sexuality, and the risk of actual death. His Foucault is a Faustian daredevil, who is willing to embark on the dangerous experimentation with his self that is one implication of the word "experience" (an implication most explicitly maintained in French). A philosophical, political, and sexual "mystic," Foucault, as Miller portrays him, knew that "the personal *was* political—and the political *was* personal—in ways that may be impossible to fathom fully."[24] He is thus the most recent figure in a tradition that Foucault himself identified and honored, a tradition that included such figures as Diogenes, Sade, Hölderlin, de Nerval, Nietzsche, Van Gogh, Roussel, and Artaud.

But Miller also understands that Foucault's notion of experience involves a retrospective fictionalization, a way to wrest coherence from chaos. Following the model of Alexander Nehamas's acclaimed study of Nietzsche, which interprets the philosopher's life as a deliberate exercise in aesthetic self-fashioning,[25] he thus struggles to find a figure in the apparently bewildering carpet that comprised Foucault's life and work. Noting the late Foucault's interest in Seneca, Marcus Aurelius, and Plutarch, Miller discerns the Stoics' project of meditation on experience in order to script a meaningful form of life, an *ethos*, in Foucault's own personal trajectory. The Foucault he constructs for us is thus self-consciously committed to the quest for limit-experiences, experiences whose intensity and multiplicity will help recapture the Dionysian oneness prior to individuation and alienation, but only in the aesthetic form that betokens Apollonian intelligibility. His, in short, is a Foucault who realizes—or dies in the quest to realize—the tragic vision Nietzsche famously saw in ancient Greece, a vision whose personal manifestation implied ultimate reconciliation with our inner *daimon*, the singular destiny that fate had assigned us.

Although in certain ways productive, Miller's reading of Foucault's life and work as a heroic pursuit of tragic limit-experiences is ultimately inadequate to the complexities of the theme. For it allows him to smooth over the tensions latent in one of Foucault's most significant distinctions, that between so-called negative and positive experiences, Miller, to be sure, acknowledges the opposition. He identifies negative experience with those "aspects of human existence that seem to defy rational understanding,"[26] such as madness, criminality, and sadomasochistic self-sacrifice. He recognizes that the valorization of negative experience is a lesson that Foucault learned largely from Bataille. But then he proceeds to reconcile it—too easily, I would argue—with its opposite, positive experience: "It was Bataille's peculiar genius," Miller contends, "to suggest that eroticism, taken to its most extreme limits in sado-masochistic practices, was a uniquely creative way to grapple with otherwise unconscious and unthinkable aspects of this 'negative experience,' turning it into something positive, enabling a person to 'say yes' in the spirit of Nietzsche—even to a recurrent fantasy of death."[27]

This reading of Bataille's influence on Foucault is problematic, because in it experience, even in its most seemingly unrecuperable negative version, becomes raw material for a higher level sublimation that restores precisely the plenitudinous presence that the annihilation of the self would seem to deny. It does so by tacitly recuperating that presence through an assimilation of negative experience to a project that recalls the quest of religious mystics for ecstatic fusion with the divine. Miller, to be sure, is able to cite passages in Bataille which do appear to endorse a "negative theology founded on mystical experience" and ones in Foucault which speak positively of an "original innocence,"[28] but in so doing, he underplays the creative tensions that are actively at work in the interview with Trombadori. As a result, we get a unified notion of experience, a specular version that implicitly duplicates the dialectical account of phenomenological *Bildung* that Lyotard and other critics of Hegelian sublation find so troubling.[29]

In other words, Miller ultimately privileges one moment in the mélange of meanings Foucault himself attributes to experience, the one which recognizes it as a post facto fiction, something written *après coup* rather than immediately lived. "In the end," Miller admits, "I was forced to ascribe to Foucault a persistent and purposeful self, inhabiting one and the same body throughout his mortal life, more or less consistently accounting for his actions and attitudes to others as well as himself, and understanding his life as a teleologically structured quest."[30] It is not clear, however, if Miller thinks he is being forced by his need as an author to find a pattern, or by Foucault's own impulse—let's call it Stoic—to script his experience retrospectively, producing an intelligibility Miller is then merely echoing, or by Miller's discovery of a teleology that was really operative at the very beginning of Foucault's project like a personal daimon assigned him by fate. But whatever the source of the compulsion, the result is a version of Foucault's life and works that is a powerful secondary elaboration. Put another way, the yea-saying Nietzschean gesture of making positive all negative experience, which Miller invokes in his account of Bataille's putative influence on Foucault, works to smooth over the palpable tensions, even contradictions, that make the concept of limit-experience so productive and fascinating.

Miller not only provides a problematic sublimation of negative into positive experience, but he also elides the peculiarly communal or nonindividual impulse in limit-experience as well. When Miller does introduce a non-individual dimension into his teleological narrative of Foucault's development, which he does especially in his attempt to write a sympathetic account of the S/M scene, he bases it on a tacitly liberal notion of consenting adults, who trust their partners to respect their dignity, even as they seem to be abusing it.[31] Possessing the "persistent and purposeful self" he attributes to Foucault, the players in the "game" or "theater" of S/M—metaphors he deliberately invokes to show that none of the cruelty is for real—are ultimately pedestrian figures, "as nonviolent and well-adjusted as any other segment of the population."[32]

We can see just how problematic such a well-intentioned exculpation is, if we investigate Foucault's debt to Bataille's notion of experience a bit more deeply than does Miller. For there is little in Bataille's life and work that lends itself to so anodyne an understanding of the concept. First, what has to be acknowledged is the impossibility of rendering that life and work into an organic, aesthetically formed whole. Significantly, the major biography of Bataille by Michel Surya has as its subtitle "la mort à l'oeuvre," which, among other things, suggests death to the work of art. The frequent reproach to Bataille by his enemies, such as André Breton and Jean-Paul Sartre, that he hypocritically preached violence and transgression, but practiced the quiet life of a librarian, provides a useful insight into his concept of experience: that it resists being totalized into a meaningful pattern in the manner of Nehamas's Nietzsche or Miller's Foucault.

Second, it must be remembered that experience was not always a privileged term in Bataille's vocabulary, and needs to be put into play with others that nuance it in important ways, such as sovereignty, nonknowledge, and communication. It emerged into prominence only during the Second World War, after Bataille's unsuccessful efforts at creating a collective intellectual *cum* political community in the Contre-attaque and Acéphale groups and at the Collège de Sociologie during the late 1930s. Perhaps because he realized that his own project had veered dangerously close to that of the fascists he was trying to combat, perhaps as a result of his health problems—he had suffered a severe recurrence of tuberculosis in 1942—or perhaps simply because the Nazi occupiers were not very tolerant of such experiments, Bataille seems to have retreated into a solitude very different from the public activity of the previous decade.[33] The result was a new emphasis on what Bataille called, in the title of the first volume in his *Somme athéologique*, begun in 1941 and published in 1943, "inner experience."[34]

Many of the themes of his earlier work—sacrifice, the sacred, violence, the *informe* (formlessness), debasement, and *dépense* (waste or expenditure)—now resurfaced in an apparently new key. One recent commentator, Allan Stoekl, has gone so far as to call it the register of the personal, in which "the experience itself is *one individual's*, and is at least related to certain meditative practices."[35] Whereas the earlier Bataille seemed to be supporting the heterodox sect in opposition to the orthodox church, now his atheological, negative religion, Stoekl suggests, rejected even sectarian solidarity in favor of the lonely path of a Nietzschean superman, whose inner experience is radically incommunicable and completely his own.

Such an understanding of inner experience, however, presupposes notions of interiority and individuality that Bataille was at pains to subvert—at least at certain moments in his text. Indeed, the text of *Inner Experience* itself, it might be argued, calls into question the ideal of personalized aesthetic redemption that underlies an attempt like Miller's to turn negative into positive experience and Stoekl's to stress its individual and personal nature. As Denis Hollier pointed out a number of years ago, *Inner Experience* is an autotransgressive book: it is not a book. It took too long to write for that. So long that one might say that time itself wrote it—is inscribed in it. Bataille wrote it with time, and in defiance of planning. He put time into it, in the literal sense. Which precludes our reading this book in any way other than in the space of textual heterogeneity outside the book. The texts composing it are not contemporary: no simultaneity ever existed among them. Their juxtaposition makes us read the gap making them different from the project that gave birth to them.[36]

Not only in formal—or more precisely, *informe-al* terms—, but in substantive ones as well, *Inner Experience* undermines any attempt to read it as a plea for positive, personal, individual, fully interiorized experience. Nor, despite Bataille's initial introduction of the terminology of mysticism with its goal of fusing subject and object in God,[37] should it be understood as a plea for a larger positive unity with the universe. For it is precisely the impossibility of such a successful fusion that Bataille suggests is one of the most powerful limits of inner experience—indeed, why inner experience at its most negative is indistinguishable from limit-experience itself. As Derrida remarked in his seminal essay on Bataille, "From Restricted to General Economy: A Hegelianism without Reserve,"

> that which *indicates itself* as interior experience is not an experience, because it is related to no presence, to no plenitude, but only to the "impossible" it "undergoes" in torture. This experience above all is not interior: and if it seems to be such because it is related to nothing else, to no exterior (except in the modes of nonrelation, secrecy, and rupture), it is also completely *exposed*—to torture—naked, open to the exterior, with no interior reserve or feelings, profoundly superficial.[38]

Although Derrida's definition of experience here is perhaps too restricted—identified, as it is, entirely with the plenitudinous presence that Bataille would call positive experience—his observations about the impossibility of full interiority in negative experience are nonetheless valid.

For Bataille expressly—if, to be sure, not at every moment[39]—repudiated any hope for the successful overcoming of the fissures and gaps of the self through totalizing experience, which would make of self and world a harmonious whole. He thus denied the complete equivalence of inner experience and the ecstasy of the mystic.[40] "What characterizes such an experience," he cautioned, "which does not proceed from a revelation—where nothing is revealed either, if not the unknown—is that it never announces anything reassuring."[41] Likewise, it repudiates the consolations of philosophy, in particular the Hegelian hope that "the highest knowledge" can be made "an extension of inner experience. But this *phenomenology* lends to knowledge the value of a goal which one attains through experience. This is an ill-assorted match: the measure given to experience is at once too much and not great enough."[42] This is not to say, however, that inner experience is simply the opposite of critical reason, as some of Bataille's critics have assumed, but rather that it cannot be ever fully reconciled with it in its positive form, in its Hegelian guise as absolute knowledge.[43]

Philosophy can never, in fact, successfully totalize because it is a part of the world of profane work, whereas inner experience ultimately derives from the sacred, a realm in which *dépense* rather than production is the ruling principle. The Durkheimian dichotomy between the sacred and the profane is a defining moment of the human condition. As Bataille was to put it in *Erotism*, "it is difficult to imagine the life of a philosopher continually or at least fairly often beside himself. We come back to the essential experience dividing time into working time and sacred time."[44]

Another solution rejected by genuine inner experience is the self-control of the ascetic, who tries to master his internal conflicts and reach a state of oneness with the divine through self-abnegation. "My principle against ascesis," Bataille writes, "is that the extreme limit is accessible through excess, not through want. . . . Ascesis asks for deliverance, salvation, the possession of the most desirable object. In ascesis, value is not that of experience alone, independent of pleasure or suffering; it is always a beatitude, a deliverance, which we strive to procure for ourselves."[45] Sovereignty, in Bataille's special use of the term, is thus the opposite of mastery, the denial of salvation through self-control.[46] Although privation along with pleasure—in the sense of *jouissance*—is an essential element of that sovereignty, it can never lead to a state of bliss beyond the anguish that feeds it. As Jean-Michel Heimonet put it, inner experience is "necessary in order to expiate the inherent will of the subject to 'become everything,' to 'become God' himself."[47]

Still another consolation negative experience denies itself is the project of action as deliberate self-fashioning. "Inner experience," Bataille explains, "is the opposite of action. Nothing more. 'Action' is utterly dependent on project,"[48] which is itself informed by discursive intentions. Not only is it problematic because it raises reflection to too high a level, but also because it situates true existence in a future state, thus undermining the moment of presence—albeit not a plenitudinous presence—that is essential to inner experience.[49] Despite its apparent similarity to the "inner experience" celebrated a few years earlier by the German writer Ernst Jünger, whose *Kampf als innere Erlebnis* (1922) had glorified war as an aesthetic, amoral escape from bourgeois normality, Bataille's version rejected heroic activism, even if it may have shared some of Jünger's fascination for the communal implications of the *Fronterlebnis*.[50]

With all of these warnings against misconstruing inner experience, did Bataille, we might well wonder, ever tell us what negative inner experience actually is? Repeating the ploy of his celebrated dictionary definition of *informe*, which claimed it was a task—the task of debasement—rather than a word with a positive meaning,[51] he, in fact, resisted turning it into a straightforward statement, preferring to see it as a kind of force instead: "The difference between inner experience and philosophy resides principally in this: that in experience, what is stated is nothing, if not a means and even, as much as a means, an obstacle; what counts is no longer the statement of wind, but the wind."[52] At once a means and an obstacle, a force not a form, negative inner experience thus signals a paradoxical relation to the self-grounding of the subject. "By virtue of the fact that it is negation of other values, other authorities," Bataille writes, "experience, having a positive existence, becomes itself positive value and authority."[53] But then he immediately adds in a footnote, "the paradox in the authority of experience: based on challenge, it is the challenging of authority; positive challenge, man's authority defined as the challenging of himself."[54]

If experience may be construed as its own authority, based on no exterior criteria such as theology or reason, it is nonetheless an authority that is always undermining itself. Even the definition of experience's goal as ecstatic oneness or mystical fusion cannot be simply affirmed because it suggests a secure knowledge that is too reassuring, too positive. In its place, Bataille put Blanchot's principle of "contestation," which produced an intransitive affirmation of nothing, as Foucault himself noted in his tribute to Bataille.[55] Because it resists coherence, it undermines all notions of specular subjectivity that seek to place the metasubject without and the microsubject within in a mirror relationship of perfect mimesis. As Kristeva, tacitly invoking Bataille's close relationship to Lacan, writes, "inner experience is a crossing that is against the grain of specularization as the initial moment of the constitution of the subject."[56]

But if it rejects the specular mimesis or ecstatic fusion of inner and outer, it also implies a breach in the absolute integrity of interiority which seems to be privileged by the very term "inner experience," a breach which allowed Derrida, as we have seen, to say that it was superficial, exposed to torture from without, and lacking in internal reserves.[57] In one sense, then, limit-experience means that there is no uncrossable boundary between subject and object, ego and alter, self and world. "In experience," Bataille writes,

> there is no longer a limited existence. There a man is not distinguished in any way from others: in him what is torrential is lost within others. The so simple commandment: "Be that ocean," linked to the *extreme limit*, at the same time makes of a man, a multitude, a desert. It is an expression which resumes and makes precise the sense of a community.[58]

Although there is no absolute exteriority beyond experience, an impossibility assured by the death of the only fully transcendent being, God, negative inner experience erases—but does not simply obliterate—the boundary between self and other. The community it founds and the communication it fosters thus necessitate going beyond the purely personal or individual.[59] As he put it in *Literature and Evil*, "I am sure about one thing: humanity is not composed of isolated beings but of communication between them."[60] Limit-experience, contrary to Miller's reading of Foucault, is not a singular exercise in aesthetic self-fashioning through experiments in transgression. It inevitably involves others, but in more complicated ways than the contractual reciprocity implied by Miller's depiction of the S/M community of role-playing, consenting adults.

Bataille's notions of community and communication have been notoriously difficult to get in focus. One recent commentator, Rebecca Comay, has suggested a comparison with Walter Benjamin's idea of *Erfahrung*:

that communifying "experience" already lost by the time of the industrial era, taken up or overwritten by the circuit of productivity and exchange. In reality, such experience had been lost long before it could ever begin. For Benjamin knew well that there was never a moment of originary plenitude to be recapitulated or "reexperienced": Erfahrung—the experience lost—is nothing other than the experience of loss. Experience reveals only the truth that there never was an "experience."[61]

To put it in somewhat different terms, the journey (Fahrt) of experience is a dangerous one without any assurance of home-coming, as the Latin root—ex-periri, which also gives us the word peril—suggests.[62]

In Comay's account, however, Heidegger even more than Benjamin provides the most useful comparison. For not only did Heidegger reject the Diltheyan notion of immediate Erlebnis and the Hegelian alternative of dialectical Erfahrung, but he also came to understand the importance of the economy of the gift in leading to the dispossession of the centred self and the subversion of the possibility of perfectly equal exchange—subverting, we might say, the civil reciprocity of Miller's consenting adult sadomasochists.

The most extensive Heideggerian reading of community and experience in Bataille can be found in Jean-Luc Nancy's The Inoperative Community.[63] Nancy understands Inner Experience as a product of Bataille's disillusionment with the nostalgic quest for mystical communion and sacred immanence Bataille had pursued in the 1930s, when he was involved with the Surrealists, Contre-Attaque, Acéphale and the Collège de Sociologie. Nancy does not, however, construe it as a retreat into personal inwardness and individual self-absorption. Bataille, he argues, is still convinced that community is vital, that "outside of community, there is no experience."[64] But it is not a community to be consciously constructed, the result of a collective project of self-fashioning. Instead, the community is what Blanchot would have called désoeuvrée (inoperative, unworked, unproduced, at loose ends, or, to borrow Ann Smock's translation, uneventful),[65] and thus unlike a poesis, a self-conscious work of art in the traditional sense of the term.

Rather than a community of pure immanence and unimpeded intimacy, in which the members are part of a plenitudinous and meaningful totality, the inoperative or unworked community is composed of finite human beings whose relations to each other are forged precisely through their mutual finitude. Bataille, Nancy writes,

> is without doubt the one who experienced, first, or most acutely, the modern experience of community as neither a work to be produced, nor a lost communion, but rather as space itself, and the spacing of the experience of the outside, of the outside-of-self. The crucial point of this experience was the exigency, reversing all nostalgia and all metaphysics, of a "clear consciousness" of separation. . . .[66]

The consciousness of that inevitable separation, of the impossibility of absolute unity, was provided, Nancy suggests, by an awareness of the awesome fact of death, the inevitability of human finitude.

Here Nancy's Heideggerian pedigree is perhaps most apparent, but it is a Heideggerianism with a twist. Whereas Heidegger's emphasis was always placed on the need for Dasein to accept its own "being-toward-death," Nancy stresses awareness instead of the death of the other as constitutive of community. "Community," he claims, "is revealed in the death of others; hence it is always revealed to others. Community is what takes place always through others and for others. . . . If community is revealed in the death of others, it is because death itself is the true community of I's that are not *egos*."[67]

Acknowledging the finitude of others is a quintessential, community-inducing limit-experience in several senses. First, it resists sublating those deaths into a meaningful, theodicy-like narrative in which they become somehow part of a larger story of redemption, elevated to the level of the infinite; instead, they remain in all their finite ineffability a reproach to the hubris of those who want to reconcile experience and absolute knowledge. Second, it provides a check to the mistaken belief that communication means specular identification, for although we can understand the death of the other from the outside, we cannot fully participate in it or experience it authentically "from within" (in the traditional sense of pure interiority). Communication also means something very different from intersubjective interaction in the Habermasian sense, because the *telos* of perfect understanding Habermas imputes to language in its pragmatic guise is ultimately specular in implication.[68]

But third, because we are reminded by the death of the other of our own mortality, thus exposing our own inevitable finitude, it prevents us from being able to turn our "own" experience into a fully meaningful narrative. For our deaths can never be integrated into our own stories through a retrospective totalization; we, after all, are no longer around to provide the secondary elaboration required.[69] Experiencing the death of the alter, even from the "outside," compels us to experience the alterity within ourselves.

Although Nancy notes that the disillusioned Bataille tended to restrict his notion of community to a "subjective sovereignty of lovers and of the artist—and with this, also the exception of darting 'heterogeneous' flashes cleanly split from the 'homogenous' order of society with which they do not communicate,"[70] he argues that an enlarged notion of community can be derived from the complicated interplay of limits that is communicated in this way. In a later work, The Experience of Freedom of 1988, Nancy presents an even more elaborate defense of the links between experience and freedom, which involves the act of founding a polity as a limit-experience (the founding of a city, he notes, sets up its limits) and which claims experience is not simply the negative of the subject, but its extension to its limits ("the peril of the crossed limit that is nothing other than the limit of essence [and therefore existence], the singular outline of shared being").[71] He also nuances what might seem the morbid stress on death in his earlier work by including birth among those experiences that are known to one only through the experiences of others.[72] Nancy's complicated and abstruse argument is beyond the scope of this essay; suffice it to say that he develops a notion of limit-experience that takes us very far away indeed from the model presented in Miller's account of Foucault.

Nancy's ruminations on experience also reinforce the point with which we began: that contrary to the dominant Anglo-American reception of poststructuralist thought, experience is a term that cannot be effortlessly dissolved in a network of discursive relations. Indeed, as Kristeva argues in the epigraph about Christianity cited at the beginning of this essay, it is precisely the reduction of experience to discourse that Bataille, and Foucault as well, cautions us against. Instead, we have to be attentive to the various ways in which different concepts of experience—negative as well as positive, limit as well as ordinary, nonsubjective as well as subjective—prevent us from ever having a simple foundational version on which to base an epistemology or from which to launch a politics.

But having learned these lessons should not prevent us in turn from asking hard questions about the limits of limit-experience itself. For even in its more problematized forms, the appeal to experience may still harbor certain problems that need to be addressed. Is it, for example, a contradiction to privilege subject-annihilating ecstatic experience and at the same time try to talk about that experience "objectively" and impersonally? Is the result, as Habermas has charged in his critique of Bataille, "an inconclusive to-and-fro?"[73] Can we prevent the ultimate transfiguration of a negative experience into a positive one, as Barbara Herrnstein Smith has claimed must happen when we give value to the seemingly valueless phenomena we call loss or waste?[74] Can, in other words, Foucault succeed for very long in preventing his "experience-books" from becoming reified secondary elaborations in the hands of others, such as Miller, who then aestheticize his life as well into a retrospectively positive form? Can negative experience with all of its denial of authority, structure, and coherence provide a basis for the building of institutions, or is it, as Richard Wolin has warned, an inherently anti-institutional ideology with unexpected similarities to the old liberal notion of "negative freedom," "freedom from" rather than the "freedom to" known as "positive freedom?"[75] Is a notion of communication based on the experience of shared finitude, of unsublatable mortality, really sufficient to generate helpful answers to the practical problems that beset the living, problems that refuse to disappear when limit-experiences miraculously disrupt quotidian existence? Is there, in fact, a danger that an elite group of experience virtuosos will become indifferent to the legitimate claims of those who lead more mundane lifes?

These and a host of other questions anxiously accompany the restoration of experience as a central concern of cultural theory at the present time. It is, however, the great merit of Foucault, Bataille, and other so-called poststructuralist defenders of its importance that they have forced us to go beyond the sterile choice between naive experiential immediacy and the no less naive discursive mediation of that experience that has for too long seemed our only alternative. The limits of limit-experience have thus in some sense become equivalent to the very limits of critical theory today.

6

No Power to the Soviets

✳

The lessons for the left of the revolutions of 1989–90 in Eastern Europe are still being absorbed, slowly and sometimes painfully. The Leninist model of building a socialist society, long bereft of any serious support outside of the party bureaucracies legitimated by it, has been conclusively discredited. No longer even able to claim that it can effectively mobilize an economy and provide for its citizens' well-being, Leninism has forfeited its pretense to be the vanguard of anything but political repression. Its philosophical weaknesses, often criticized by a host of critics from all sectors of the political spectrum, have finally been pragmatically confirmed; the Marxist dream of unifying theory and practice has ironically been realized.

The demise of the Leninist model is lamented by virtually no one, on either the left or right. In fact, for many leftists, it has seemed to clear the air, allowing a more hopeful alternative to emerge in its aftermath. Without the need to provide elaborate justifications for a system that always required a certain *sacrifizio d'intelletto*, the left can finally free itself from the embarrassment of having to rationalize away its own doubts. Or at least so it has seemed to many who have resisted the temptation to abandon all of their radical hopes and critical indignation about the evils of capitalism.

Still, the window of opportunity has appeared much smaller and harder to open than might have been thought before the changes. In East Germany, in particular, the non-Leninist left, exemplified by figures like the novelist Christa Wolf, was singularly unsuccessful in turning the events to its purposes in the days after the Wall crumbled. Even the Social Democrats found themselves left behind by the nationalist desire for reunification.

Perhaps after the passage of time and the romance with free market economics sours, the pendulum will swing a bit in the other direction, but it is difficult to muster much enthusiasm about the results. For Leninism was not the only socialist casualty of the recent events; no less called into question, at least implicitly, was another model of emancipatory organization, and one that had occupied a central role in the socialist imaginary for more than a century.

This alternative model was that of the workers' council or soviet, which has often functioned as the utopian counterpoint to the "realistic" Leninist stress on the party.[1] Preserved in name only in the title of the Soviet Union, it remained nonetheless a vital rallying point for libertarian socialist critics of authoritarian, bureaucratic, statist communism. Rooted in the syndicalism of the nineteenth century, councils became historically important at various moments in the revolutions of our own—1905 and 1917 in Russia, 1918 to 1920 in Germany, Austria, and Italy, and 1956 in Hungary.[2] Along with the soldiers' councils formed within the disintegrating armies at the end of World War I, they provided the stimulus to a general proliferation of direct democratic organizations. Even intellectuals like Kurt Hiller and Heinrich Mann briefly fashioned themselves into a *Rat der geistigen Arbeiter* (Council of Brain Workers) in the early Weimar years.

The councils, to be sure, were never able to establish themselves for very long as the basis of a stable system. But rather than a drawback, their being largely untested proved a kind of boon. For uncompromised as they were by the exigencies of power, they could remain the repository of phantasmic hopes as the political and economic organizational form that would realize rather than betray the promise of socialism. Their prefigurative function was thus ironically enhanced by their practical defeat.

As such, the councils served as the stimulus to a remarkable tradition of intellectual creativity. Antonio Gramsci during his *Ordine Nuovo* period, Georg Lukács before he repudiated his "left infantilism," the Dutch "Council Communists" Anton Pannekoek and Herman Gorter, Karl Korsch, Otto Rühle, Max Horkheimer, Cornelius Castoriadis, André Gorz, Paul Mattick, the Yugoslav *Praxis* circle, and a wide variety of other heterodox Marxists all at one time or another posited the council as the foundation of the new society. For what can be called the "redemptive" impulse in socialist theory, the council often provided the antidote to the bureaucratic state.[3] In fact,

Western Marxism as a whole, it has been suggested by Russell Jacoby,[4] had its roots in the "left communist" enthusiasm for the councils in the immediate post–World War I era.

Although the era after the Second World War lacked any comparable revolutionary ferment, the council ideal did not die. When Tito set out to chart his own path to socialism, he launched—to be sure, from above rather than below—workers' councils in 1950. In May 1968, belief in their virtues served as the litmus test of true radicalism for militants of such movements as the International Situationists or *Socialisme ou Barbarie*, as well as for many Marxists with a Human Face in Czechoslovakia. As late as the brief and abortive rise of Eurocommunism in the 1970s, the councils retained their talismanic allure. Until very recently, dissident and emigré Eastern European intellectuals continued to find them attractive.[5] Even non-Marxists like Hannah Arendt could find in the councils, stripped to be sure of their irrelevant economic function, the modern incarnation of the dream of political freedom first embodied in the Greek polis.[6]

What made the councils so attractive was a combination of putative virtues. Unlike the trade union, which was a defensive organization of workers still enmeshed in the wage relations of capitalism, they prefigured the day when self-management would mean the producers had full control over the means and the fruits of their production. Because of their relatively small size and autonomous governance, they presented a challenge to centralizing statist versions of socialism based on a command economy in which all the decisions were made from above. Drawing on urban traditions of communal self-rule, which had reasserted themselves during the Paris Commune, they permitted a leftist appropriation of the powerful yearnings for *Gemeinschaft* that had been so successfully exploited by the right.[7] More than merely economic units operative on the factory level, they were also taken to be embodiments of direct political democracy at its most participatory. Indeed, their all-encompassing structure promised to end the very estrangement of the political realm from the economic that was one of the defining characteristics of capitalist alienation.[8] In short, Lenin's slogan "All power to the soviets," although cynically betrayed in the USSR remained a potent source of opposition to the Leninist party state.

Or at least it did until the events of 1989–90. For unlike Budapest in 1956 or Prague in 1968, let alone the more turbulent revolutionary era from 1917 to 1920, no significant attempt has been made, to my knowledge,[9] to create councils as a viable alternative to the demise of the Leninist party state. No spontaneous uprising of autonomous workers has emerged from the rubble of the toppled bureaucracy and sought to proclaim the virtues of absolute self-management. No significant cries have been heard for a utopian overcoming of the distinction between politics and social or economic life. Instead, the revolutions of 1989–90 have paradoxically accepted, even sought, a certain measure of heteronomy in their willingness to hazard entry into the world economic market with all the risks that entails. And instead of calling for a decentralized federation of councils bridging the gap between state and society, they have sought to resurrect the old notion of civil society in creative tension with a no longer omnipotent state. Within that society, the trade union, with Solidarity as the exemplary instance, takes pride of place, not the council.

No explanation of this development could ignore the sheer exhaustion with socialism of any kind that marks the populations of Central and Eastern Europe. So much pernicious nonsense has been said and done in its name that it will take a long time for the stain to be wiped away. But the reasons for the eclipse of the workers' council model are deeper still. They extend well beyond the sorry legacy of what used to be called "actually existing socialism." First, there has been a general reappraisal of democratic theory, which has moved beyond the sterile dichotomy of direct versus representative.[10] Although the ideal of maximizing participatory involvement has by no means been abandoned, the necessity of some institutional framework mediating between rulers and the ruled is now widely accepted. However we understand the public sphere and its role in influencing policy, it is no longer possible, pace Hannah Arendt, to conceptualize it simply in terms of the Greek polis.

With all of its flaws, what the left used to sneer at as "bourgeois democracy" has shown itself more resilient and responsive to the needs of its constituency, or at least large chunks of it, than other alternatives. As commentators like the Italian political theorist Norberto Bobbio have persuasively argued, once the myth of the withering away of the state is left behind, the necessity of a more articulated political structure becomes obvious.[11] Although a great deal can be done to restructure both the state and civil society in more genuinely democratic directions, the overcoming of the distinction between the two in the name of a unified political cum socioeconomic community based on one form, that of councils, sets few hearts aflutter.

Second, the privilege given to workers in the council system, which always troubled commentators like Arendt, has come to seem ever more problematic at a time when the productivist bias of traditional Marxism has come under widespread attack. That is, the contention that the mode of production is the center of the totality of social relations and that workers should therefore be the prime movers in a system of self-management has been challenged by theorists as different as Habermas and Baudrillard. Ecological critics of productivism have joined with feminist critics of the traditional male figuration of the laborer to denounce the reduction of democracy to workplace self-management.[12] Others have emphasized the new importance of what Mark Poster calls the "mode of information" in generating and disseminating meanings through technologies of communication that render direct interaction in councils obsolete.[13] The willing embrace of a measure of heteronomy rather than autonomy mentioned before may reflect as much a desire to get access to the international communications network as the international market. Whatever one makes of the sometimes no less exaggerated claims made by adherents of these newer theories, they have served to undermine confidence in the assumption that socialism can be built from the shop floor up.

Finally, the very concept of the self at the root of notions of self-management has undergone radical revision. The redemptive model of an unalienated, collective subject totally in control of its decisions and their outcomes now seems highly problematic. One need not be a card-carrying poststructuralist to recognize that unified identities, individual or collective, are much more questionable in normative terms than council communist theory assumes. "Subject positions," to use the current jargon, are irreducible to self-constituting agents. Rather than shedding extraneous, "ideological" self-understandings and adopting that of a producer first and foremost, today's selves defiantly resist any one-dimensional definition. The very boundaries of a coherent self seem more porous than before and what is even more important, less threatened by the permeation of its frontiers. Thus, gender issues cut across those of class and cultural identifications complicate economic ones, as the reinvigoration of nationalism in Eastern Europe makes abundantly clear. Victims of ecological disasters also know no distinction between producer and consumer. The very equation of human agency with a strong sense of sovereign subjecthood no longer compels automatic approval.[14]

Even before the revolutions of 1989–90, socialist theory had been struggling to make sense of these changes, as the heated controversy over the post-Marxist redescription of hegemony in discursive terms by Ernesto Laclau and Chantal Mouffe testifies.[15] But whatever the outcome, it is clear that the old reliance on workers' councils as the placeholder of redemption will no longer suffice. Whether the socialist imaginary can be sustained without them is, to be sure, an issue of some concern, at least for those who resist the smug conclusions drawn by Panglossian defenders of capitalist modernization as the best of all possible worlds. The upheavals of the past year have marked an unmistakable watershed in the long history of socialism. What looms on the other side is still uncertain, but neither the bureaucratic statism of Leninism nor its libertarian antithesis seems destined for survival. The soviets died in practice a long time ago; now they are likely to die in theory as well. The challenge of the left in the years to come is to articulate an adequate alternative to the present system without recourse to the council model; from all indications, the task won't be an easy one.

7

Who's Afraid of Christa Wolf? Thoughts on the Dynamics of Cultural Subversion

✳

"Why not?" asked our driver, as he jumped the curb and drove his little Trabant onto the thin strip of paved road between the still forbidding outer ramparts of what since 1961 had been known simply as "The Wall." It was now July 1990, eight months after it had been breached and the city it had separated reunited, but this was the first time he had been tempted to enter the former *Todesstreifen* or "deathstrip" that had encircled West Berlin. What only a short time ago was a no-man's-land patrolled by watchdogs and guarded by border police with automatic weapons was now open to anyone with the curiosity to wander into it and a car as small as a Trabi able to negotiate its narrow road. Except for a listless group of teenagers resting on their motorcycles, we were the only ones who seemed to seize the opportunity that summer afternoon.

As we passed toppled watchtowers and bales of rolled up barbed wire, taking note of the fresh graffiti that now covered previously untouchable sections of the interior faces of the walls, we felt at once exhilarated and uneasy. Scarcely more than a half year before, our act would have invited imprisonment or even death; now it was a harmless adventure with nothing but the rattling of the tinny car on the uneven pavement to cause us concern. What would have once been a reckless gesture of defiance, perhaps even subversion if it had been a prelude to escape, was now an innocuous excursion for tourists fascinated by the detritus of a crumbling political order.

Our driver was a young and talented professor of English at the Humboldt University in East Berlin, a Shakespeare scholar who had made his first visit to the West only a few months before. He had been our guest in Berkeley and was now graciously showing us his city in return. As we drove through the deathstrip, he ruminated on the uncertain future of East German academics, indeed of his compatriot intellectuals in general. Although he had not actively aided the Stasi (as had the historian with whom we had lunch earlier that day), he frankly admitted that he had not been an outspoken dissident either. Like many others with careers to make and families to support, he had succumbed to the pressures of the system in which he found himself, without, he hoped, committing moral outrages. Now it was unclear if his past would be held against him, especially if job-hungry West German scholars were parachuted into East German universities to take over departments. Would they be able, he wondered, to distinguish between the hacks and time-servers, who deserved to be sacked unceremoniously, and the genuine scholars, whose gifts were thwarted by the inability to publish freely?

That his anxiety was not groundless, he pointed out, was shown by the controversy then swirling around Christa Wolf, East Germany's most distinguished novelist, which followed the publication of her short autobiographical story, *Was bleibt*, in the spring of 1990. Written a decade earlier, but kept in her drawer until the fall of the GDR, it told of her surveillance by the secret police in 1979 and the anguish it caused. Why only now, her critics in newspapers like *Die Welt*, *Frankfurter Allgemeine Zeitung*, and even the liberal *Die Zeit* were asking, did she choose to disclose her persecution? Had she, in fact, been only a pseudocritic of the regime, whose mild, often indirect reproaches were never really very hostile to the system? Was she perhaps a kind of house critic, providing a fig leaf for Communist tyranny by allowing herself to be used as an example of its alleged tolerance of criticism? For if she were genuinely subversive, why hadn't she been forcibly expatriated like the singer and poet Wolf Biermann, who was expelled in 1976? Worst of all, hadn't she benefited from her role by being granted privileges, such as the right to travel abroad, denied other citizens of the GDR?

Such questions evoked others in our East German friend. How representative were these attacks, he worried, of the reception in the new Germany awaiting academics and intellectuals from the wrong side of the Wall? Was there a witch-hunt in the works, as old scores were settled and new recriminations invented? Would humiliating, ritual self-criticisms of the type so common in Communist societies now ironically be demanded in a post-Communist Germany? How clean must the hands be of those who wished to continue their careers after the change? Who, in fact, would be empowered to examine those hands for signs of indelible stains?

Soon after our trip through the deathstrip a somewhat reassuring answer to these anxious questions was forthcoming, as outcries of indignation came from West German defenders of Wolf's integrity. In a long interview in Der Spiegel, Günter Grass angrily deplored the "inquisitorial and pharisaical tone"[1] of her critics. The leader of the West German PEN, Walter Jens, dubbed the attack an example of "postmodernist McCarthyism."[2] The author of such deeply unsettling novels as The Quest for Christa T (1968) and Cassandra (1983), they insisted, needed no lessons in resistance from comfortably placed writers in the West who risked nothing by attacking Communism.

Wolf's dogged insistence on remaining in the GDR, they further argued, could be explained by her hopes, now proven vain, for a genuinely socialist future. Her poignant plea on November 4, 1989, five days before the Wall fell, to the 500,000 demonstrators in East Berlin's Alexanderplatz to stay in the GDR reflected her belief that despite everything, something might still be salvaged from the forty years of "actually existing socialism." Wolf's fantasy, "Imagine it is socialism and no one leaves,"[3] may have been naive, they acknowledged, but it expressed the integrity of a writer whose motives were anything but self-protective.

"The Wolf case," as it quickly became known, was especially heated because it recalled for some a similar debate that split refugees from Nazi Germany and the "inner emigres" who remained at home. In May 1945, Thomas Mann had written an open letter from America to Walter von Molo in which he claimed that all books composed in Germany between 1933 and 1945 were "worse than worthless. . . . a stench of blood and disgrace clings to them; they all ought to be pulped."[4] Mann was vigorously answered by writers like Frank Thiess, who praised the inner emigres for "staying at their posts" and suffering the regime in dignified silence. German public opinion rallied around Thiess and Mann's reputation in his former homeland was badly damaged, at least in the short run until Thiess's pro-Nazi past was exposed.

Now, ironically, Wolf was being cast in the role of the compromised inner emigre and her West German critics were playing that of Thomas Mann. There was, however, a major difference, as her defenders were quick to point out, between the Nazi regime and the GDR after its Stalinist period. The latter was by no means as unequivocally evil as the former and could honestly have been interpreted as containing the potential for a progressive evolution. Wolf, moreover, had not remained silent, but had been involved in various forms of public protest, including speaking out when Biermann was expelled, which led to her demotion in the League of Writers. In addition, her strong feminist stance, evident in her essays on Karoline von Günderrode and Bettina von Arnim,[5] also challenged the East German status quo.

Wolf herself refused to respond to the charges, but in an interview in 1982 had presciently anticipated them. Asked to comment on the reluctance of nineteenth-century women writers to publish under their own names, she replied,

> Probably that can be understood in terms of the atmosphere of the time. I think there are certain things we refrain from doing nowadays, some of them consciously, that won't be understood later. Not even if we would explicitly describe them. Because a lot of taboos must actually be understood not in terms of what is stipulated, but the whole ambience and mood of the time, and the limits in one's self—a mixture of all these things, and I imagine that's the way it must have been for those women, who had dreadful external restrictions to endure. . . .[6]

To fault Günderrode for publishing under a masculine pseudonym was thus unjustly anachronistic, and by extension so too was attacking Wolf herself for not taking *Was bleibt* out of her drawer earlier. It was as foolish as failing to recognize that our friend's question "Why not drive into the deathstrip?" would evoke a different response in July 1990 from the one it would have demanded a year before.

Wolf's West German critics were not entirely blind to these considerations; Ulrich Greiner, for example, willingly acknowledged differences between Nazism and East German Communism.[7] But he insisted that one of them was the important role intellectuals like Bertolt Brecht, Anna

Seghers, Arnold Zweig, and indeed Christa Wolf had played in legitimating the Communist regime, a function rarely played by comparable figures from 1933 to 1945. It was therefore absolutely necessary that such intellectuals humbly atone for their mistakes and accept the responsibility for their misdeeds. Otherwise, the reproach made against Germany's failure to "master" its Nazi past could just as easily be made in regard to its four decades of Communism.

Behind the moralizing arguments of Wolf's critics, however, could be seen other agendas. Wolf, along with the writers Stefan Heym and Christoph Hein, represented resistance to what seemed to be the swallowing of the GDR whole by the Federal Republic. In this they were clearly not typical of the population of East Germany, which was unmoved by their pleas to make a revolution from below. The now-celebrated (or notorious) transformation of the democratic cry "We are the people" into the nationalist "We are one people," which presaged the unexpectedly rapid reunification, symbolized the vanity of their hopes. The attacks on Wolf were in part intended to make sure the unification remained what it had become by the spring of 1990: a revolution from above, a German tradition as old as the Reform era of the early nineteenth century. In addition, they were aimed at a target in the Federal Republic itself, the remnants of its demoralized and chastened left. For in criticizing Wolf's hopes of finding a residue of genuine socialist emancipation in the wreckage of the GDR, they were also striking out at similar hopes among West German intellectuals.

From the perspective of an outsider, the "Christa Wolf case" may seem oddly overblown. But once its tangle of motivations, emotional overtones, and historical resonances is unraveled, its importance can easily be seen. Wolf herself, I suspect, will survive the controversy undamaged, as her record is scrutinized and her personal integrity better appreciated. By the end of the summer of 1990, the French minister of culture Jack Lang could still award her a prize and defiantly defend her against her defamers. Significantly, unlike in the case of Mann and the inner emigres of the Third Reich, those who chose to leave or were expelled from the GDR were not the ones throwing the rocks at those who stayed.

As for the fate of less prominent academics, there can be no doubt that many nonteaching members of the East German Academy of Arts and Sciences, whose numbers were in the thousands, will find themselves looking for new work. Many seemed to have enjoyed sinecures without much compulsion to engage in serious scholarship. Those who have been actually teaching may find it easier to remain in place, especially if their subjects are now in demand. Professors of English, like our friend at Humboldt University, are likely to do a lot better than philosophers whose specialty was dialectical materialism. But even among academics in more innocent fields, those who were clearly complicitous with the old system at its most authoritarian may be shunted aside. Still, if one remembers the spotty and inconclusive de-Nazification process after 1945, it is hard to believe that much more will happen now that Communism has ended. For despite the furor over the need to "master the second German totalitarian past," there is little anxiety that Communist attitudes remain to poison the new Germany even to the extent that Nazi ones threatened the Federal Republic after the war. If anything, the threat comes from unmastered residues of the hypernationalist past, allowed to fester for forty years, rather than, *pace* Greiner, the remnants of Stalinism.

2

Whatever the ultimate outcome of the "Wolf case" and everything surrounding it, there is perhaps a larger question raised by this story, a question that can be said to touch on recent debates in American academic life. I am taking about the issue of what constitutes genuine or false "subversion." If Wolf's work and public activity before the fall of the Wall can be retrospectively damned as pseudocritical, if, to up the ante, her pseudocritical work can be construed as inadvertently functional in maintaining the repressive system it purported to challenge, then the question arises, what would a genuine critique have looked like? How, moreover, can we judge the potential gap between critical intentions and the effects they may or may not produce?

In the late 1970s, when radical American intellectuals were still bathing in the backwash of the previous decade, this precise issue was addressed by a small group of Frankfurt School disciples who talked of the transition from "one-dimensional society" to what they called the "age of artificial negativity."[8] Herbert Marcuse's celebrated claim that late capitalism had successfully suppressed any negation, any second dimension dialectically opposed to the status quo, was, they argued, no longer valid. Instead, the "system" now reproduced itself by the secretion of pseudonegations, whose artificiality was judged by the fact that they didn't really challenge it on any fundamental level. Apparently oppositional movements from feminism to the counterculture were all covertly functional in preserving the system, however much they wanted to subvert it. Even the culture industry no longer needed to control all dissident currents; instead it tolerated, even nurtured, apparently independent initiatives, which nonetheless were impotent to challenge the logic of the system as a whole.

Although the criteria distinguishing "organic" from "artificial negativity" were never satisfactorily developed by the proponents of this argument, who also failed to demonstrate how their own work was exempt from the charge of artificiality, the doubts they expressed about the contradiction between the manifest and latent functions of oppositional movements have continued to bother many observers. In the past decade, they have, for example, often informed debates about the political implications of poststructuralist thought. Is deconstruction as radically subversive as its defenders like to claim, or does it leave things shaking, but still standing, as its critics often charge? Is Foucault's notion of power so totalizing that it precludes any alternative to the eternal recurrence of the same? Is the "New Historicism" beholden to a model of containment that suggests all alleged transgressions really preserve the laws which they seem to challenge? Does the "post-Marxist" abandonment of "classist" social analysis lead to a reliance on marginal phenomena that in no way disrupts late capitalism at its core?

A great deal of energy and ingenuity has been expended on trying to answer these questions, as virtually no one wants to be found guilty of espousing a pseudosubversive position that functions to preserve the status quo. No one willingly accepts the charge of co-optation by the system hurled by their critics. Even those who insist they have given up all thoughts of a metanarrative of emancipation take pride in subverting the illusions of those who do, often claiming as well that they are calling into question the totalitarian implications of a totalizing analysis.

How valid all these claims and counterclaims may be is not my concern now. What I want to highlight instead is the widely shared topos of genuine versus false subversion, which draws on the model of manifest and latent functions. For despite the fact that the German critics of Wolf come predominantly from the right, whereas the Americans who espouse the artificial negativity argument and worry about the implications of poststructuralism are broadly speaking on the left, they both operate with the same fundamental assumption: that one can tell confidently the difference between what really subverts and what does not.

If there is any lesson of the "Wolf case," however, it is the difficulty of making this distinction. It is especially difficult to make in advance, before the outcome of actions are clear. Indeed, if we take seriously the claim that history never reaches its final state, then there can perhaps never be a vantage point from which this clarity is perfectly evident. In 1990, it may seem that Wolf was foolishly naive to believe that socialism could be reformed or that German unity entirely on Kohl's terms was avoidable, but from some later perspective, perhaps she will be understood to have anticipated future trends. Thus her "compromises" with the system may not seem so unwarranted, after all. In other words, there is an inevitably temporal moment in judgments about subversion, an infinite deferral, if you will, of the final balance sheet.

There is also what might be called a spatial problem underlying the genuine/false subversion distinction. That is, what is the relevant unit of analysis whose subversion is at stake? What are the boundaries of the system which is being challenged or maintained, and how can we circumscribe them? As Gerald Graff has rightly noted, "a point is reached at which almost anything can be praised for its subversiveness or damned for its vulnerability to co-optation, for there is always some frame of reference that will support either description."[9]

In the case of the GDR, the boundaries were easier to discern than they are for "late capitalism" or the society of "artificial negativity"; there is no physical Wall, after all, separating the latter from an alternative system. But even in the GDR's case, there were no visible walls rigidly defining its internal landscape, no markers keeping the false from the genuine subversives apart. Rather than pretend to see a clear-cut distinction between the two, it is thus perhaps wiser to be attuned to the multiple ambiguities of words and deeds that resist reduction to one function alone. From the lofty vantage point of a fully redeemed utopian order, efforts to ameliorate the status of individuals or groups in the current society may seem like counterproductive diversions. But from that of the people involved, meaningful changes in their lives and those of others may result.

It is thus imperative to be sensitive to the contextual possibilities defining the choices available at the time. Entering the deathstrip is suicidal at one moment in history, a lark the next. Deconstructing texts may at times call extratextual authority into question, at others, it may serve to reinforce the status quo. The choices we make cannot be judged by some ultimate standard of subversiveness, based on an intransigently maximalist conception of the system that has to be overthrown. Consider, for example, the well-known dilemma of the leaders of the Jewish Councils during the Holocaust, whose horrible choices no one lucky enough not to face them can presume to judge. Only those comfortably outside a complicated situation can afford to cast aspersions at the Christa Wolfs who fail to live up to some notion of absolute opposition.

This is not to deny the existence of time-servers, who pretend to agonize over moral issues, but are really concerned with prospering no matter how awful the compromises they make. But what cannot be held against them is the failure to adhere to the logic of genuine versus false subversion, organic versus artificial negativity. More traditional moral criteria must also be introduced to complicate our judgments. Those who thought such criteria could be abandoned in the name of the world court of history—the Merleau-Ponty of *Humanism and Terror* comes to mind as an obvious example—have often come to regret their decision. For history has a way of subverting the logic we impute to it. Among its victims are the belief that participants and even historians can know what genuine and artificial negativity, real and pseudosubversion, actually are.

8

Postmodern Fascism? Reflections on the
Return of the Repressed

✳

The still escalating debate over the relation between Martin Heidegger's philosophy and his embrace of Nazism took a new and startling turn with the publication in 1992 of Ernst Nolte's *Martin Heidegger: Politik und Geschichte im Leben und Denken.*[1] Unlike Heidegger's increasingly beleaguered apologists, Nolte willingly concedes that fundamental aspects of Heidegger's thought and important dimensions of Nazi politics were indeed closely related. But then he reaches the extraordinary conclusion that this was not entirely to the philosopher's discredit, for Nazism in the 1930s had a certain historical legitimacy as the only plausible bulwark against Communism. As a result, Heidegger was not fully wrong in sympathizing with it.

Such a breathtaking contention did not catch entirely off guard those who had followed Nolte's dubious role in the so-called *Historikerstreit* (Historians' Dispute) of the mid-1980s, when, along with Andreas Hillgruber and Michael Stürmer, Nolte sought to relativize both the Holocaust and the Nazi experience by setting them in the context of other horrors of the twentieth century, and even argued that the Jewish "threat" to Germany was such that the Nazis had a plausible justification for undertaking a war against the Jews. Nor was it surprising to those who knew of Nolte's personal relationship to Heidegger—he had known the philosopher since his student days in Freiburg in 1944—to find him providing so audacious a defense of his hero. From the perspective of the late 1980s, Nolte's nuanced sympathy for Nazism and Heidegger's defense of it were not therefore completely unexpected.

For those who remember Nolte's role in the 1960s, however, the period when he first came into international prominence as a historian, it still remains an extraordinary shock to discover that he could so strongly defend Nazism's historical legitimacy. For in 1963, he had published a very different kind of book entitled *Der Faschismus in seiner Epoche: Die Action Franççis, Der italienesche Faschismus, Der Nationalsozialismus*, which was translated by Leila Vennewiz two years later as *Three Faces of Fascism*.[2] Although not without its detractors, who distrusted its overly philosophical underpinnings or worried about its emphasis on biographical accounts of the movements' leaders, the work quickly established itself as a classic in the interpretation of fascism in general and Nazism in particular.[3] The dustcover on the paperback edition boasts an encomium from Fritz Stern, a liberal historian and certainly no friend of the Nazis, which compares it with Hannah Arendt's *Origins of Totalitarianism* as one of the "most thoughtful discussions of the entire fascist phenomenon." George Lichtheim, despite several reservations, could tell the readers of the *New York Review of Books* that "we shall not soon have a better account of the political and spiritual factors that went into the European catastrophe between the wars."[4] Even as late as 1989, Saul Friedländer, who had vigorously denounced Nolte during the Historikerstreit, could still call the book a "monumental study," which placed Nolte squarely in the "intentionalist" rather than "functionalist" camp in explaining the Holocaust.[5]

Its author's appalling recent pronouncements should not, therefore, prevent us from returning to this extraordinarily stimulating work. Indeed, doing so may provide us with useful guidelines in the quest to gauge the possibilities of a renewed fascism in the 1990s and beyond. For Nolte's analysis transcended the purely descriptive and posed fundamental questions about the deeper roots of fascism, questions that, alas, now seem necessary to ask once again.

Nolte's complex argument in *Three Faces of Fascism* is directed against several targets. First, it opposed the totalitarian analysis so fashionable during the Cold War era, the essential conflation of right- and left-wing extremism into one anti-liberal democratic model by theorists like Arendt, J. L. Talmon, and Carl Joachim Friedrich. Instead, Nolte claimed fascism was essentially a counterrevolutionary rival to communism, rather than its twin. Or more precisely, to cite one of his major formulations: "fascism is anti-Marxism which seeks to destroy the enemy by the evolvement of a radically opposed and yet related ideology and by the use of almost identical and yet typically modified methods, always, however, within the unyielding framework of national self-assertion and autonomy."[6]

Second, Nolte sought to contextualize the Nazi experience by setting it within the larger context of fascism rather than totalitarianism, a category in which he included Mussolini's Italy and the Action Française of Charles Maurras, a movement that never came to power but was important in France in the period after the Dreyfus affair. By beginning his analysis with the Action Française, Nolte was able to tie fascism to the earliest counter-revolutionary and counter-Enlightenment traditions. In so doing, to be sure, it might seem as if he were tacitly anticipating the relativization of the Holocaust, which so dismayed his opponents during the Historians' Dispute. This conclusion might be given added credence by Nolte's explicit repudiation of what he called "the Jewish interpretation, which is based on the most appalling of all human experiences,"[7] an interpretation that stressed the utter uniqueness of Nazism. Nolte did, however, acknowledge that from the point of view of the importance of anti-Semitism, the Nazis had no peer; it was just that fascism as a whole could not be reduced to a generalized version of its most virulent exemplar.

It is, however, the third general argument of the book that is most pertinent to our larger theme, because it provided a very ambitious, philosophically informed explanation of fascism, which nonetheless sought to situate it in a specific historical era. According to Nolte, fascism could be understood within its own epoch in terms of three basic dimensions. The first is what he calls the "life-and-death struggle of the sovereign, martial and inwardly antagonistic group,"[8] which he sees as latent in virtually all of history, but fully manifest in the fascist movements of the twentieth century. By sovereign, he means the deliberate exclusion of other people; by martial, the employment of warlike methods to achieve its goals; and by inwardly antagonistic, the existence of internal stratification, class or status, which then leads to the projecting of conflict outward by engaging in or threatening foreign wars. Such manifestations of group self-assertion, he concedes, are widespread throughout history, but are especially evident in twentieth-century fascism.

The other two dimensions of fascism are, however, more specifically related to the epoch of its efflorescence. One involves the crucial role of Marxism, which as we've already noted, Nolte construed as the primary target of the fascist counterrevolutionary impulse. Although Nolte agreed that fascism learned some of its practical methods from Marxism-Leninism, which gave some weight to the totalitarianism analysis he wanted to undermine, the important point is that fascism could emerge after World War I only in response to a vigorous and expanding radicalism of the left. George Lichtheim could thus entitle his appreciative review of the book the "European Civil War," because Nolte had correctly highlighted the death struggle between the radical left and the radical right at a time when a viable center seemed in danger of almost totally disappearing. The implication is that fascism could emerge only in reaction to an aggressive and totalizing Marxism.

The third and most complicated dimension of Nolte's analysis concerns the process he calls transcendence, which has two dimensions, the practical and the theoretical. At its most fundamental level, fascism emerged only as a response to both kinds of transcendence. Practical transcendence is, roughly speaking, Nolte's term for what is often called modernization: the bureaucratization of the world, the spread of the commodity and market forms of capitalism, the abstraction of social life, rapid urbanization, the growth of the impersonal state, the centralization of political power, and so on. Fascism, Nolte argues, is a distorted protest against these trends in the name of lost immanence: the restoration of community, particularity, rootedness, and the concrete as opposed to alienation and abstraction. It is thus able to attract those people who feel left behind in the process of practical transcendence, such as the members of the lower middle class or peasantry.

In addition, fascism also expresses a resistance to theoretical transcendence, by which Nolte means the attempt to grasp the world in intelligible concepts, conceive of it as a totality which can be understood by reason, and make it available for humanist intellectual appropriation. In this respect, fascism can be understood as a response to what might be called the hubris of intellectual species imperialism, the ambition of certain movements to make sense of the world in universal and abstract categories for the purpose of its domination. It was Maurras who anticipated this aspect of the fascist project in his critique of "anti-nature" and suspicion of the originally religious notion of divine transcendence, which began with monotheism (one reason why the Jews could be seen as the prime culprit in the process of theoretical transcendence). But it was Nietzsche, according to Nolte, whose "philosophy of life" was "the first to give voice to that spiritual focal point toward which all fascism must gravitate: the assault on practical and theoretical transcendence, for the sake of a 'more beautiful' form of 'life.' "[9] To the extent that the Faustian drive in Western culture always to transcend led to a kind of infinite striving that drew humankind further and further away from its roots in the here and now, it engendered an inevitable yearning for the restoration of immanence. On the left, Marxism represents a similar yearning—Nolte claims the goal of the classless society is precisely to replace theoretical transcendence—which is why it is so much a competitor to fascism.

Although Nolte never mentions Heidegger in his discussion of transcendence—in fact, one commentator was led to believe his adoption of a "phenomenological" method meant he was actually a Hegelian[10]—it is not difficult to hear echoes of Heidegger's lament about the humanist forgetting of Being and loss of a "world" in which humans are at home. It is for this reason the book concludes with a nuanced—and at the time somewhat puzzling—expression of "sympathy" for fascism, which in retrospect can be understood as prefiguring Nolte's later advocacy of a more explicit justification of its historical legitimacy: "It is precisely in this broadest of all perspectives that the observer cannot withhold from fascism that 'sympathy' of which we have spoken. . . . For transcendence, when properly understood, is infinitely remote from the harmlessness of safe 'cultural progress'; it is not the couch of the finite human being, but in some mysterious sense his throne and his cross."[11] Whereas Nolte, alas, now seems to express some sympathy for the answers fascism provided to the challenge of practical and theoretical transcendence, *The Three Faces of Fascism* suggests only that the questions it addressed were the right ones for its age.

Are they, however, appropriate for our own? That is to say, does the precise constellation of factors that Nolte adduced to explain the rise of fascism in interwar Europe, the Europe fighting a civil war between radical right and radical left, still obtain today? To begin to answer these questions, I want to turn to a widely discussed recent book, which although never directly speaking to the issue of fascism's return, nonetheless, when taken together with Nolte's claims in *Three Faces of Fascism*, has some illuminating insights on its likelihood: Fredric Jameson's *Postmodernism: Or, the Cultural Logic of Late Capitalism.*[12] According to Jameson, cultural modernism can be understood as the aesthetic correlate of a still unfinished modernization process, whereas postmodernism registers the virtual completion of that process and the near universalization of those developments that Nolte identified with practical transcendence and the Marxist in Jameson would prefer to call reification: bureaucratization, the expansion of the centralized state, the spread of the market and commodification, and so on. It is significant that in an earlier work that focused on the English writer Wyndham Lewis, Jameson had argued that both Lewis's fascist politics and his modernist aesthetics could be understood as "a protest against the reified experience of an alienated life."[13] That is, during the transitional era, resistance was still possible in the hope of restoring something lost called nature or tradition, or of achieving a future utopian order in which immanence would be restored with new means.

Postmodern culture, in contrast, reflects a period in which the process of modernization has finally been completed and significant resistance to technological, instrumental rationality, market-commodity relations, bureaucratization, and so on has virtually disappeared. Postmodernism has lost or somehow repressed much of the anxiety produced by the traumas of modernization; the groups left behind by it are no longer sufficiently numerous to present a problem. When postmodernists appeal to history or tradition as an antidote to excessive practical transcendence, they do so only in the form of self-conscious, polyvalent pastiche; when they invoke something called "nature," they do so with the full knowledge that it is an artificial construct, rather than a genuine state of prelapsarian grace to which we might somehow return. Even when they utter the talismanic word "community," they know that the image of a homogeneous, meaningful gathering of benignly cooperative people in face-to-face proximity is little more than an exercise in nostalgia in the age of e-mail and virtual reality machines. In short, there is far less yearning today for a lost immanence than there was when what Nolte calls the protest against practical transcendence was at its height.

As for the threat of theoretical transcendence, postmodern theory—with all its distrust of foundational quests and totalizing projects—may be defined precisely as the acceptance of a kind of perpetual limbo between complete immanence and complete transcendence, a willingness to give up both grand, totalizing narratives and all ambitious projects of complete theoretical abstraction, on the one hand, and the contrary yearning to return to a fully meaningful, entirely concrete lifeworld, on the other. Thus today, Nietzsche is no longer read as the defender of immanence and a more beautiful form of life, but rather as the inspiration for poststructuralist critiques of the very possibility of plenitude, presence, and totalized meaning. Even Heidegger tends to be appreciated these days less for his nostalgia for plenitudinous Being than for the stimulus to the questioning of that very goal.

There is, I would concede, an element of exaggeration in Jameson's argument, which may not be as globally applicable as he suggests. Understood in different terms from the ones he invokes, say those of Jürgen Habermas, modernity may still be an "uncompleted project," which need not be equated with the maximization of abstraction. But in many respects, it is hard to gainsay Jameson's claim that, however we judge its implications, something new has arrived that means we are beyond the moment when modernization in most of its guises was radically changing the face of Europe. As such, Jameson's model helps provide the beginning of an answer to the question raised by Nolte's path-breaking work of the 1960s: Are we still broadly speaking in the "epoch of fascism," as recent, troubling events in post–Cold War Europe might suggest? The answer, to put it simply and with full awareness of the dangers of complacency, is that we are not. For if we have moved past the point of maximum anxiety about practical transcendence, if we have abandoned the project of theoretical transcendence, and if we are no longer faced with an aggressive Marxism that can provide the stimulus and model for an equally aggressive fascism, then its resurgence in the 1990s and beyond is not likely to be the genuine thing. We still, to be sure, have our share of "sovereign, martial, inwardly antagonistic groups," some of which will doubtless find it convenient to recycle the scape-goating appeals of fascism; what after all is the agenda of "ethnic cleansing"? But by and large, the postmodernization process is destined to engender new political forms, which will require still unimagined analytical categories and, alas, new strategies of defense. As is often remarked, fascism was utterly absent from the political vocabulary of the nineteenth century, which would have been deeply astounded by the course of events in our own century. If we can be confident of anything, it is that the twenty-first has some surprises in store for us as well. We ought not to prepare for them by holding on too tightly to the lessons of a past epoch that is, thankfully, no longer our own.

9

Educating the Educators

✳

It will be old news by the time this is printed, but on January 30, 1993, it merited an eight-column headline in all the California papers. "Honig Guilty on All Counts," screamed the *San Francisco Chronicle*, whose lead sentence read "State schools chief Bill Honig, a nationally recognized leader of the school reform movement, was found guilty yesterday of using his elected post to direct money to a private educational program run by his wife." State conflict-of-interest laws were invoked to convict Honig of felonies for placing four school principals, who were paid $337,509 in state funds, with the Quality Education Project headed by Nancy Honig and headquartered in their San Francisco home. Besides whatever penalties the courts might inflict on him, Honig was required to leave the post as California superintendent of public education he had held since 1982.

For anyone who had followed Bill Honig's dramatic rise to prominence—shortly after he left the obscurity of his job as Marin County superintendant of schools, he was touted as a prospective gubernatorial candidate or a future secretary of education—his fall was a bitter reminder that educational policy is one of the most hotly contested arenas in today's cultural wars. For Honig's undoing was not merely his questionable judgment in allowing what everyone concedes was a laudable initiative in parent involvement in education to be tainted by the overly close involvement of his wife. He was also an implicit victim of the zealousness of right-wing Republican attorney general Dan Lungren and conservative members of the state board of education, who were angered by his refusal to countenance creationist "science" in California textbooks and his support for bilingual education. Honig was done in as well by the ruling of a judge who dismissed as irrelevant all evidence concerning his good intentions—a man of considerable wealth, he was not in it for the money—in granting the contracts.

Honig's departure was greeted with dismay by most advocates of education in California. He had used his office to forge a coalition of Democrats and many Republicans around increased funding for schools, curriculum reform, and more rigorous teacher training and testing. Although his policies were liberal and inclusive, he was respected by those who wanted to maintain high educational standards, which he insisted could be meaningfully applied to all of the state's ethnic groups. His earnest, idealistic, hortatory style was a refreshing departure from the bureaucratic petty-mindedness that often comes to characterize those beaten down by the endless struggle over educational policy and practice.

✳

I invoke Honig's story now, however, neither to rehearse the arguments for or against his conviction nor to repeat the lamentations of his supporters, justifiable as they may be. I want instead to use it to introduce a more general issue, the vexed relationship between "high" intellectual life in America and the general educational process through which virtually all of our children pass. For Honig was himself, as I know from personal experience, deeply concerned with precisely this theme. How, he wanted to know, can the abstruse developments at the cutting edge of intellectual life have an impact on schooling? How can ivory tower dwellers mingle effectively with those in the streets below?

The personal experience to which I allude occurred just before Honig became superintendant of California's public schools. He called me in the fall of 1980 to ask if I were willing to construct and teach an informal course for him and his friends on the current cultural crisis. Although I did not know who he was at the time, I agreed to meet and discuss the possibility. Honig's evident enthusiasm for ideas and his promise of interesting participants won me over, and the following spring we met fortnightly at his house for twelve discussions of texts I hoped would provide a range of opinions about the pressing cultural issues of the day. The group was, as he had pledged, a stimulating mix of lawyers, businessmen, and educators, all of whom were actively shaping a world that academics study from afar. One, the banker Anthony Frank, would in fact later become United States postmaster general.

Although the course was designed to focus on the American scene, it began with Carl Schorske's newly published *Fin-de-siècle Vienna*, to provide a comparative framework for an analysis of the link between political crisis and cultural turmoil. We then moved to selections from Robert Nisbet's *The Sociological Tradition*, which carefully unpacks the meaning and history of such keywords as "community," "authority," and "alienation." Along with Nisbet's essentially conservative reading of the debates around these terms, I assigned Herbert Marcuse's classic Frankfurt School text, "The Affirmative Character of Culture," Hannah Arendt's "What Is Authority?" from *Beyond Past and Future*, and Raymond Williams's chapter, "Culture" in *Marxism and Literature*.

Our subsequent readings included Michel Foucault's *Discipline and Punish*, Steven Lukes's *Individualism*, John Murray Cuddihy's *The Ordeal of Civility*, James Ogilvy's *Many-Dimensional Man*, Fredric Jameson's *Prisonhouse of Language*, Richard Schacht's *Alienation*, and Daniel Bell's *The Cultural Contradictions of Capitalism*. In retrospect, the absence of texts dealing with gender or multicultural issues or by minority authors may seem embarrassingly apparent—only the Cuddihy thematized the issue of particularism and universalism in its treatment of Jewish intellectuals in Europe and America— but the works we did read certainly stimulated wide-ranging and lively discussions.

I wouldn't presume to know whether Honig and his friends got what they wanted from the course, but from my point of view, the experience was very illuminating. My Fabian-like fantasy of influencing the movers and shakers of society came up against the reality of the gap between academic (or more precisely, intellectual) discourse and that of even the most well-informed lay persons. The supposition that the "chattering classes," as the English like to call them, can chatter in the same way about the same issues was not borne out. Call it a difference in habitus, institutional matrix, or cultural field, there was no escaping the baggage each of us brought with us. The gap, interestingly enough, was not evident merely in differences in jargon or familiarity with the current fads in intellectual life. Instead, it reflected a fundamental disparity in outlook, which can be encapsulated, if in somewhat simplified form, in the dichotomy between critique and affirmation.

Whereas my most fundamental inclination was to problematize the self-evident, complexify the simple, and unpack the apparently solid, leaving many questions still unanswered, theirs was to analyze and act, to move beyond paradox and ambiguity to positive programmatic resolution. In the vocabulary of a university academic, words like "subversion" and "disruption" had become by 1981 the god-terms that needed no apology, "to critique" or "to deconstruct" the verbs that packed the most punch. What Paul Ricoeur had called the "hermeneutics of suspicion" had clearly won out over the "hermeneutics of recollected meaning." Accordingly, the subterranean agenda of the course, as I conceived it, was to unsettle some of the group's assumptions about the implications of honorific terms like "community," "authority," and "culture." Although in some vague way the ultimate goal was meaningful change, I was not bent on providing pragmatic solutions of my own to the problems before us.

The role of critical gadfly has, of course, been one of the most seductive self-images of the intellectual. Marx's famous call for "the ruthless critique of everything existing" is echoed in such manifestoes as Kurt Tucholsky's "Wir Negativen" of 1919, with its truculent insistence that "we cannot yet say Yes."[1] In a widely remarked essay of 1969, the English historian J. P. Nettl went so far as to define true intellectuals as opposed to professional academics precisely by the former's propensity to perennial dissent.[2] Although there have been contrary examples of mandarin affirmation, when intellectuals have succumbed to the temptation to become yea-sayers, they rarely replace for very long the more congenial intellectual stance of negativity. It was not by chance that the sociologist Alvin Gouldner could call the fundamental discriminating factor indicating membership in what he saw as an intellectual New Class an embrace of "the culture of critical discourse."

Honig, on the other hand, still maintained what might be called a quasi-Arnoldian faith in a more ennobling version of a noncorrosive high culture and a belief in the importance of extending its reach to those now outside its purview. Going beyond the German notion of Bildung, with its emphasis on merely personal cultivation, he endorsed Arnold's faith—transmitted through twentieth-century figures like Leavis and Trilling—in the beneficial social effect of the pursuit of perfection, a stress that assumed the universal significance of at least certain cultural norms. Not surprisingly, the text that was received with the most hostility in the class was Marcuse's essay on "affirmative culture," with its attempt to debunk the transcendent idealism of the Arnoldian tradition.

The stance of faithful preserver and disseminator of the cultural riches of the past and the nurturer of new—but not too new—cultural creation has, of course, frequently been seen as the pedagogue's main function. Such a function, not surprisingly, often accompanies a sense of public responsibility tinged with moral uplift. Critical sociologists of education—those who associate themselves with the model of dissenting intellectual limned above—have as a result been swift to foreground the complicitous role such pedagogy plays in creating docile citizens of the modern nation-state, treating education as a prime example of what Althusserians liked to call an "ideological state apparatus." Even what may have originally functioned in a subversive manner in the hands of critical intellectuals can become affirmative, they note, when it enters the school curriculum, two obvious examples being Marxism in the former Soviet empire, aesthetic modernism in the West.

It would, of course, be a mistake to reify the distinction between critical intellectuals and constructive pedagogues. The tension between critique and construction is, after all, itself sometimes played out in educational policy terms. Is the main task, pedagogues wonder, to instill critical skills or to nurture the talent for constructive creativity and problem-solving? Can an overemphasis on the former lead to corrosive and cynical skepticism, while an excessive reliance on the latter promotes a lack of judgment or an attitude of status quo–preserving, utilitarian pragmatism, which never questions its deeper premises? Is culture, however we define it, a treasure from the past to be transmitted reverentially or a living, on-going process that must devour that past, actively forgetting in order to create anew? These are issues that often preoccupy intellectuals and pedagogues alike. Still, there is a kind of tendential division of labor between yea- and nay-sayers that was very much in evidence during the course of the class.

❋

Now, however, more than a decade later and after Honig's spectacular rise and fall, a number of ironies about such a division have become increasingly apparent. For unexpectedly, both positions have in a way been outflanked by a third, that being the powerful rise of a curious variant of popular or mass culture that is itself deeply hostile to received pieties, indeed of any pieties at all. In the past, both a high-minded traditional culture and a critical avant-garde could dismiss as mindless kitsch a mass culture that seemed conformist, affirmative, and lacking in any value except entertainment of the most debased kind. Congratulating themselves for possessing a reflective distance from the seductions of the spectacle and the lure of escapist fiction, they could denounce the naive gullibility of those who were controlled by the masters of mass cultural manipulation.

Now both of these standpoints—let's call them elite and adversarial cultural criticism—are themselves on the defensive against an assault by a generation that sees them, sometimes explicitly, sometimes not, as ideological justification for the cultural power of a pseudo-universal "intellectual class," whose seeming differences cover over a commonality of interest. There is, as one of the celebrants of this new sensibility, Andrew Ross, has put it, "no respect" left for either position. We are thus unlikely to recognize, he tells us, "what is fully at stake in the new *politics of knowledge* if [we] fail to understand why so many cultural forms, devoted to horror and porn, and steeped in chauvinism and other bad attitudes, draw their popular appeal from expressions of disrespect for the lessons of educated taste."[3]

Now ironic reflection, camp parody, and awareness of manipulation have themselves become part of mass culture, which is no longer predominantly grounded in seductive immediacy and the deliberate fostering of what Herbert Marcuse ironically dubbed the "happy consciousness" of "repressive desublimation." What seems to prevail today instead is what the German theorist Peter Sloterdijk has called "cynical reason," which he defines as "enlightened false consciousness," a "hard-boiled, shadowy cleverness that has split courage off from itself, holds anything positive to be a fraud, and is intent only on somehow getting through life."[4]

This transformation means that the most disturbing impulses no longer emanate from a critical intelligentsia at war with a cultural establishment, but rather from a much more unsettling mix of inchoate forces that have emerged "from below." These include everything from computer hackers to body piercers, postmodernist performers to underground "zine" cartoonists, skater dudes to cyberpunk bands, gangsta rappers to queer activists. Not all of these can be simply labeled quietistic or defeatist—the militancy of the last mentioned is anything but—and yet they also manifest evident impatience with the critical pretensions of the radical intellectuals who have for so long occupied the anti-establishment highground in the cultural landscape. Heroic attempts like those of Greil Marcus in *Lipstick Traces* to discern a latent utopianism in their apparent nihilism come up against the overwhelming evidence of their loss of faith in radically holistic solutions.[5] And certainly, they have no use for the Arnoldian vision of cultural sublimation that inspires idealist pedagogues like Honig.

In short, in a world in which Beavis and Butt-head have replaced Horkheimer and Adorno as the reigning champions of negation, the old conflict between adversarial intellectuals and affirmative pedagogues seems somehow dated. Neither camp seems to have its finger on the pulse of a generation whose education appears more and more of an impossible challenge every day. Sadly, a well-intentioned reformer like Honig has to contend with kooks who think Darwin is the Anti-Christ, while radical intellectuals schooled in the sixties recycle critiques that seem more and more remote from what is really happening thirty years later. In short, whoever seeks to educate the educators today will have to come to grips with a strange, new world of cultural creation—and demolition—unlike any we have experienced before. If there is anyone out there up to the task, I would welcome a copy of the reading list.

10

The Aesthetic Alibi

✴

In a recent essay decrying the General Services Administration's dismantling of his site-specific public sculpture, Tilted Arc, in 1989, Richard Serra
made his case in terms of what he called "moral rights" against property
rights.[1] Although the government had paid for the work, he argued, it had
no right to destroy it, for the result was to override "the right to freedom of
speech, the right to freedom of expression, the right to protection of one's
creative work."[2] Instead of "maintaining the integrity of its artworks,"[3] the
government was exercising a kind of censorship, which threatened to introduce political considerations into the realm of art.

More than a reaction to the special case of "public art" like Tilted Arc,
Serra's alarm was fueled by an increasing number of challenges to the
unhindered expression of transgressive ideas and symbolic actions in the
past few years. Such a development in the United States seems especially
ironic at a moment when elsewhere in the world, most notably the former
Soviet bloc, restrictions are being relaxed. At times the threat has been
directed at "high art," as in the case of Serra's sculpture, at others against
"low" or "popular art," as exemplified by the reaction to performances by
the rap group 2 Live Crew. Sometimes the charge has been obscenity, as
with the photographs of Robert Mapplethorpe, or the corruption of mi-
nors, in the case of Jock Sturges's photos of nude children, or something
akin to blasphemy in the case of Andres Serrano's infamous Piss Christ.

Politically, the menace has usually been identified as coming from the
right, with figures like Jesse Helms, Patrick Buchanan, and Donald Wild-

mon the major culprits; but with the hysterical (and often hypocritical) inflation of "political correctness" into an equally ominous threat, it has also now become linked at times to the left.[4] No less variable have been the threatened punishments, which range from the destruction of already existing works and the imprisonment of offenders against standards of decency to the loss of funding from the National Endowment for the Arts or the General Services Administration. But whatever the justification, source, or penalty, a pattern has emerged in which freedom of expression seems very much under siege. With the Ayatollah's death threat against Salmon Rushdie as the reductio ad absurdum of this trend, artists and their supporters have recognized how high the stakes can get in the struggle. As a result, the ghost of Senator McCarthy has been sighted with greater frequency than at any time since he seemed to be mercifully buried in the 1960s.

Sorting out all the complex issues raised by these events would be an impossible task in the modest compass of this column. Even venturing yet another attempt to discuss the limits of free speech seems foolishly ambitious, especially for someone with no expertise in the intricacies of the law. What I would prefer to do instead is focus on one aspect of the debate, which concerns the question of what is normally called "artistic freedom." For in the response to efforts at restricting free speech, the assumed special right of the artist has frequently been claimed. Serra may talk loosely of "moral rights" and worry about free expression in general, but it is clear that, say, a "non-signature" architect with no artistic pretensions who protested against an alteration to a house he designed would get nowhere. Even Madonna in *Truth or Dare* could brazen her way out of a threat to close her concert down for public lewdness in Toronto only by righteously wrapping herself in the flag of *artistic* free expression.

Broadly speaking, artistic freedom can be defined as a special case of freedom of speech, which raises it to a more purified level. That is, the restrictions on free speech in a liberal society are generally relaxed still further when that speech (or any symbolic action) is deemed to have aesthetic value. It may be prohibited to shout "fire!" from the audience of a theater, because of the panic it will engender, but there is no problem with the same cry on the stage, just as long as it remains understood as part of the play. For as speech-act theorists have been telling us for some time, the "perlocutionary" impact of the same words, their ability to make something happen, varies with the context. What would be libelous or offensive in everyday life is granted a special dispensation, if it is understood to take place within the protective shield of an aesthetic frame.

One of the distinguishing marks of liberal, secularized Western societies is precisely our claim to recognize such a protective shield. When it is pierced, and works of literature or art are burned for their repugnant ideas, transgressive language, or distasteful imagery, we grow indignant at the failure to observe what seems to us almost a natural boundary. Although we may disagree over what justifiably can claim protection under the doctrine of aesthetic freedom, virtually all of us honor the distinction between art and its other, and are willing to tolerate in the former sphere what would be troubling in the latter. We even invent new categories like "performance art" to permit behavior that without its protection would in all likelihood threaten the perpetrator with immediate incarceration in a mental institution, if not a jail.

The ideal of "artistic freedom," it can safely be said, is one of the most sacrosanct in our culture, and we relish any opportunity to reaffirm its value. Not for us, we tell ourselves proudly, are there exhibitions of "degenerate art" designed to humiliate artists who fail to conform to the state's authoritarian tastes. Not for us are there laws forcing heterodox writers to circulate their work in samizdat editions or seek exile abroad. Even postmodernists, who pride themselves on challenging the liberal pieties of the Enlightenment tradition, can find ammunition for the defense of aesthetic freedom in the claim of Jean-François Lyotard that a radical incommensurability—a "differend" in his vocabulary—exists between art and other "regimes of phrases."[5] The right to free aesthetic expression is in fact so much a part of our self-understanding that it often seems to have its own intrinsic justification going beyond that provided to free speech in general by the first amendment.

What, however, makes all of this appeal to artistic freedom so paradoxical, what in fact should force us to reconsider its self-evident truth, is that the challenge to its integrity has come not only from the troglodytes who fail to understand the rules of the aesthetic game, but also from another source, and one far more difficult to dismiss out of hand. That is, it comes from within the discourse of the aesthetic itself, or more precisely from those artists and intellectuals who have called into question the very idea of a distinct and inviolable realm of experience called "art." For if they are right and we are no longer permitted to assume that such a realm exists, a realm radically apart from other spheres of life, then it becomes highly problematic to grant what used to be thought of as contained within its boundaries any special dispensation.

The critique of the integrity of the aesthetic has come, broadly speaking, from three directions, which we may designate historical and sociological criticism, avant-garde practice, and poststructuralist theory. The first of these has established the chronological origins of the idea of what the literary critic M. H. Abrams calls "art-as-such,"[6] which rather than being an eternal cultural given, came into being only in the eighteenth century in England and Germany. Encompassing the so-called fine arts, enjoining an attitude of contemplative appreciation akin to religious worship, defining works as autotelic, disinterested, and autonomous, this new appreciation of a generic category called "art" generated a discourse called "aesthetics" developed with great power by writers like Shaftesbury, Burke, and Addison in England and Baumgarten and Kant in Germany. Its practical value was perhaps first put to the test during the French Revolution, when the art treasures of the discredited monarchy were saved from the iconoclastic fury of the mob and protected in the Louvre, itself thus wondrously transformed from a king's palace into a museum preserving the artistic patrimony of the nation.

The subsumption of discrete artistic crafts under the generic category of art, and the discursive isolation of aesthetics from ethics, metaphysics, epistemology, and other philosophical fields, was accompanied by the institutional creation of networks of evaluation, preservation, and commodification, which invested the idea that art was a realm apart with social rather than merely cultural force. In an age when traditional hierarchical standards were under pressure, the concept of aesthetic taste and the market judgments of value that went along with it provided new ways to distinguish high from low, worthiness from worthlessness. Bourgeois pretensions to distinction through aesthetic connoisseurship went hand in hand with the substitution of the marketplace for aristocratic patronage systems.

Along with these changes went the construction of the creative genius as a figure of unconstrained power, who produced art by breaking rather than following rules. Although often heroized as a victim of bourgeois philistinism, the genius was ironically in large measure a function of the aesthetic system engendered by the same changes that led to the market demand for his creations. Like art itself, the genius was often construed as unbound by nonaesthetic considerations—cognitive, ethical, or whatever. His pursuit of aesthetic perfection could, to be sure, lead to a chilling indifference to more conventionally humane concerns, an attitude brilliantly captured in Oscar Wilde's observation that "when Benvenuto Cellini crucified a living man to study the play of muscles in his death agony, a pope was right to grant him absolution. What is the death of a vague individual if it enables an immortal work to blossom and to create, in Keat's words, an eternal source of ecstasy?"[7] By and large, such attitudes were tolerated as the cost of untrammeled artistic freedom.

There is a great deal more that could be said about the historical construction of the category of Art and the aesthetic discourse surrounding it, a topic of considerable current scholarly interest.[8] But suffice it to note for now that once we have come to appreciate "art's" contingent, historical roots, it has inevitably grown more difficult to defend free aesthetic expression as if it were a self-evident truth. Indeed, in the hands of sociologists like Pierre Bourdieu, an awareness of the historical construction of aesthetic value can lead to a denial that art in any way transcends its institutional roots in the system of social distinction that it helps maintain.[9] In this reading, culture becomes "cultural capital' and artistic freedom is little more than the right to assert hierarchical superiority in a more "tasteful" way than mere money or breeding would allow.

From a very different perspective, that of the so-called avant-garde movements of the late nineteenth and early twentieth centuries, a complementary assault on the integrity of the aesthetic was launched. Dadaist manifestations, Duchamp's ready-mades, Surrealist automatic writing and found objects, all of these challenged the ideology of the creative genius and the permanent, transcendent value of the works he created. Although at times descending into a nihilist "anti-art for anti-art's sake," the avant-garde by and large held on to a belief in the redemptive potential of art. Here the value of art as a realm of autotelic and autonomous disinterestedness was not challenged per se; what was at issue instead was the continued separation of that realm from everyday life. As Peter Bürger has argued, the avant-garde often sought to infuse everyday life with the emancipatory energies of art.[10] That is, it sought not the abolition of the separate sphere of the aesthetic as much as the realization of its "promise of happiness" in the realm of quotidian existence. Unlike the modernists, who Bürger claims remained within the institution of art and disrupted only conventional notions of the artwork, the avant-garde actively sought to heal the wound that split art from life.

The emancipatory outcome they sought has not, to be sure, been realized, surviving only in the parodic form that we can identify with the postmodernist version of reintegrating art and life. Nor has their own "work" successfully escaped being reaestheticized by the powerful institutions of collection and preservation that still determine what is art and what isn't. What Walter Benjamin made famous as the aura around works of art has not dissolved as easily as he and others in the heyday of the avant-garde had hoped. But in challenging the integrity of the institution of art and debunking the claim that artists are creative geniuses above the law, they have also helped undermine the premises of the discourse on which the idea of aesthetic freedom is based.

Still a third stimulus to this debunking has been more recently provided by the theories loosely called poststructuralist. Jacques Derrida's *Truth in Painting* is perhaps the best-known locus of an argument that has been elaborated by others in the same camp, such as Philippe Lacoue-Labarthe, Jean-Luc Nancy, and Paul de Man.[11] For Derrida, the absolute distinction between the work, or *ergon*, and its surrounding frame, or *parergon*, is impossible to maintain. Intrinsic and extrinsic, text and context, cited words in quotation marks and "direct" words spoken without them,[12] all of these are intertwined in ways that undercut the ideal purity of the aesthetic realm. Aesthetic discourses, such as Kant's Third Critique, are likewise invaded by the parergonal cognitive and ethical considerations they try to keep at bay. Thus, although deconstruction is often taken to mean the imperialism of the aesthetic, because of its refusal to segregate literal from metaphorical meanings and rhetoric from philosophy, it might be understood just as well to imply a belief in the opposite: the pollution of the pure realm of art by "extraneous" considerations from outside. It is not surprising that something called the "aesthetic ideology" has been its target as often as it has in the work of Marxist cultural critics like David Lloyd or Terry Eagleton.[13]

As a result of these and comparable critiques, the integrity of the institution of art no longer seems as inviolable as it did from the era of, say, Matthew Arnold to that of Clement Greenberg. This is not to suggest, however, that it has simply collapsed or is even on its last legs. For the social and economic exigencies that called it into being are still very potent. The ironic complicity between commodification and the ideology of unique genius can scarcely be doubted in an age of $50 million Van Goghs. But what has become dubious nonetheless is the practice of evoking artistic freedom by those who must surely know that the ground on which they base their case has turned into quicksand.

Interestingly, this is not the first time such inconsistencies have appeared. Take, for example, a celebrated episode in the history of Surrealism, the furor surrounding Louis Aragon's poem "Front Rouge."[14] Containing the memorably lyrical lines, "Shoot Léon Blum, Shoot Boncour Froissard Déat, Shoot the trained bears of social democracy," the poem caused Aragon to be indicted on charges of incitement to murder and provocation of desertion in the army in January 1932. André Breton and the Surrealists rallied to his defense, organizing a giant petition on his behalf, which some 60,000 people signed. Many who did were won over by the Surrealists' invoking of the general principle that a poem should not be confused with a political tract. Falling back on what can be called "the aesthetic alibi" for what he acknowledged was only a mediocre "poem of circumstance," Breton wrote, "I say that this poem, by its situation in Aragon's work on the one hand and in the history of poetry on the other, corresponds to a certain number of formal determinations which do not permit the isolation of any one group of words ('Comrades, kill the cops') in order to exploit its literal meaning, whereas for some other group ('The stars descend familiarly on earth') the question of this literal meaning does not come up. . . . The meaning and significance of the poem are *different* from the sum of all that the analysis of the specific elements it involves permit to be discovered in it. . . ."[15]

Here we have the peculiar spectacle of one of the leading avant-garde critics of art for art's sake, one of the most dogged believers in transgressing the barrier between art and life, resorting to traditional notions of the inviolable integrity of the organic work, the formalist distinction between form and content, and the radical distinction between literal and metaphorical uses of language. Not surprisingly, Breton was roundly attacked as a hypocrite by writers like André Gide and Romain Rolland, who claimed that symbolic action inevitably had moral and political consequences, which could not be so easily evaded. To claim a special immunity on the part of the poet, they furthermore argued, was to raise him above the common man, whose prosaic challenges to authority were unprotected by the alleged disinterestedness of the aesthetic realm.

Aragon, for his part, ultimately repudiated Breton's defense, partly because the Surrealist pamphlet contained subtle criticisms of the Communist Party, to which he soon gave his uncontested loyalty. The "Aragon Affair," as it became known, ended with Aragon, against whom all charges were dropped, leaving behind his Surrealist affiliation entirely and Breton sputtering with rage at the betrayal. What he seems to have been a bit less outraged by was the betrayal of his own principles by the appeal to aesthetic purity he had made on behalf of the ungrateful Aragon. The interpenetration of art and everyday life, he seemed to be saying, was only a one-way affair; it was justifiable when art sought to influence the everyday or made raids on it of its own choosing for inspiration, but should everyday concerns invade the sacrosanct realm of the aesthetic, then its freedom was being violated.

Today, the same logic seems to prevail among those who most piously defend artistic freedom against the incursion of the state, the church, or social groups offended by what they see or read. It is tempting as a result to repeat the charges of Gide and Rolland and simply dismiss the appeal to a special dispensation for artistic expression as self-serving and hypocritical. Salman Rushdie, we might be inclined to conclude, was right to disappoint his defenders and accept some responsibility for the offense his book caused Muslim believers. Madonna, by the same token, should have been woman enough to shoulder the blame (or accept the credit) for the fact that her material challenged the sensibilities of the good citizens of Toronto.

And yet this is a temptation that must be resisted. For what then would be left, the nagging worry remains, to protect us from the censorious efforts of the Helms, Wildmons, and Khomeinis of the world, if the fiction of aesthetic integrity were utterly abandoned? How might we fend off the wholesale invasion of the aesthetic realm by those who want to subordinate it to nonaesthetic considerations—moral, political, economic, and so on. This concern, I agree, is not an idle one, as threats to free expression (artistic or otherwise) should never be taken lightly. The recent disclosures about the explicit political pressure on decisions at the National Endowment for the Arts shows how easily such threats can be translated into action.

There are, it seems to me, three ways to preserve what the doctrine of artistic freedom in its naive form can no longer be expected to protect. The first draws on a solution recently suggested by feminists concerned about the problematic practical consequences of deconstructing the centered subject, female or otherwise. Rather than accepting the dissolution of subjects entirely into discursive systems, with the accompanying danger of robbing women of their potential for self-realizing agency and the solidarity of their group identity, theorists like Gayatri Chakravorty Spivak and Rosi Braidotti have introduced the idea of "strategic essentialism."[16] Acknowledging that collective subjects like "woman" are ultimately artificial constructs rather than natural givens, they have claimed that it is nonetheless permissible to adopt an essentialist discourse when it is strategically useful in combatting discrimination against people who are the victims of negative essentializing.

Although the parallels are not perfect, perhaps a similar strategic essentialism might seem warranted in the case of artistic freedom. That is, even though it may be impossible to ontologize the aesthetic as a separate realm apart from mundane values and interests, it may be useful in certain circumstances to claim that it is such a realm in order to provide a bulwark against the pressures to subordinate what we normally include in "the aesthetic" to what is extrinsic to it. Such an approach, however, may well invite the rebuke that fictions can work only so far as they remain persuasive to the people who hold them. If those who defend the integrity of "art" know it to be no more than a concocted category, what is to keep this knowledge out of the hands of those who attack that integrity? How long can a strategy effectively operate that is built on a distinction between those who are privy to the truth (which they only pretend to forget) and those who are not?

A second, possibly more fruitful defense arises from the observation

made above, that despite all the efforts to historicize, deconstruct, or render obsolete through realization in the lifeworld the differentiated realm of
art, it nonetheless survives as an ideology because the social and economic
reasons for its existence persist. That is, just because we can de-naturalize a
category like the aesthetic and expose it as historically relative does not
mean it necessarily goes away. Nor does showing its boundaries to be
porous mean that they are entirely effaced. Art may no longer be legitimated in traditional terms, but if it successfully functions as "cultural
capital," then it is likely to be around for a long time to come.

If this is the case, then why not still draw on some of the residual power
of the category, without foregrounding its deeper socioeconomic function,
to protect transgressive symbolic action? Although such a solution, like
that of strategic essentialism, may seem a bit duplicitous, it does seem to
keep the less theoretically astute thought police at bay. Or at least so one
might conclude from the trial of the Cincinnati museum exhibition of the
Mapplethorpe photographs, when the jury accepted "expert testimony" (by
eminent "cultural capitalists") as to their artistic merit.

A final, somewhat more candid alternative would be to accept the collapse (or at least moribund status) of the category of the aesthetic and fall
back on a more general defense of free speech of all kinds. Such a solution
would spare us the embarrassment of saying that an elite of soi-disant
artists can claim more protection than the average citizen. It also would
avoid the no less elitist implications of the first two defenses, based as they
are on the difference between those disabused of the aesthetic ideology and
those still in its thrall. Such a defense, to be sure, would do little to help in
cases such as Serra's Tilted Arc, where something more fundamental has to
be assumed to justify the continuing rights of the "creator" after he or she
has sold the work created, but on other instances, it might be sufficient to
resist censorship.

Here a potential problem arises, however, at a time when challenges to
the absolute exercise of free speech, whether through the invocation of
community as opposed to universal standards or the controversial critique
of "fighting words," threatens to narrow the definition of the permissible.
The 1973 Supreme Court decision in the case of Miller v. California opened
the possibility of local juries deciding what was obscene or offensive. More
recent opinions, I am told, suggest that a broader category like the univer-

sally construed "public sphere" may get us beyond the potentially stifling judgments of narrowly defined "communities," which never, pace the Helms and Wildmons of the world, have any one shared set of standards. But there is still no reason to assume that the offensive and transgressive symbolic action hitherto defended on aesthetic grounds will automatically survive, because there remains the inevitable struggle to define who has the power in such a public sphere to decide what is permissible and what isn't. And as the recent Supreme Court decision curtailing free speech in publicly funded abortion clinics suggests, this power may well be wielded by the current court with a narrow definition of what is permissible.

It may therefore be necessary to draw on all of the defenses outlined above—and still others yet to be invented—to resist the implications of the unraveling of the aesthetic alibi. "The freedom of the artist," like the ideology of l'art pour l'art on which it rests, may be a myth in its classical form, but without some less vulnerable version of the same notion, we are in danger of losing more than a faded ideal. For insofar as the category of "art" provides a shelter not only for cathartic and consoling experiences of beauty, but also for experiments in cultural transgression and innovation, it serves a vital future-oriented function that transcends its status as mere capital in the cultural economy of our day. It is perhaps for this reason that we stubbornly hold on to its privileged status, even as we have paradoxically come to recognize that it is built on foundations of extremely porous clay.

II

Mimesis and Mimetology: Adorno and Lacoue-Labarthe

✳

Mimesis, Roland Barthes insists in S/Z, produced a sickening feeling in his stomach, a kind of nausea that came from its conservative reproduction of already existing signs.[1] For the resolutely anti-representational Barthes, any straightforward imitation of the external world, any aesthetic practice based on reference and repetition rather than the free play of signs, was inherently inadequate. A semiotic approach, he argues, must attend to the semantic play in the system, which undoes the closed economy of mimetic imitation. Likewise, in "The Double Session," Jacques Derrida disapprovingly asked if traditional literary criticism, with its search for univocal hidden meanings and the thematic kernels of text, was not "a part of what we have called the *ontological* interpretation of mimesis or of metaphysical mimetologism?"[2] For Gilles Deleuze and Félix Guattari, mimesis is "radically false," a part of the paranoid order of spatial stasis they call the "copy" as opposed to the liberated, nomadic space of the "map."[3] Jean-François Lyotard identified mimesis with the "masters' law" and praised Diogenes' "cynical body" for defying it.[4] And Paul de Man dismissed mimesis as merely one literary trope among others, a trope, moreover, whose alleged naturalness needs to be deconstructed, for "what we call ideology is precisely the confusion of linguistic with natural reality, of reference with phenomenalism."[5]

For these theorists, and for many others normally labeled, for better or worse, poststructuralist, a conventional aesthetic privileging of mimesis or what is taken to be its synonym, imitation, is an ideologically suspect recirculation of the readymade, a false belief in the fixity of meaning and the possibility of achieving full presence, a language game that fails to see itself as such. Lacan's warnings against the misrecognitions of the mirror stage would be yet another instance of this critique. Whereas in the much older Platonic critique of mimesis its danger was understood to be the undermining of a stable notion of truth, which is threatened by duplicitous copies of mere appearances, here it is precisely the opposite worry that is at work: the anxiety that mimesis means privileging an allegedly "true" original over its infinite duplications.[6] Or rather, at least in the case of Derrida, it involves that worry and its apparent contrary: that the mimetic "double" may itself be taken as self-sufficient, needing no external referent at all. That assumption, which underlies certain modernist aesthetic practices, implies a no less dubious belief in the full ontological presence of the simulacrum itself.

In apparent contrast, the competing intellectual tradition known as the Frankfurt School found much in mimesis to praise. Although no less suspicious than poststructuralism of the naive referentialism of naturalist and realist aesthetics, Critical Theory valued mimesis as a valuable resource in its struggle to counter the reigning power of instrumental rationality in the modern world. Drawing on Walter Benjamin's suggestive ruminations of 1933, "On the Mimetic Faculty" and "The Doctrine of the Similar,"[7] and Roger Caillois's 1938 book Le mythe et l'homme,[8] Max Horkheimer and Theodor W. Adorno mourned the loss or withering of a primal and inherently benign human capacity to imitate nature as the dialectic of enlightenment followed its fateful course.[9] Although they recognized the sinister potential of mimetic behavior when combined with the instrumental rationality it generally opposed—a potential realized precisely in the mocking Nazi mimicry of the Jews and duplicated in the culture industry at its most repressive—by and large, mimesis served as an honorific term in their vocabulary.[10] In his Aesthetic Theory, Adorno could thus call the mimetic behavior that is precariously preserved in art "a receptacle for all that has been violently lopped off from and repressed in man by centuries of civilization, during which human beings were forcibly subjected to suffering" and "the endeavour to recover the bliss of a world that is gone."[11]

Not surprisingly, a significant secondary literature has arisen around the enigmatic concept of mimesis in Critical Theory, especially in the thought of Adorno, which one commentator has gone so far as to call the "obscure

operator" of his entire system and another has called "a foundational concept never defined nor argued, but always alluded to, by name, as though it
had preexisted all the texts."[12] Commentators have carefully unraveled
its overdetermined origins in anthropological theories of shamanism and
sympathetic magic, zoological analyses of animal mimicry, psychological
theories of compulsive repetition, and aesthetic ideas of representation.
However, no one, to my knowledge, has attempted the formidable task of
thinking about Adorno's positive evocation of mimesis in the light of more
recent poststructuralist commentary on the same theme.[13]

Such a task becomes all the more intriguing when we realize that several
thinkers in the poststructuralist camp are less unequivocally hostile to
mimesis than the picture painted above would suggest. That is, despite the
animadversions against naive referentiality in the work of theorists like
de Man, Lyotard, and Barthes, mimesis in a more complicated sense has
played a positive role in certain poststructuralist theory. A case can be
made, in fact, for the Derrida of "The Double Session,"[14] but it is in the
work of Philippe Lacoue-Labarthe in particular that the most profound
poststructuralist meditation on the implications of the concept can be
found. After a brief sketch of Adorno's complicated use of the term, I want
to pass on to how mimesis figures in Lacoue-Labarthe's work, most notably the texts recently collected in Typography.[15] By then comparing the two, I
hope to provide a new perspective on the significance of this extraordinarily vexed term.

I

A first approximation of Adorno's use of mimesis, whether in aesthetic,
philosophical, anthropological, or psychological contexts, would necessarily stress its relational character, its way of bridging but not collapsing
differences. These differences are not, however, simply between a representation and what is represented, as the dominant tradition of thought
about mimesis assumes, nor between one producing subject and another
(the genius, say, imitating divine creation), as a subordinate tradition assumes.[16] The crucial difference is rather between what are traditionally
called subjects and objects (or at least the "other" of subjects) in the world.
Conceptual thought can be understood as an act of aggression perpetrated
by a dominating subject on a world assumed to be external to it; it sub-

sumes particulars under universals, violently reducing their uniqueness to typifications or exemplars of a general or essential principle. Mimesis, in contrast, involves a more sympathetic, compassionate, and noncoercive relationship of affinity between nonidentical particulars, which do not then become reified into two poles of a subject/object dualism. Rather than producing hierarchical subsumption under a subjectively generated category, it preserves the rough equality of the object and subject involved.

More precisely, it assimilates the latter to the former in such a way that the unposited, unintended object implicitly predominates, thwarting the imperialist gesture of subjective control and constitution that is the hallmark of philosophical idealism. "Mimetic behaviour," Adorno insists, "does not imitate something but assimilates itself to that something."[17] The word "imitation" (Nachahmung), he implies, suggests too active a role for the subject, whose making alone cannot be the source of the meaning it finds in the mimetic relation with the other.[18] Instead, Adorno prefers the verb anschmiegen (to snuggle up or mold to) to stress a relationship of contiguity.[19] In a way, he is returning to the original Greek use of the term, for example, in the Delian hymns or Pindar, when "mimesis" meant the expression of an inner state through cultic rituals rather than the reproduction of external reality, rituals that included music, dance, and mime.[20] Although in these instances, "mimesis" meant an outward expression of something inward rather than a relation between subject and external object, in both cases, the mode was more like benign assimilation than domination.

In more passively assimilating itself to the other, the subject of mimesis also preserves the sensuous, somatic element that the abstractions of idealist reason factor out of cognition or sublate into a higher rationality. Precisely which senses are most involved I will examine shortly, but for now suffice it to say that mimesis necessarily entails a crucial role for the body in the interaction between self and world. Equally important, it is the body as both the source of pleasure and the locus of pain.

Yet mimesis, as Adorno develops it, is not to be understood as the simple opposite of reason, as it sometimes has been.[21] It is closer to what Habermas once called a "placeholder" for a "primordial reason," which, however, cannot be satisfactorily theorized without betraying its preconceptual status.[22] As Adorno explains in Aesthetic Theory:

The continued existence of mimesis, understood as the nonconceptual affinity of a subjective creation with its objective and unposited other, defines art as a form of cognition and to that extent as "rational." . . . What the stubborn persistence of aesthetic mimesis proves is not that there is an innate play instinct, as some ideologues would have us believe, but that to this day rationality has never been fully realized, rationality understood in the sense of an agency in the service of mankind and of human potentials, perhaps even of "humanized nature" (Marx).[23]

Although initially manifest in the context of what Sir James Frazer calls "sympathetic magic," mimesis should thus not be reduced to "the superstitious belief in the ability to have a direct impact on things."[24] Nor is it simply an appreciation of the uncanny similitudes that supposedly already exist in nature, those wondrous astrological, physiognomic, or graphological correspondences, the "secret language of things" that Benjamin in his more anti-modern moods finds so intriguing. In aesthetic mimesis in particular, what is preserved—as well as transformed—is the sedimented "material" of past artistic endeavors, which suggest a historical and natural "other" worthy of assimilation. Moreover, mimesis partakes of nonmagical forms of knowing, in part through its preservation of some of the cognitive power of intuition, as opposed to conceptual appropriation, the intuition Kant sees as a hallmark of aesthetic experience.[25]

Its nonmagical status also follows from the complicated relationship mimesis has to expression, by which Adorno means something more than revealing the psychological interiority of the individual artist. Instead, what is expressed is a dissonant resistance to the harmonizing impulses of affirmative art, a resistance that is grounded in a remembrance of the sedimented suffering of the past and the continuing suffering of the present—the suffering of the object as well as the subject, of what might be called "nature" as well as humankind.[26] "Expression in art is mimetic," Adorno claims, "just as the expression of living creatures is the expression of suffering."[27] Mimesis is thus a check to the ideological overcoming of real pain in the idealist art of consolation or the realist art of reconciliation.[28] Hence mimesis remains vital to the uncompromisingly dissonant modernist art, for example, that of Beckett or Kafka, Adorno so vigorously championed (for reasons that were thus diametrically opposed to Barthes's semiotic celebration of the alleged free play of signifiers).[29]

Perhaps most important, the rational moment of mimesis paradoxically follows from its own need to be supplemented by—or, rather, placed in a force field with—precisely that very conceptuality it seems to spurn. In aesthetic experience, Adorno insists, mimesis is never sufficient unto itself, but always needs to be juxtaposed in a constellation with the constructive impulse of "spirit."[30] "In art," he writes, "mimesis is both inferior and superior to spirit: it is contrary to spirit and yet the cause of spirit's being kindled. In artworks spirit has become the principle of construction. For spirit to live up to its telos means that it must well up from the mimetic impulses, constructing them by assimilation rather than external decree."[31] Spirit and mimesis, construction and expression, thus exist in a creative tension in works of art, a tension that should be preserved. Although they infiltrate each other—"To represent the mimesis it supplanted," Adorno wrote in Negative Dialectics, "the concept has no other way than to adopt something mimetic in its own conduct, without abandoning itself"[32]—the two cannot be simply identified at some higher level of unity.

Precisely because works of art preserve rather than falsely reconcile such tensions, they also stage what might be called a negative dialectic of imitation in relation to what exists outside their apparently self-enclosed boundaries. Adorno presents this negative dialectic as an unavoidable antinomy. On the one hand, works of art—or at least modernist ones that take seriously the "art for art's sake" credo—strive for autotelic self-sufficiency, which allows Adorno to say that "the mimesis of works of art is their resemblance to themselves."[33] As Lambert Zuidervaart points out, this claim implicitly answers the Platonic fear that art is duplicitous because it fails to imitate a higher reality; for Adorno instead, "similarity with itself separates the artwork from a false reality, where nothing is really real because everything obeys the law of exchange."[34] That is, by refusing to imitate, or be assimilated entirely to, a bad external reality—by paradoxically honoring, one might say, the Jewish taboo on graven images—works of art hold out the hope for a more benign version of mimesis in a future world beyond domination and reification.

On the other hand, the actual failure of such works to achieve absolute self-identity, a failure produced, inter alia, by their always being made for those who enjoy, exchange, or consume them, bears witness to the still-unredeemed quality of life in the social world. That imperfection necessarily infiltrates the work and mocks the illusory claim to completion. As such, it also bears witness to bodily pain, the unhealed wounds of damaged life that are indirectly represented in the artwork's dissonant fissures. The very illusory quality of art, its deceitful claim to present the absolute in sensuous terms, is thus at once a protest against the inadequacies of the world it refuses to imitate and an expression of the inability to transcend those inadequacies through aesthetic means alone.

Adorno, to be sure, was aware that the delicate balance he admired in certain modernist works was threatened by the increasing hegemony of spirit and construction, understood in essentially instrumental rationalist terms, over mimesis or expression. The withering away of the sensuous moment in late modernist art meant that all that was being imitated was the reified social relations of the administered world, a conclusion he amplified in his critique of Schoenberg's move from atonalism to the twelve-tone row.[35] Its effects were felt outside the realm of art as well, Adorno insists, for "the contemporary loss of any subjective capacity for experience is most likely identical with the tenacious repression of mimesis today."[36] And when the repressed does return, Adorno laments, it often does so in the distorted form of a sadistic mimicry that shows its subordination to the ends of instrumental, dominating rationality.

To combat that repression is no easy task, but one modest effort is discerned by Fredric Jameson in Adorno's own, idiosyncratic prose style. Without ever reducing philosophy to a variant of literature, Adorno seeks to subvert the dominating, homogenizing power of conceptual thinking by introducing a mimetic element in his own writing. According to Jameson, this moment appears in those moves in Adorno's prose that can be called narrative. That is, his writing stages the conflicts and tensions of a story over time, with various theoretical terms and philosophical arguments playing the roles of actors, a procedure that tacitly undercuts the atemporal impulse of conceptual reason. "This micro-work of the sentence on the isolated concept," Jameson writes, "is, then, what undermines its apparent rational autonomy and pre-forms it . . . for its multiple positions in the larger movement of the constellation or the 'model.' The mimetic or the narrative may be thought to be a kind of homeopathic strategy in which, by revealing the primal movement of domination hidden away within abstract thought, the venom of abstraction is neutralized, allowing some potential or utopian truth-content to come it to its own."[37]

Whether or not the term "narrative" is fully appropriate here—it may suggest too linear an emplotment to capture the chiasmic logic Jameson himself recognizes as Adorno's main trope—the importance of Adorno's stylistic mimesis of mimesis is worth taking seriously, for it goes beyond a mere external staging of dialectical conflicts. Perhaps a more fruitful way to bring it to the surface would be to follow Adorno's own praise for the stylistic device that he finds best resists conceptual synthesis: paratactic rather than hypotactic syntax.[38] By resisting the imperative to arrange ideas hierarchically, parataxis both undercuts the mediating logic of conceptual subordination and bears witness to the crisis of meaningful experience (Erfahrung in Benjamin's well-known sense, rather than Erlebnis) in the modern world.

In his discussion of Hölderlin, Adorno acknowledges, to be sure, that language, unlike music, cannot avoid some conceptual homogenizing: "by virtue of its significative element, the opposite pole to its mimetic-expressive element, language is chained to the form of judgment and proposition and thereby to the synthetic form of the concept. In poetry, unlike music, a conceptual synthesis turns against its medium; it becomes a constitutive dissociation."[39] In the later poetry of Hölderlin, this dissociation is especially "striking—artificial disturbances that evade the logical hierarchy of subordinating syntax."[40]

Precisely because he remains true to the unsublatable tension between the synthetic and the dissociative impulses in language, however—to what we have seen Adorno call elsewhere the spiritual/constructive and the mimetic/expressive moments in art—Hölderlin produces an aesthetic instantiation of negative dialectics. As such, he resists the mythologizing reading based solely on the putative content of the poems that Heidegger wants to force on him as the simple antithesis of idealism, the gnomic prophet of prereflective Being. The same resistance might be discerned in Adorno's own writing, which never one-sidedly pits mimesis or sympathetic magic against conceptual rationality, synthetic domination, or theoretical reflection in a nondialectical opposition.

2

To invoke Adorno's admiration for, and arguably mimetic appropriation of, Hölderlin's paratactic style provides a convenient bridge to Lacoue-Labarthe, who finds in Hölderlin—albeit more so in the dramatic works like *The Death of Empedocles* and the translations of Sophocles than in the later poetry—a profound lesson on the same issues. In "The Caesura of the Speculative," one of the central essays in *Typography*, Lacoue-Labarthe, in fact, approvingly cites Adorno's text, claiming that its author is justified in "comparing the 'parataxis' characteristic of Hölderlin's late style with the writing of Beethoven's last quartets."[41]

Lacoue-Labarthe's target in this piece is what he sees as the speculative dialectic at work in both tragedy, understood in a certain way, and absolute idealism, a speculative dialectic he identifies with what Heidegger calls "the ontotheological in its fully accomplished form."[42] He finds, underlying that dialectic, "the guiding thread of a primary and constant preoccupation, of a single question—none other than that of *mimesis*, at whatever level one chooses to examine it (whether it be that of 'imitation,' in the sense of the 'imitation of the Ancients,' of mimesis as a mode of *poiesis*, i.e., Aristotelian mimesis, or even—and this does not fail to enter into play—of mimesis in the sense of 'mimetism' or *imitatio*)."[43] According to Lacoue-Labarthe, only mimesis provides the means to transfigure negativity into positive being through representation; only mimesis allows the tragic pleasure that overcomes a visceral feeling of horror at the terrible events reproduced. This economy of specular transfiguration is precisely what underlies idealist philosophy as well, indeed philosophy in general. As such, it is the basis of what Derrida calls a "mimetologism," the imitation of the same in a closed system of ultimate higher reconciliation, a system in which what is mimetically re-presented is the putative unity of the logos itself, a logos that is identified with the truth.[44]

Lacoue-Labarthe is careful to deny that Hölderlin consciously transcends this economy, at least at the level of his own theoretical understanding, which is "speculative through and through."[45] Indeed, he implies that a complete extrication from the mimetological, speculative economy would be impossible.[46] But what Hölderlin's work does accomplish is a kind of internal dislocation of it, an exposure of a caesura in its smoothly working operation (as in the alexandrine), like the pause in poetic meter. And he does so by regressing behind Aristotle's affirmative understanding of mimetic representation to reveal what "haunts Plato under the name of mimesis and against which Plato fights with all of his philosophical determination until he finds a way of arresting it and fixing its concept."[47] Rather than expelling the troubling implications of the mimetic duplication of the same—an expulsion Lacoue-Labarthe calls the speculative "denegation" of mimesis—Hölderlin allows it to fester in the midst of his own tragic dramas, producing a kind of endless oscillation between proximity and distance that denies sublation and reconciliation and that cannot rest content at either pole.

More precisely, the dialectical structure of speculative recuperation and the infinite oscillation coexist in an uneasy equilibrium, the melodic and the rhythmic impulses of the work never coming together completely. The caesura in the work is thus mimetic representation itself, the space between the original and its duplicate the hiatus rather than either pole. For this reason, Lacoue-Labarthe is able to conclude, with an implicit nod to Benjamin, that Hölderlin's dramas come closer to the baroque Trauerspiel than to classical Greek tragedy.[48] Whereas the structure of speculative dialectics that underlies the latter is like the completed work of mourning, which in German is Trauerarbeit, the Trauerspiel keeps the "play" of mourning going forever without any final reconciliation or working through, keeping, that is, the "play" in the system from achieving any terminal stasis.[49]

If it follows any logic, it is that of paradox, which Lacoue-Labarthe dubs "hyperbologic." Expatiating in the other essays in his collection on its meaning, Lacoue-Labarthe points to the ambivalence at work even in Aristotle's notion of mimesis, at once a duplication or copy of what already exists and a supplement or addition to fill the lack in what exists. Whereas the former is reproductive, the latter is productive. Whereas the former assumes nature is sufficient unto itself, the latter implies the need for a substitution. The paradox follows from the fact that mimetic substitution means both the need to imitate what already exists and the realization that what exists is itself insufficient and must be supplemented by the imitation.

As Diderot shows in his discussion of actors who can imitate the identity of a character precisely because they themselves lack all fixed character, the result undercuts the notion of a proper, self-possessed identity. "The paradox," Lacoue-Labarthe writes, "states a *law of impropriety*, which is also the very law of mimesis: only the 'man without qualities,' the being without properties or specificity, the subjectless subject (absent from himself, distracted from himself, deprived of self) is able to present or produce in general."[50] Plato also grasps this paradox but denounces the hypocrisy he sees as its issue, whereas Diderot—and Lacoue-Labarthe—appreciate it precisely for its destabilizing effect, its active unsettling of reified selfhood (indeed even of the fragile notion of the self that underpins Adorno's notion of mimesis as the expression of suffering).

Significantly, Lacoue-Labarthe connects the hyperbologic of the mimetic paradox to that of semblance or illusion (*Schein*) in general, a category Adorno also privileges in his writings on aesthetics.[51] "The division between appearance and reality, presence and absence, the same and the other, or identity and difference," Lacoue-Labarthe argues, "grounds (and . . . constantly unsteadies) mimesis. At whatever level one takes it—in the copy or the reproduction, the art of the actor, mimetism, disguise, dialogic writing—the rule is always the same: the more it resembles, the more it differs."[52] For Adorno as well, it is aesthetic illusion that resists mimetological closure, or what he calls the "general mimetic abandonment to reification, which is the principle of death."[53] Even certain variants of modernist art had succumbed to that principle through a simple presentation of external reality without aesthetic transfiguration into illusion: "Ever since the beginning of modernism art has absorbed objects from outside," Adorno remarks, "leaving them as they are without assimilating them (e.g., montage). This indicates a surrender by mimesis to its antagonist, a trend which is caused by the pressure reality exerts on art."[54] Lacoue-Labarthe's hostility to the ideology of the genuine or authentic original, which mimesis merely duplicates, is thus explicitly shared by Adorno, who warns in *Minima Moralia* against "the concept of genuineness as such. In it dwells the notion of the supremacy of the original over the derived. This notion, however, is always linked with social legitimation. All ruling strata claim to be the oldest settlers, autochthonous."[55]

Perhaps more than Lacoue-Labarthe though, Adorno is willing to retain an emphatic notion of truth in relation to works of art, for "the definition of art in terms of illusion is only half correct: art is true to the degree to which it is an illusion of the nonillusory (*Schein des Scheinlosen*). In the last analysis, to experience art is to recognize that its truth content is not null and void."[56] But it was precisely Adorno's point—and here he tacitly antici- pates Lacoue-Labarthe's defense of the hyperbologic paradox—that such truth is manifest only in the nonsublatable, negative dialectic of illusion and nonillusion itself. As such, it could be understood as comparable to a permanent allegory without symbolic reconciliation.[57]

Significantly, it is the yearning for totalized reconciliation that Lacoue- Labarthe, in an essay written with Jean-Luc Nancy, claims was at the root of "the Nazi myth."[58] Myth, they claimed, "is the mimetic instrument par excellence,"[59] because it seeks absolute identification through typified exis- tence (real "experience" through the realization of racial types). Although arguing that the Germans' need for mimetic mythologizing was stronger than elsewhere, because their imitation of the Greeks was itself an imita- tion of an earlier French mimesis of the ancients, they darkly conclude, in a way reminiscent of Horkheimer and Adorno's *Dialectic of Enlightenment*, that "this logic, with its double trait of the mimetic will-to-identity and the self-fulfillment of form, belongs profoundly to the mood or character of the West in general, and more precisely, to the fundamental tendency of the *subject*, in the metaphysical sense of the word."[50] Like the Frankfurt School theorists, they acknowledge the complicity of mimesis in one of its guises—in their case, that of the nonallegorical search for perfect identity, in that of Horkheimer and Adorno, the "organized control of mimesis"[61] by instrumental rationality—in the realization of nightmare politics. Even the Heidegger from whom Lacoue-Labarthe and Nancy had learned so much is not exempt from this critique: "an unacknowledged mimetology seems to overdetermine the thought of Heidegger politically," Lacoue- Labarthe admits, after the growing scandal about Heidegger's politics in the 1980s.[62]

The victims of Nazism, in contrast, are those who adhere to a non- mimetological variant of mimesis, which resists mythic closure. "All in all," writes Lacoue-Labarthe in his book *Heidegger, Art and Politics*, "the Jews are infinitely mimetic beings, or in other words, the site of an *endless mimesis*, which is both interminable and inorganic, producing no art and achieving no appropriation."[63] Although the claim that Jews have never produced art may seem perverse (as well as inaccurate), it is meant in a flattering way to the extent that "art" suggests symbolic sublimation of the unreconciled fissures of existence. Horkheimer and Adorno make a similar claim in *Dialectic of Enlightenment*, when they argue that for all the Jews' complicity in the millennia-long process of dominating nature, "they did not eliminate adaptation to nature, but converted it into a series of duties in the form of ritual. They have retained the aspect of expiation, but have avoided the reversion to mythology which symbolism implies."[64]

3

Much more could be done to tease out the telling similarities between Adorno's and Lacoue-Labarthe's general notions of mimesis, but I want to turn now to the specific issue of the sensual element in their accounts. In the essay just discussed, "The Nazi Myth," Lacoue-Labarthe and Nancy claim that the Aryan type is the product of "a construction and conformation of the world according to a vision, an image, the image of the creator of forms. . . . [T]he *anschauen*—'seeing' as vision and intuition piercing to the heart of the things and *forming* being itself, the 'seeing' of an active, practical, operative dream—is the heart of the 'mythicotypical' process."[65] Privileging vision, in other words, is understood to be in the service of the speculative, theatrical, theoretical version of mimesis, which elsewhere Lacoue-Labarthe damns as mimetological.[66]

A similar argument informs his consideration of the psychoanalytic theory of the self in "The Echo of the Subject," included in *Typography*. Its targets are Lacan's privileging of vision in the mirror stage and in the Imaginary and René Girard's notion of mimetic rivalry, both of which depend on a conceptualization of the subject in narcissistic terms. Preferring a notion of aural to visual mimesis—the Greek nymph Echo to that of her love object, Narcissus—he turns to the analyst Theodor Reik's discussion of voice and rhythm, in *The Haunting Melody*, for help in constructing a nonidentical, uncanny version of the self. He calls it "allobiographical"—"the 'novel' of an other (be it a double)"[67]—rather than autobiographical. Such a self, he claims, is not based on specular reflection, on the imitation of the same, but rather on the *unheimliche*, rhythmic repetition of an original that never existed in itself, a perpetual spacing without end. Rhythm, in fact, "establishes the break between the visible and the audible, the temporal and the spatial (but also the inscribed and the fictive), thus resisting the hold of such partitions and bearing a relation to *archi-écriture* in the

Derridean sense of the term."[68] As such, perhaps it remains, as Derrida himself says in his introduction to *Typography*, "outside the order of the sensible. It belongs to no sense."[59] And, I might add, it rejects the Platonic realm of pure intelligibility as well.

Although one might discern a certain similarity between this argument and Benjamin's faith in "nonsensuous correspondences"—for example, those between heavenly constellations of stars and human destiny claimed by astrology—as the basis of a benign notion of mimesis, for Adorno, such a parallel is harder to discern. Despite his oft-proclaimed embrace of the Jewish taboo on graven images and his recognition that, of all the senses, smell is perhaps the most mimetic Adorno never completely denigrated visuality per se or sought a realm prior to both the senses and intelligibility.[70] As Gertrud Koch and Miriam Hansen have recently shown, even when it came to the mass cultural phenomenon known as film, Adorno could posit an emancipatory potential in the medium itself.[71] However much Hollywood films are part of the ideological culture industry, the cinematic mimesis of expressive bodies suggests a prelinguistic experience prior to the conscious articulations of the ego.

In *Aesthetic Theory*, Adorno specifically defends the importance of a visual moment in art, which is another way to say the intuitive as opposed to the purely conceptual: "the desideratum of visuality [*Anschaulichkeit*] seeks to preserve the mimetic moment of art."[72] But rather than fetishizing that moment into the essence of art per se or rigidly opposing sensuality to spirituality, Adorno also argues that "mimesis only goes on living through its antithesis, which is rational control by artworks over all that is heterogeneous to them. . . . Art is a vision of the nonvisual; it is similar to a concept without actually being one."[73] Once again, it is the constellation of mimesis and rationality, expression and spirit, that defines the unsublated aesthetic prefiguration of the utopia that Adorno refuses to abandon.

Perhaps because of that refusal, Adorno never finds rhythmic repetition without end, that infinite spacing and perpetual deferral so characteristic of deconstruction, as unambiguously congenial as does Lacoue-Labarthe. One of the central charges against Stravinsky in Adorno's celebrated invidious comparison of his music with Schoenberg's was directed precisely against the Russian composer's over-reliance on rhythmic composition: "even in those cases where the Schoenberg school operates with such rhythms, they are for the most part charged with melodic and contrapuntal content, while the rhythmic proportions which in Stravinsky dominate the musical foreground are employed solely in the sense of shock effects."[74] These shocks are simply absorbed by the numbed and overpowered musical subject, who no longer expresses the suffering of modern life, let alone has the will to resist it. Unlike Lacoue-Labarthe, Adorno never relegates to the margins of his analysis the expressive moment of mimesis, which reveals the body—natural as well as human—in pain.

Adorno's suspicion of the value of rhythmic repetition derives, it might be speculated, from the link he sees between it and what Freud had understood as the functioning of the death drive. In fact, as Josef Früchtl rightly argues, the ambivalence toward mimesis that can at times be detected in Adorno may be explained in part by his recognition that reconciliation and destruction are closely intertwined.[75] That is, the radically anti-narrative structure of the death drive, its compulsion to repeat in the service of restoring a state of undifferentiated stasis that can, however, never be realized short of actual death, lends to nonmimetological mimesis a melancholic tone that anti-utopian poststructuralists like Lacoue-Labarthe find congenial, but which Adorno does not.

Adorno, however much he may have been a practitioner of a "melancholy science," never gleefully embraces the masochistic self-shattering that defenders of the repetition compulsion claim is a release from the ideological mystifications of subjecthood.[76] He understands that the radical reduction of ego strength through the mimetic duplication of the inorganic world—what Caillois calls psychasthenia, in his study of insect mimicry—could also mean the triumph of reification. As his frequent denunciations of surrealism demonstrate, Adorno remains suspicious of an aesthetic that is based on the uncanny evocation of compulsive beauty by a depersonalized subject who ultimately reveals itself as "inanimate and virtually dead."[77] Although Jameson may overstate the case by saying that it is narration itself that Adorno hoped mimesis would rescue in its conflict with conceptuality, it is nonetheless true that he never damns narrative coherence *tout court* as merely another instance of the speculative suppression of nonidentity that is, in Derrida's terms, a version of mimetologism. He does, to be sure, acknowledge that any attempt to restore it, under the present circumstances, is necessarily ideological—telling a story could only be based on the very continuity of experience (*Erfahrung*) that had been lost in the modern world—but he does not rule out the possibility of a future in which it might once again be meaningful.[78]

It is perhaps such historical hopes, which despite everything Adorno never lost, that most distinguish his meditations on this theme from those of Lacoue-Labarthe, who seems to defend an endlessly oscillating mimesis that is based on a paradoxical hyperbologic that steadfastly resists ontological stability, subjective integrity, and speculative representation, all of which are seen as evidence of mimetological closure. In contrast, Adorno places mimesis, also understood as susceptible to, but not identical with, mimetology, in a tense constellation with its apparent opposites: rationality, spirit, narrative coherence, and subjective construction. Neither *Trauerarbeit*, in the sense of a fully triumphal mastery of otherness through a higher level sublimation like that of classical tragedy, nor *Trauerspiel*, in the sense of a perpetually melancholic resistance to any closure, defines his delicately nuanced position. Instead, Adorno practices a *trauerliche Wissenschaft*, a "melancholy science," in which the noun is no less important than the adjective. As a result, mimesis may be a necessary element in his utopian vision, but it is by no means sufficient unto itself.

4

What have we learned by this comparison between the uses of mimesis in Adorno and Lacoue-Labarthe? First, it is clear that the most interesting contemporary debate over mimesis has little to do with the issue of referential representation versus the autoreferentiality of sign systems. Nor can it be reduced to a mere synonym for imitation. Despite the easy dismissal of mimesis by the thinkers cited at the beginning of this paper, it survives in important and unexpectedly similar ways in both poststructuralism and Critical Theory.

Second, it is no less obvious that the word itself is polysemic, even catachrestic, with meanings that carry with them the residues of their separate origins in anthropological, psychological, aesthetic, philosophical, and zoological discourses. So, too, the value of the "original" model to be mimetically duplicated—variously identified with nature as a nonsubjective other, the active producer of that nature, the cultural tradition of the ancients, or the reified relations of the modern world—inevitably inflects the judgment about the process itself. If, then, there is an economy of mimesis, what Derrida calls an economimesis, it is difficult to reduce it to a circulation or equilibrium of identical acceptations.[79] Instead, the term changes its meaning and often its evaluative charge depending on the context in which it appears. It is for this reason that even mimicry, which often seems to be related to the mocking and demeaning imitation of victims, can turn around and become a tool of resistance, as postcolonial theorists like Homi Bhabha and postmodernist feminist artists like Cindy Sherman have recently demonstrated.[80]

Third, that context often involves the complex relation between mimesis and rationality or conceptuality. What the poststructuralists call mimetology involves subordinating mimesis to a deadening logic of sameness or sublation, a theoretical/theatrical logic based on visual reproduction, which they see as typical of the Western ontotheological project in general. Mimesis understood as rhythmic repetition without closure, an infinite oscillation between original and copy, is posited as the—to be sure, never fully successful—hyperbological antidote to mimetology, as the uncanny caesura in a speculative system that seeks to stifle its playful uncertainties.

In the case of Adorno, mimesis becomes problematic when it is in league not with reason per se but with the instrumental rationality of the modern world. Then what it imitates is the *nature morte* of a world of reified relations, in which the suffering of both humans and nature is no longer expressed. But as his discussion of the interaction between mimesis and rationality in art indicates, Adorno feels that both are necessary to avoid surrendering to the potential in mimesis alone to ape the repetitive rhythms of the death drive. Despite his occasional adoption of a rhetoric of nostalgia for a lost paradise of mimetic affinities, Adorno posits a constellation in which reason and mimesis each make up for the deficiencies of the other.

Finally, we have seen that both Adorno and Lacoue-Labarthe share an appreciation for the function mimesis can play in decentering the strong constitutive subject, opening a place for otherness and nonidentity and enabling a nondominating relationship between the human and the nonhuman. Although Adorno never goes so far as Lacoue-Labarthe in marginalizing the suffering subject or advocating the surrender of its ego strength, he recognizes that such a subject has to be put in a constellation with the other victims of domination rather than given absolute pride of place. What in Roland Barthes produces feelings of nausea, in Lyotard, a denunciation of the "master's law," and in Deleuze and Guattari, a nomadic flight from paranoid despotism turns out in the two theorists I have examined to be a potential source of healing and solace. Which of these opposing attitudes we should ourselves imitate is a conclusion I let each reader draw for himself or herself. Unlike concepts that coerce, mimetic affinities should, after all, operate only through sympathetic attractions whose power cannot be imposed by theorists from the outside.

12

The Academic Woman as

Performance Artist

✳

"She walked into the room," my informant sardonically remembered, "wearing nothing but warpaint and a tampax." The speaker, whose anonymity under the circumstances might be wise to preserve, was referring to one of the new breed of academic women who emerged into prominence in the 1980s and remain powerful presences today. Willing to shock, eager to discomfort, skilled at the arts of intimidation, they gain attention as much by who they are—or how they stage "who they are"—as by what they are arguing. The traditional decorum of the lecture hall is shattered as they insistently foreground their refusal to play by the rules of the game. Mindful of the importance of what speech-act theorists call the performative as opposed to constative dimensions of truth claims, they know that audiences are there to be worked on or worked over, not merely persuaded by cool logic and the weight of irrefutable evidence. As a result, they deliberately blur the distinction between the charismatic authority of the speaker and the warranted assertability of her message; like performance artists, they make themselves—and the uproar they cause—into works of art.

Such shenanigans are not, to be sure, unprecedented. Think, for example, of Oscar Wilde's triumphal lecture tour of America in 1882, launched by his famous answer "nothing but my genius" to the customs officer's question if he had anything to declare. More recently Stanley Fish has become a household name by behaving more and more like Morris Zapp, the fictional character David Lodge originally based, so it is said, on Fish himself. Certain prominent African American scholars, like Henry Louis

Gates Jr. and Cornel West, have effectively marshaled the resources of black rhetorical traditions, such as "sign fying," which with a slight twist find their way as well into rap music. There are even whiffs of performance artistry in the jacket photos on certain academic books, the most notorious examples being the beefcake shots of the literary critics Frank Lentricchia and D. A. Miller, which occasioned an earnest comparative discussion a few years ago in the pages of *Critical Inquiry*.[1]

What, however, makes the recent spate of academic performance artists different is the clear dominance of women among them. Let me name a few of the obvious candidates: Judith Butler, Jane Gallop, Avital Ronell, Eve Kosowsky Sedgwick, and Gayatri Chakravorty Spivak. Each has an identifiable style: Butler's streetwise, tough girl dyke, Gallop's sexual predator, wearing her notorious skirt composed of men's ties, Ronell's exaggeratedly polite punk, Sedgwick's straight woman writing about gay sexuality and "coming out of the closet" about her weight problem and love for spanking, and Spivak's Third World Woman (via Paris) with a score to settle. Each has what can be called a major attitude, and each has successfully disrupted the assumptions of traditional academic discourse.

In fact, as shown by Ronell's audaciously stylized and imaginatively produced *Telephone Book* and *Crack Wars*,[2] they sometimes even rewrite the rules for scholarly publishing as well. And as demonstrated by Gallop's notorious cover photo for her 1988 collection *Thinking through the Body*, which unflinchingly depicts an infant's head being extracted by an obstetrician at the moment of birth, they can also brilliantly exploit techniques of visual self-presentation to shock and unsettle.[3]

What makes their disruptions more than mere fodder for common room gossip or the titillation of *Lingua Franca*'s readers, however, is the consistency between style and substance in their performance. That is, they have instantiated rather than merely enunciated a challenge to the prevailing pieties of what the sociologist Alvin Gouldner used to call "the culture of critical discourse."[4] According to the rules of that culture, only better ideas should prevail in a setting of perfect neutrality, an abstract contextless context. Here the authority of the personal name is abandoned for the authority of the argument, or as I've put it elsewhere, name-dropping is replaced by dropping names.[5] This ideal type, which has been the ostensible basis of the scientific method ever since Horace's "Nullius in verba" (in the words of no one) was adopted as the motto of the Royal Society, has come under increasing critical scrutiny. Not only has it been shown to be often betrayed in actual practice, including that of the "hardest" natural sciences, but it has also come to be attacked for positing a universal, transcendental, and disembodied subject of knowledge, which does not, indeed cannot, exist in the real world.

The women academic performance artists have contributed to the subversion of this model in several different ways. At times, they have adopted a confessional mode, which seems to say let's cut through all the crap and speak sincerely from the heart. No more closets, no more subterfuges, they defiantly assert; we're big girls now with tenure, and we won't knuckle under to your outmoded rules of civility. Even when you enter the public realm, they remind their audience, you don't lost your gendered, desiring, ethnically marked bodies and become a disinterested mind. Here the so-called identity politics underlying multiculturalism in certain of its guises finds a concrete embodiment through what, to cite the title of a recent book by Nancy K. Miller, can be called "getting personal."[6]

At other times, however, they have rejected the mode of self-revelation as itself a problematic residue of the belief in an authentic self to be revealed. Instead, they have engaged in a deliberately strategic mobilization of typical female stereotypes—the woman as avenging virago, castrating Medusa, seductive vamp, exotic temptress, and so on—to confound the expectation that there is a straightforward particular self behind the universal self assumed by traditional academic discourse. Adopting the strategy of self-fashioning most frequently perfected by male dandies, they have engaged in a dazzling practical display of the deconstructive theory many of them find so congenial.[7] Valorizing the self-conscious duplicities of masquerade, they have challenged not only the transcendental subject of traditional theory, but also the allegedly "authentic" subject of concrete experience. Like Cindy Sherman's postmodernist photos, they efface the boundaries between artifice and life, thwarting the desire to put them once again "in their place."

In her recent recollection of a 1982 presentation to the prestigious International Poetics Colloquium at Columbia, in which she was self-conscious about being the only female speaker Jane Gallop claimed this strategy was a serendipitous discovery:

> I dressed in a manner that bespoke the body as style, stylized sexuality. I wore spike heels, seamed hose a fitted black forties dress and a large black hat. I was dressed as a woman, but as another woman. If my speech signaled an identification with a woman of another place, my clothes bespoke an identification with a woman of another time. I was in drag. My clothing drew attention to my body but at the same time stylized it, creating a stylized body, what in the paper I called a poiesis of the body. The fit between the paper and the look, the text and the performance, was articulated unconsciously, and it worked.[8]

A decade later, unconscious luck has become calculated contrivance.

Another of its explicit functions has been to call into question the distinction between high and low culture which tends to inform conventional educational practice as well. The performance artists' disdain for traditional decorum and willingness to assume cultural roles normally stigmatized as "vulgar" has, it should be noted, a specific gender implication. For the high/low dichotomy was a fundamental assumption of an aesthetic modernist discourse that often figured avant-garde art as male and mass culture as female.[9] By refusing to respect the difference between esoteric works of art and exoteric kitsch, performance art, both in and out of the classroom, seeks to subvert by deed as well as rhetoric the domination of male models of cultural superiority.

In so doing, the academic performance artists make explicit what the dandies always knew: that behind social or cultural interaction lies a struggle for power. No longer the passive object of male gazes, they look back shamelessly and without apology, as if the role of hysteric in Charcot's celebrated amphitheater at Salpêtrière is now to be played by Manet's brazen Olympia. Foucault's lesson that the will to power is more potent than the will to truth is apparent in their shrewd manipulation of the guilt feelings of their predominantly conventional audience, which often is cowed into a kind of uneasy silence. Who, after all, wants to risk combat with someone wearing nothing but warpaint and a tampax? Looked at benignly, the result is to empower previously marginalized people, who were in some sense at a disadvantage when the rules of decorum were set by others. Now not only can the subaltern speak, but she does so on her own terms and in her own idiom.

Looked at with a less forgiving eye, however, the implications of academic performance artistry can appear somewhat more problematic. For there is a risk in undermining the assumptions of the culture of critical discourse too thoroughly, and that risk can be summarized in two words: Camille Paglia. I am not claiming that the figures mentioned above are somehow responsible for making the world safe for the likes of Paglia, but they may have helped warm up her audience. Still, the differences between them are worth stressing. Whereas they have found ways to combine substance and style in creative and unsettling ways, she has managed to evacuate virtually anything substantial from her cynically overwrought public persona. Instead, she betrays an almost clinical need for exhibitionism, which drives her to extremes of freakishness that seem too bad to be true. Combined with a take-no-prisoners willingness to belittle anyone or anything that stands in her way, her tawdry self-exposure has garnered her lots of easy publicity, but virtually no respect. Her pronouncements on such issues as feminism, French theory, or political correctness, for all their glittering packaging, often prove to be about as original and scintillating as those of Phyllis Schlafly.[10] At least Madonna, who is Paglia's explicit role model, knows how to sing and dance. Hurricane Camille, as she likes to call herself, turns out to be like the many destructive tropical storms: lots of sound and fury surrounding an empty center.

The descent of the academic performance artist from, say, Gayatri Spivak or Jane Gallop to Camille Paglia is a little like the trajectory followed by transgressive comedians from Lenny Bruce to Andrew Dice Clay. The media initially loves *agents provocateurs* who subvert the positions they claim to uphold, but ultimately even they see through the posturing. Paglia's first book, *Sexual Personae*, was taken seriously by some commentators; her second, *Sex, Art, and American Culture*, was savaged by virtually all who could get through its overheated, self-inflated prose. When Oscar Wilde insolently declared his genius, many people nodded approvingly; when Paglia no less insolently declares hers, almost everyone coughs in embarrassment and turns away.

What will remain once the hurricane blows itself out is the cautionary example of what happens when scholarly discourse is transformed into nothing but performance art. It is one thing to transgress boundaries and call categories into question, thus unsettling the comfortable assumptions of the dominant discursive model with its tacit underpinning of heterosexual male entitlement. It is something else, however, to efface those boundaries entirely and reduce one practice entirely to another. The neutral culture of critical discourse in which persuasive ideas come before personal authority and disembodied minds argue without reference to their corporeal ground may be a utopian fantasy in its purest form, but it still provides a regulative ideal, which we abandon at our jeopardy. For without it we are at the mercy of grand guignol performers who don't know the difference between acting up and acting out, and in the process trivialize the very important issues raised by disrupting but not entirely rejecting the much-maligned routines of academia.

13

Abjection Overruled

❋

Who Comes after the Subject? asks the title of a recent collection of essays by leading contemporary French thinkers.[1] Whether or not the postmortem is premature, there can be no doubt that the "subject," however we may want to define it, has been in serious, perhaps terminal, crisis now for many years. Its supposed autonomy has been undermined, its integrity violated, its capacity for agency called into question. Neither the transcendental/species subject beloved by the Kantian tradition, the historical/class subject championed by Hegelian Marxists, nor the individual/contingent subject defended by liberals has been spared the withering fire of a wide range of critics, who grudgingly acknowledge only "subject positions" in discursive fields. It has come to the point that you don't even need to place "bourgeois" or "Cartesian" before the word "subject" to express derision; it is the subject *tout court* that is, to cite the title of another typical book, "in question."[2]

One result has been a palpable weakening of faith in the collective projects that were presumably to emerge from the realization of subjective intention, the collaborative exercise of power that Hannah Arendt liked to call "acting in concert." Any attempt to nurture integral forms of solidarity seems suspect in some quarters because such integrity is bought at the necessary cost of excluding others. For theorists like Jean-François Lyotard, dissensus is preferable to consensus because it preserves the radical incommensurability of the positions prior to the attempt to reconcile them. It is thus hard to disagree with the philosopher J. M. Bernstein's recent lament: "the 'we' that would sustain political judgment and praxis has disappeared from direct view; 'we' do not know, directly or immediately, who 'we' are. Our 'we' has gone underground, appears only through the theoretical tracing of the fate that has rendered us strangers to one another."[3]

One obvious source of the disappearance of the confident collective subject is the realization that those who claim to speak for it are often, in fact, far less representative than they pretend to be. "What do you mean 'we,' white man?" the famous riposte to the Lone Ranger's observation, "we're in trouble, Tonto!" when they were surrounded by hostile Indians, has become the rallying cry of minorities everywhere. In addition, as many feminists have been quick to point out, it is only male chauvinist piggies who cry " 'we, we, we' all the way home."

Even the more particularist communitarian model of subjectivity now favored by multicultural tribalists has not been spared serious criticism. As the historian David Hollinger has argued in a recent essay entitled "How Wide the Circle of the We? American Intellectuals and the Problem of the Ethnos since World War II,"[4] ethnocentric definitions of collective subjectivity—even generous ones like Richard Rorty's equation of the relevant ethnos with American citizenship—come up against the problem of conflicting affiliations, which cut across any coherent notion of solidarity. No one, after all, is just, say, a worker, a Catholic, a woman, a heterosexual, an Italian-American, and so on, but at the unstable nodal point of such overlapping identities, all of which may pull in different directions. Hollinger's own "postethnic" alternative, which treats ethnic identity as a problem rather than a given, opens the door for a chastened universal subject to return. But, as Hollinger is the first to point out, it is not clear how much of the old humanist "I" can find its way back.

Rather than speculate myself about defensible notions of individual or collective subjectivity, a task that has occupied too many contemporary thinkers to enumerate, I want instead to take seriously the question "who comes after the subject?" I want in particular to consider the credentials of one prominent candidate, who (which?) has suddenly gained serious attention in a number of circles. For the crisis of the subject has cleared the way for a competing cultural figure, whom we might ironically call, following the literary critic Michael André Bernstein, the "abject hero."[5]

In fact, abjection in general has recently burst into prominence as a cultural category of uncommon power, "a fertile theoretical incitement," as one enthusiastic commentator put it, "to literary and aesthetic reflection."[6] Journals like the trendy bilingual (English and Portuguese) *Lusitania: A Journal of Reflection and Oceanography* devote entire, elaborately produced issues to "The Abject, America," which include articles praising "the party of affirmative abjection."[7] Visual artists as well as cultural theorists join the chorus. In 1993, the Whitney Museum of American Art mounted a show of selected items from its permanent collection under the rubric "Abject Art: Repulsion and Desire in American Art." Its organizers, who were—oh, delicious irony—"Helena Rubinstein Fellows" at the Museum, could rightly boast that "the concept of abjection, encompassing investigations of discursive excess and degraded elements as they relate to the body and society, has emerged as a central impulse of 1990s art."[8]

Why, I want to ask, has abjection now become so powerful a source of cultural value, when it served for so long as its antithesis? What are the stakes involved in privileging what has traditionally been debased? How coherent are the arguments, implied if not explicit, on its behalf? How successfully, in short, can the abject hero serve as the successor to the discredited subject as a—paradoxically idealized—image of the human condition?

By common consent, the publication in 1980 and translation two years later into English of Julia Kristeva's *Powers of Horror: An Essay on Abjection* put the concept on the cultural map.[9] Although there had been anticipations in some of the scattered work of Georges Bataille,[10] Kristeva's wide-ranging psychoanalytic, anthropological, religious, and literary ruminations on the centrality of abjection made it a leading candidate in the search for what comes after the subject. As Kristeva described it, the abject—from the Latin *abjicere*, to throw away—has both biological and cultural dimensions. It encompasses all of those bodily wastes—excrement, pus, menstrual blood, mucus, vomit—that anticipate the culminating moment when the total body becomes waste through its transformation into a corpse. It is also manifest culturally in tabooed food, "perverse" or incestuous sexuality, violent crime, and religious notions of abomination and sacrilege—in anything in fact that threatens rigid boundaries and evokes powerful fears of filth, pollution, contamination, and defilement.

Distinguishing the abject not only from the subject, but also from the object, which faces the subject and can be named, Kristeva defines it as

' the violence of mourning for an 'object' that has always already been lost. The abject shatters the wall of repression and its judgments. It takes the ego back to its source on the abominable limits from which, in order to be, the ego broke away—it assigns it a source in the non-ego, drive, and death.[11] As such, it provokes contradictory emotions of horror and fascination, which signal the uncanny return of something primordial the "healthy" ego finds repellent.

In linguistic terms, it involves a breakdown of the communicative, symbolic function of language, and the restoration of something more fundamental, which Kristeva identifies with a primal body language—in her vocabulary, the "semiotic" as opposed to the "symbolic"—that expresses the conventionally inexpressible. In psychological terms, it means the reappearance of a relationship to the maternal body, which patriarchal culture through the "healthy" resolution of the Oedipus complex has tried to repress, or more precisely, throw out of the psyche entirely. Instead of the radical, indeed violent, separation from that body that ultimately produces an integral, "mature" centered ego, the abject recalls a primal fusion, or at least a confusion, of boundaries, which undercuts the self-sufficiency of the subject, allowing more basic forms of communication prior to the symbolic exchanges of intersubjectivity. In short, abjection points back to a time before individuation, just as it signifies the time after when the body becomes a mere corpse.

But in addition to these extreme states, abjection can manifest itself in the interactions of everyday life as well, in, for example, the transgression of religious taboos and dietary regulations. Perhaps even more important, Kristeva argues, the power of abjection can also appear in literature, where it inspires writing that transgresses normal conventions of symbolic discourse and disrupts the sublimating pieties of aesthetic idealization. Her privileged examples are the novels and manifestoes of Louis-Ferdinand Céline, whose viciously immoral and politically objectionable content are endurable because of the daring and brilliance of his style, "where any ideology, thesis, interpretation, mania, collectivity, threat, or hope become drowned."[12]

In larger cultural terms, Céline's abject rhapsodies, Kristeva tells us, are literary instances of the carnivalesque tradition of reversal and transgression, which Mikhail Bahktin famously explored in writers like Dostoyevsky. The dialogic heteroglossia of such texts undermines the authority of the sovereign author and the univocality of his or her enunciations. "To the carnival's semantic ambivalences, which pair the high and the low, the sublime and the abject," Kristeva also notes, "Céline adds the merciless crashing of the *apocalypse*."[13]

Kristeva's foregrounding of the apocalyptic moment in Céline alerts us to one of the sources of the current power of abjection in a cultural climate such as our own, which has more than its share of apocalyptic winds blowing from many different directions.[14] At a time when many traditional cultural codes have lost their ability to constrain or inspire and a pervasive cult of victimization feeds resentment and rancor, abjection—along with other "jections" like "de-" and "re-"—seems to many a more forthright way to characterize "our" forlorn state than any artificially cheerful alternative.

But there are also more positive reasons for its appeal, which go beyond a shared sense of despair. There is, for example, the evident affinity between abjection and the heady, if overwrought, language of *délire*, which so many recent critics have both praised and emulated.[15] For deconstruction in particular, the transgression of categorical boundaries and contamination of binary oppositions is an evident virtue. Derrida once, in fact, explicitly privileged vomit as the disgustingly unassimilable "other" of the beautiful and the moral, serving philosophy therefore as "an elixir, even in the very quintessence of bad taste."[16] Insofar as delirious language—the language of radical desublimation—is moreover seen as somehow closer to the body with all of its creaturely imperfections and dark torments than to the soul or mind with their pretensions to lucid transcendence, it functions as yet another candidate in the perennial search for a more authentic, poetic, or revelatory mode of expression—even on the part of those who explicitly eschew the rhetoric of authenticity and revelation.

In terms of visual language, a similar motive can be easily discerned. A recent exhibition at the MIT List Visual Arts Center featuring the abject art of Louise Bourgeois, Robert Gober, Lilla LoCurto and William Outcault, Annette Messager, Rona Pondick, Kiki Smith, and David Wojnarowicz was entitled "Corporal Politics." Here the unflinching representation of dismembered body parts, tortured flesh, and infected bodily fluids is defended precisely in terms of its truth-telling—and thus politically liberating—subversion of the idealized body of formal perfection that for so long

dominated Western artistic representations of the nude.[17] Francis Bacon's
"prosthetic grotesques" were valuable, Allon White likewise argued in
explicitly Kristevan terms, because they offered us diagnostic revelations of
"the phobic substratum of a social formation chronically unable to manage
its communal symbolic life. Bacon's solitary abjects bear witness to a
society bereft of the basic ritual forms necessary to mediate cultural production: hysteria became the most authentic bourgeois equivalent to the
carnivalesque."[18]

A no less explicitly political implication can be drawn from the challenge
to the metaphor of purification that underlies the celebration of the abject.
Here, however, the point is not that abjection tells us the horrible truth
about the grotesquely hysterical underpinnings of bourgeois order, but
rather that a certain kind of impurity may itself be a valuable goal. That is,
at a moment when the word "cleansing" seems always to be preceded by
the ominous adjective "ethnic," a little tolerance for what is cast out as
impure seems worth promoting. From this perspective, the resurgence of
communal tribalism and identity politics in the contemporary world seems
less like a progressive restoration of lost roots than a warrant for intercom-
munal warfare based on the narcissistic repudiation of the alter within.

Kristeva's explicitly gendered reading of the implications of abjection,
although by no means universally shared by all feminists, also helps explain its seductive power. For by identifying the abject with the maternal
body, perhaps even the pregnant woman's body prior to parturition, she is
able to align it with those forces that patriarchal oedipalization seeks to
contain and repress. As Elizabeth Gross has pointed out, this linkage also
expresses the general denigration of subjectivity that has allowed abjection
to emerge so strongly as an alternative: "the maternal is not to be confused
with the position and role of a *subject*, for it is a process without a subject.
Pregnancy, for example, does not involve the mother's agency or identity. If
anything, it is the abandonment of agency. 'Becoming mother' implies an
abrogation of subjective autonomy and conscious control."[19]

Even for those theorists of gender who find Kristeva's celebration of the
maternal body too essentialist, abjection has become a privileged term.
Thus Judith Butler in her recent *Bodies That Matter*, notes that all positive
notions of sexual identity require the abjection of a contrary identity. "The
forming of a subject," she tells us, "requires an identification with the

normative phantasm of 'sex,' and this identification takes place through a repudiation which produces a domain of abjection, a repudiation without which the subject cannot emerge." The task of "queer theory" is to mobilize abjection against this process, "as a critical resource in the struggle to rearticulate the very terms of symbolic legitimacy and intelligibility."[20]

✳

With all of these positive as well as negative reasons, it is not difficult to see why abjection has garnered such recent attention. But a closer look suggests troubling implications as well. The attraction of queer theory to the abject hero(ine) over the subject is one obvious place to begin. For in the era of AIDS, when we all live under the threat of a virus which apparently works by pollution and contamination, the straightforward overturning of conventional value hierarchies, especially purity over the impure, seems simplistic. The contributors to the *Abject Art* catalogue have, in fact, evident difficulty in sorting out the contradictory implications of privileging abjection. One explicitly considers the potentially homophobic implications of the art "because, in joining images of homosexuality and abjection, even if to empower, they risk reinscribing the homosexual as abject." He concludes nonetheless that the risk is worth taking, but does so by smuggling in precisely the strong notion of subjecthood that the concept of abjection is designed to undermine: "by authoring the subject position of the abject homosexual from within, gays and lesbians are able to problematize, diversify, and resignify that abject position for themselves and others. . . . That abject identifications are effective in disrupting 'normativeness' suggests that power exists for those who (re)claim it."[21]

Another contributor, describing the sinks made by the gay artist Robert Gober shortly after the onset of the epidemic, remarks: "Due to the absence of any plumbing fixtures, faucets, and pipes, the sinks (symbolic of cleansing and purification) were dysfunctional, conveying the lack of any possibility of cleansing—signifying, according to the artist, the lack of a cure for AIDS."[22] In other words, instead of celebrating impurity and defilement, such works explicitly lament their dire consequences, at least on the level of medical science. And in so doing, they force us to distinguish between different modes of abjection, some more benign, some more dangerous than others. What is normally seen as sexual abjection—the polymorphous perversity stigmatized by conventional morality—is to be embraced as inherently liberating, but its medical counterpart is harder to accept, for maintaining the taboo against pollution may well be functional in preserving the very bodies whose ecstatic desublimation the other abjection valorizes.[23]

If such distinctions can be made, then perhaps the adequacy of the general category of abjection as a primordial condition subtending so many different phenomena, psychological, cultural, literary, religious, anthropological, and so on, needs itself to be questioned. "For all its local insights," Michael André Bernstein warns, "the sweep of Kristeva's account elides its specificity, so that her abject is hypostasized, functioning as a global concept that, depending on the circumstances, can be regarded, as at once a force, a condition, a drive, or a kind of frantic reaction in the face of mortality. . . . an analysis of abjection that can move without hesitation from Oedipus at Colonnus to taboos associated with menstruation, and then to the Holocaust, seems to me to abandon, by overextension, the explanatory force of the term."[24]

Another way to make the same point is to wonder about the implications of assimilating biological categories too easily to cultural ones. Is the repulsion we feel at rotting corpses or the bodily fluids of AIDS sufferers, which may harbor genuinely harmful substances, really the same as our food taboos or sexual distastes, which protect us from more imagined disasters? Should we eschew safe sex, move to the Love Canal, and gulp in second-hand cigarette smoke because overcoming the phobia of abjection of whatever kind is somehow intrinsically emancipatory? Although the boundary between biology and culture is not as firm as was once imagined and many overlapping discourses structure both, it is by no means clear that they are simply equivalent. Indeed, to acquiesce in the categorization of culturally stigmatized groups of people in the same terms used to condemn bodily wastes may well contribute to the diminution of their dignity, rather than enhance it, contrary to the strained reasoning cited above. Although it is clear that the hope is that by reversing the normal hierarchy, such a benign outcome will ensue, it is surely a risk to assume it necessarily will. Even the apotropaic, preemptive invocation of abject symbols as a way to defuse their power of horror is not certain to have the desired result.

A no less troubling question arises from the paradoxical incorporation of abjection into the realm of the aesthetic. For how can the artist avoid the sublimating elevation of abjection into precisely the idealized state it is supposed to undermine? In other words, is "abject art" perhaps an untenable oxymoron, little more than an eye-catching label in the never-ending search for new ways to accrue cultural—and perhaps economic—capital? Although the quasi-sacred space of the museum can be apparently contaminated by introducing real (or even simulacral) excrement, impure bodily fluids, severed body parts, and the other examples of abjection and base materialism, its institutional power is such that the abject object is nonetheless transfigured into an aesthetic one. In 1964, Sam Goodman and Boris Lurie exhibited several piles of tromp-l'oeil shit at the Gallery Gertrude Stein in New York and John Miller and Mike Kelley did something similar twenty years later. But however much these gestures succeeded in stretching the boundaries of the aesthetic, they somehow still remain within them.

If, as we have noted, Kristeva distinguishes radically between objects and abjects, and defines abjection in terms of mourning for an impossible, always, already lost object, can the objective realization of an artist's notion of abjection ever fail to betray his or her intentions? "The various means of purifying the abject—the various catharses—make up the history of religions," Kristeva remarks, "and end up with that catharsis par excellence called art, both on the far and the near side of religion."[25] In her contribution to the recent roundtable discussion of abjection in October, Rosalind Krauss contends that even Kristeva was unable to keep the distinction straight: "Kristeva's project is all about recuperating certain objects as abjects—waste products, filth, bodily fluids, etc. These objects are given an incantatory power in her text. I think that move to recuperate objects is contrary to Bataille."[26] From Krauss's point of view, Bataille's notion of the informe is preferable because it is more structural and functional than Kristeva's idea of abjection, an unending performative process rather than a fully realized result.

Whether or not such a distinction is fully fair to Kristeva, it points to the paradoxical implications of representing abjection through substantively positive, visually present objects, however repellent, in the space of the museum or on the pages of an exhibition catalogue. Denis Hollier's response to the Abject Art exhibition gets to the core of the problem: "What is abject about it? Everything was very neat: the objects were clearly art works. They were on the side of the victor."[27] Calling for a "party of affirmative abjection" in the pages of a slickly produced, lavishly subsidized, bilingual journal certainly qualifies as a prime example of being "unclear on the concept." Besides being instances of bad faith, such artistic reifications, one might add, unwittingly produce the aesthetic equivalent of the identity politics that certain supporters of abjection, those raising the banner of queer theory, have been at pains to challenge.

They also pose the related question of the primordial authenticity that supposedly underpins the preference for desublimated abjection over sublimated subjectivity. Kristeva herself seems to mobilize this rhetoric with her claim that abjection refers back to a presymbolic state of semiotic fusion prior to separation from the mother. In discussing the power of Celine, she notes his ability to have us "believe that he is true, that he is the only authentic one, and we are ready to follow him, deeply settled in that end of night where he seeks us out.'[28]

There are, however, two fundamental problems with the rhetoric of primordial authenticity as applied to abjection. The first concerns the myth of originary plenitude, prior to the very split between subject and object, that abjection itself sometimes seems to recall. Such myths, we are now used to being told, are ideological exercises in nostalgia for a past that never was or yearnings for a utopian future that will never be. Bataille once tellingly criticized Jean Genet for wanting to turn his own abjection into a positive state of oneness: "Genet wants abjection even if it only brings suffering. He wants it for its own sake, beyond the commodities he finds in it. He wants it because of a vertiginous propensity towards an abjection in which he loses himself as completely as the ecstatic mystic loses himself in God."[29] But it was precisely such a successful union with the divine, Bataille knew, which the unsublatable split between subject and abject always keeps at bay. Put differently, there can never be a state of perfect desublimation, which somehow frees itself entirely of some power of restriction and distinction, whether we call it symbolic language, patriarchal law, or the formal organization of the body.

The second reason the rhetoric of primordial authenticity is wanting is pointed out by Michael André Bernstein, who shows the extent to which the abject hero is himself a tropic construction with a long pedigree. Tracing its origins in the literature of the Roman saturnalia, he probes its modern incarnations in Diderot's *Rameau's Nephew*, Dostoyevsky's novels, and the heterogeneous works of a Celine whose violent fantasies he refuses to justify on stylistic grounds. A similar point might be made about the visual abject, which draws on a self-conscious tradition of the grotesque as old as the Renaissance.[30] As Allon White concedes in his discussion of Francis Bacon, "we may trace the prosthetic grotesque through Van Gogh, Goya, Callot, Breugel, and Bosch,"[31] even if the atrocities of the twentieth century added literal horrors unimagined even in their most feverish fantasies.

It is, moreover, precisely because of the tropic prefiguration of the type that the abject hero's dreams of authenticity remain necessarily frustrated. "The self-contempt of figures like Jean-François Rameau or the Underground Man," Bernstein observes, "is due to their haunted sense of only acting according to 'type,' of lacking authenticity even in their suffering, where they most need to feel original."[32] The result is the fueling of their *ressentiment*, which can never be assuaged by a realization of their yearnings for authentic life.

Bernstein's attentiveness to the psychological tone underlying the power of abjection helps explain its attraction in an era of ubiquitous victimization. Moving beyond literary invocations, he suggestively demonstrates how the template of abject heroism functions as well in the public response to real monsters like Charles Manson and his "family," allowing their audience to share in the self-abnegating, but allegedly truth-telling fantasy that has for so long allowed identification with literary abject heroes. Bernstein goes as far as to suggest that the themes of abjection have themselves become so commonplace in our culture that it would be more accurate to say that "what is repressed . . . is the force of the prosaic, the counter-authenticity, if you will, of the texture and rhythm of our daily routines and decisions, the myriad of minute and careful adjustments that we are ready to offer in the interest of a habitable social world."[33]

Bernstein's own evocation of a "we" whose "daily routines and decisions" are worth valorizing may, to be sure, seem too beholden to the comfortable rhetoric of the universal subject whose crisis helped prepare the way for the current celebration of abjection. *Ressentiment*, moreover, will always seen like an unwarranted emotion from the point of view of those on top of the hierarchy, who are its target. But Bernstein's alarm—and that expressed by critics like Krauss and Hollier from a very different perspective—at the current, uncritical celebration of abjection is worth taking seriously. For there is a danger in what might be called the romance of inclusivity, which argues that any exclusion, repudiation, or alienation is necessarily evil. That danger is the substitution of a quantitative notion of value for a qualitative one: the greater the number of things valorized and accepted, the better. From this perspective, any vertical hierarchy is seen as oppressive and any horizontal leveling somehow emancipatory. What is forgotten is the inevitability of creating some new value hierarchy on the ruins of the old; indeed, depending on the context, what may be construed as valueless on one scale may turn out to be the opposite on another (as the magic transformation of abject human waste into "night soil" makes clear).

The risk in pointing out this difficulty is that it can always be scorned as yet another conservative *rappel à l'ordre*, a reestablishment of the stifling logic of patriarchal, symbolic, idealizing sublimation, which neutralizes genuine subversion and represses the base materialism of our abject bodies. But as the example of the contradictory status of abjection in the response to AIDS shows, it is necessary to make some sort of hierarchical distinction in order to avoid the untenable conclusion that no pollution whatsoever is to be resisted. A similar point might be made about Kristeva's stylistic defense of Céline, which covertly draws on one version of aesthetic redemption, even as it condemns another. Why, after all, should it be so easily assumed that the ability to fend off feelings of disgust or repulsion is somehow a mark of distinction, when in fact, such things might simply be a sign of anaesthetic insensitivity? Why must the only form of armoring be that of the oedipalized subject, when another, more malign version might well be apparent in the incapacity to feel anything but diffuse *ressentiment* and identification with abjection? The "body in pieces" so beloved by anti-Oedipal critics of sublimation may, after all, prove a bit too scattered to come up with anything approaching an ethical response to challenges to the human dignity it tries so hard to subvert.

The real task, it might be argued in conclusion, is to find a way beyond the increasingly sterile dichotomy that pits order against subversion, law against transgression, rigidity against destabilization, and the subject against the abject. Some anthropologists have shown that carnivalesque reversals are less a genuine threat to stability than a safety valve that keeps the system going. Abjection may well function in the same way, as a necessary impulse in an economy of subjective constitution, which feeds off precisely what it seems to reject in a kind of endless game of *fort-da*, a game in which every Jesse Helms creates his own Robert Mapplethorpe and every David Wojnarowicz needs his own Patrick Buchanan. The idealized version of the subject entirely free from its allegedly ignoble other—the base materialism of its body—has been successfully exploded by the new attention paid to abjection; to this extent, it cannot be simply overruled, as my cheeky title may suggest. But the no less one-sided exaltation of the abject as a liberating antidote to the repressive subject must now also be questioned. Otherwise there is no hope for finding or constructing some sort of viable "we" who will resist the powers of horror, powers whose reach extends well beyond the covers of a novel or the walls of a museum.

14

The Uncanny Nineties

✳

For reasons that will become clear shortly, the title for this column was to be "The Unheimlich Manoeuvre." But regrettably, I was beaten to the punch last winter by a clever editor of the *New York Review of Books*, who used it to adorn a review of several recent horror novels. Initially chagrined by being scooped, I then came to realize that there was something strangely fitting in the fact that what I thought was an original idea was actually anticipated by someone else. For it is precisely the issue of the uncertain status of originality and the haunting of what seems new in the present by the residues of the past that is my theme. The term that best captures that feeling is, of course, the "uncanny" (or in German, *das Unheimliche*), which has become one of the most supercharged words in our current critical vocabulary. What, I want to ask, are the implications of its present power? Why now in the 1990s has the uncanny become a master trope available for appropriation in a wide variety of contexts? What are the possible drawbacks of granting it so much explanatory force?

By common consent, the theoretical inspiration for the current fascination with the concept is Freud's 1919 essay "The Uncanny," which used E.T.A. Hoffmann's short story "The Sandman" as an occasion for an exploration of the effects of "something which is secretly familiar, which has undergone repression and then returns from it."[1] Identifying that something with castration anxiety, whose displaced effects he noted in the fears of blindness expressed in Hoffmann's story, Freud also pondered the etymology of "unheimlich," which he followed Schelling in defining as "the name for everything that ought to have remained hidden and secret and has become visible." Its linguistic contrary, which the English translation "canny" (originally from the Latin for "to know") fails to register, is "heimlich" or "homey." What "ought to have remained secret" therefore is somehow related to a conflicted desire to return "home," an overcoming of the split or alienation that is expressed as anxiety about castration (either imagined in the past or feared in the future). At its deepest level, the desire is for reunion with the mother's body.

The experience of the uncanny is itself both disturbing and pleasurable, an involuntary repetition that expresses in displaced form what Freud would analyze in greater detail in the work he completed the following year, *Beyond the Pleasure Principle*, as the "death instinct." The uncertainty produced by the uncanny concerning the boundaries between our living selves and our dead, automatonlike simulacra demonstrates the link. Its troubling power Freud would experience in his own life in the strange feeling he had toward putative "*Doppelgänger*," those doubles who evoked an earlier stage when his self was still not fully differentiated from others (and also anticipated the stage after death, when dedifferentiation would return with a vengeance).

For a half century, Freud's seminal essay "The Uncanny" seems to have occasioned little comment. You will look in vain for a serious discussion of it in such standard accounts as Philip Rieff's *Freud: The Mind of a Moralist* or Richard Wollheim's *Freud*. Radical Freudians of the 1960s like Norman O. Brown and Herbert Marcuse paid it no heed, and it is still unremarked in recent works by Peter Gay and Frank Sulloway. Lacan treated it in a 1962–63 seminar on *L'angoisse*, which remained, however, unpublished. Only in the early 1970s did it finally emerge into the light in essays by Hélène Cixous and Jacques Derrida, the latter included in his widely read collection, *Dissemination*.[2] A slew of dense, complex, often brilliantly imaginative discussions by poststructuralist thinkers, such as Sarah Kofman, Philippe Lacoue-Labarthe, Neil Hertz, Samuel Weber, Friedrich Kittler, and Françoise Meltzer, quickly followed, and the "uncanny" had arrived, at least among leading literary critics. There it remained for a while, however, exercising only a select group of commentators.

But in the past few years, the concept has migrated from the ghetto of poststructuralist literary criticism first to the visual arts, and now to cultural studies in general. In 1992, Anthony Vidler published a remarkable

collection entitled *The Architectural Uncanny*, which demonstrated its interpretative yield when applied to urban space and built form.[3] The following
year saw two books on Surrealism, Hal Foster's *Compulsive Beauty* and
Margaret Cohen's *Profane Illumination*, which probed the ways in which the
Surrealist notions of objective chance, convulsive beauty, and the mar-
velous were informed by a compulsive fascination with the uncanny, a
fascination already noted in Rosalind Krauss's studies of Surrealist photography.[4] The Surrealist object, they point out, is forever the lost object
whose desired recovery can never be realized. The postmodernist recycling
of the Surrealist and Dadaist repetitions, evident for example in the work of
Sherrie Levine, has been understood as a kind of meta uncanniness, a
repetition of the repetition compulsion itself.[5] Even more recently, a comparable analysis has begun to infiltrate film criticism and cultural studies
as well.[6]

Significantly, virtually all of these authors have found in Walter Benjamin's celebrated ruminations on the modern city a powerful stimulus to
their extension of the concept of the uncanny into the new territory initially
reconnoitered by Surrealism. Benjamin, in fact, had once written an essay,
"Demonic Berlin," based on his secret childhood reading of Hoffmann's
uncanny tales, as Jeffrey Mehlman has recently noted in his resurrection of
Benjamin's radio scripts of the 1930s.[7] Benjamin's sensitivity to the residues of the archaic and the natural in the future-obsessed modern city of
restless change has allowed a new appreciation for the value—perhaps even
the utopian potential—of what modern urbanism thought it had banished.
With Benjamin as inspiration, it has become possible to extract the unheimlich out of its purely psychological or aesthetic context and make it
into a category with larger social and cultural implications, indeed one
with a certain critical charge. Mehlman himself had made a start in this
direction with his 1977 account of "revolution and repetition" in Marx,
Hugo, and Balzac.[8]

It is thus not surprising to find that when Derrida, after so many years of
hesitation, finally got around to treating Marx directly in lectures he gave at
the University of California, Riverside, in 1993, he was able to do so only by
foregrounding the uncanny, "spectral" quality of Marx's current status.[9]
Now that Marx was being unceremoniously buried by former friends and
foes alike, Derrida was able to make the self-consciously "untimely" ges-

ture of resurrecting the corpse, or more precisely its ghost. "At a time when a new world disorder is attempting to install its neo-capitalism and neo-liberalism," Derrida noted, "no disavowal has managed to rid itself of all of Marx's ghosts. Hegemony still organizes the repression and thus the confirmation of a haunting. Haunting belongs to the structure of every hegemony."[10]

Derrida's resuscitation of Marx is perhaps less significant for his analysis of the continuing relevance of Marx's actual arguments—although he has some striking insights worth taking seriously—than for his insistence on the structure of uncanny haunting itself exemplified by the ghost's return—or more precisely, a sense of waiting for that return. Protesting against the rhetoric of one-directional temporality captured in the endless parade of "posts" that mark our cultural moment, Derrida defends a repetitive time that is perpetually "out of joint." Noting that the seemingly positive category of the "heimlich," which implies a safe haven to be restored, is itself deeply fraught in Freud's discussion of its implications, Derrida adds that Heidegger's description of Dasein's relation to the world expresses the same structure of unfulfilled longing for an eerily familiar home that, however, was never really inhabited and therefore can never be regained. No interior can be made safe from the incursion of the alien other. Ultimately, then, the alternative between the uncanny and the canny is, for Derrida, undecidable.[11]

This typically deconstructionist conclusion Derrida then applies to what he calls Marx's "spectrology," which also denies the plenitudinous presence of full emancipation. Plural specters are needed to prevent the homogenization of the human project into a totalized metaghost or singular *Geist* (which is another way to describe the dominating power of Capital itself). What Georg Lukács had famously bemoaned as the "transcendental homelessness"[12] of modern man and sought to end through a socialist revolution, Derrida declares is instead the hidden telos of Marx's own project, which he finds especially evident in *The German Ideology*. Historical materialism is precisely a protest against the dissolution of the contingent subject into an effect of the *geistige* metasubject, whether understood as the abstracting power of Capital or the no less abstract notion of a universal class, which is merely its inverse image.

Juxtaposing what he dubs a "hauntology" to the more traditional ontology of metaphysics, Derrida argues that "it is necessary to introduce haunting into the very construction of a concept. Of every concept, beginning with the concepts of being and time. That is what we would be calling here a hauntology. Ontology opposes it only in the movement of exorcism. Ontology is a conjuration."[13] Thus, the uncanny becomes not a source of terror and discomfort—or at least not that alone—but also a bulwark against the dangerous temptations of conjuring away plural specters in the name of a redeemed whole, a realization of narcissistic fantasies, a restoration of a true *Heimat*.

To introduce the connotatively rich word *Heimat* is, of course, to foreground the political stakes in this resurrection of the uncanny, for historians have long recognized the talismanic power of that word in a Germany that yearned for the secure, communal identity that modernization seemed to destroy.[14] Although there were some Marxists, most notably the utopian Ernst Bloch, who sought to harness its power for leftist purposes, by and large, *Heimat* served as rallying cry for a nostalgic right that sought its home in a national or *völkisch* community. It still continues to set some hearts aflutter, as evidenced by the success of Edgar Reitz's epic film of the same name. Much of the deconstructionist valorization of the uncanny is in fact aimed at a new version of the same desire in the integral nationalisms that have emerged in the wake of Communism's collapse. Here Derrida repeats the gesture he has made in many different contexts of identifying with the wandering, nomadic Jew rather than the settled, autochthonous gentile. In so doing, he expresses his solidarity with the displaced and exiled, the permanent members of a global diaspora that continues to grow with the internationalization of the labor market and the frightening upsurge of communal conflicts.

There is, however, a certain irony in the embrace of the uncanny as an antidote to phantasmatic notions of home. For one salient form of the return of the repressed in the current scene is, after all, precisely the purifying nationalism and ethnonarcissism that hopes to exorcise the alien within and achieve authentic cultural integrity. Similarly, the recent campaign to restore respect for Victorian values and solutions to social problems by the Newt Gingrichs and Gertrude Himmelfarbs of the world betokens a desire to restore an alleged lost moral wholeness and cozy domesticity. All of the fundamentalist restorations, religious as well as secular, that bedevil our fin-de-millennial world show how widespread this phenomenon is. Not every ghost who comes back is like that of the anti-totalizing Marx whose untimely virtues Derrida now defends.

There is, in other words, a danger in the valorization of uncanny repetition without resolution and the power of haunting per se. For in celebrating spectral returns as such, the precise content of *what* is repeated may get lost. As Jeffrey Mehlman once pointed out, "what is *unheimlich* about the *unheimlich* is that absolutely *anything* can be *unheimlich.*"[15] Hauntology, like ontology, is not a unified phenomenon, but has, we might say, many different shades (even Marx, Derrida agrees, has himself become more than one ghost). Some of these are ironically themselves strong expressions of the very homesickness that the acceptance of "transcendental homelessness" as a value in itself seeks to subvert. Their all too successful return threatens the hauntological project with precisely the ontological solidity it tries so hard to undo.

It may therefore not be enough to say that hegemonic attempts at closure necessarily call up their spectral others and thus can never be total, when those others are themselves no less—and may be more—problematic versions of the same desire for wholeness. Perhaps this is what Derrida himself covertly acknowledges when he points out the ultimate undecidability between the "unheimlich" and the "heimlich." But maybe it is still worth trying to distinguish, as Benjamin certainly thought we could, between the utopian and dystopian moments in the repetition of the outmoded. Otherwise we risk accepting all incursions of death into life, all residues of the mortified past and inanimate nature in the lifeworld of the present, all returns of the repressed as inherently liberating to the extent that they free us from the false hope for a fully lived presence.

A second difficulty with elevating spectral uncanniness to an inherently benign solvent of narcissistic self-absorption and premature closure emerges if we return to the etymological issue again and pit the literal against the metaphorical meaning of "heimlich." Whereas the latter implies a desire for a womblike state of ontological security prior to symbolic castration, the former simply means having an actual place in the world you can call your own. Derrida himself employs the word in this more prosaic sense when he rails against one of the evils of the new world order: "the massive exclusion of homeless citizens from any participation in the democratic life of States, the expulsion or deportation of so many exiles, stateless persons, and immigrants from so-called national territory already herald a new experience of frontiers and experience—whether national or civil."[16] Although this sentence might be stretched to mean that it is no disadvantage to be homeless, stateless, or in exile, unless you are deprived of political rights as well, it is hard to imagine Derrida being so callously indifferent to the distinction between the literal and metaphoric "unheim-lich." Anthony Vidler, for his part, explicitly concedes that "faced with the intolerable state of real homelessness, any reflection on the 'transcenden-tal' or psychological unhomely risks trivializing or, worse, patronizing political or social action."[17]

Still, what is left unacknowledged in such disclaimers is the unsettling effect of the "unheimlich manoeuvre" itself, which works so tirelessly to undermine the hard and fast distinction between the metaphoric and the real, the symbolic and the literal, the animate and the inanimate. Failing to make such distinctions can have its costs, however, for as Hal Foster has warned, it may well be the case that in the postmodern world, "our forest of symbols is less disruptive in its uncanniness than disciplinary in its delirium."[18] Now that the commercial marketplace as well as the political arena has discovered the appeal of the retro, even the dead are not safe from exploitation, their images revivified to sell soft drinks and shake the hand of Forrest Gump. It is now the height of canniness to market the uncanny.

Perhaps one way out of this impasse is to say that whereas there can never be a perfectly secure home, a domestic interior impervious to incur-sions from without and the return of what has been excluded from it, the alternative should not be actual or even metaphorical homelessness per se. Here one is making a virtue out of what normally has been seen as a source of distress simply by reversing the valences. Perhaps we should strive instead for the strength to dwell in perpetually haunted houses, learning to live with the spooks that periodically invade them, but we should make sure that they have roofs literal enough to keep the rain off our heads.

The nineties, we might note in conclusion, are turning out to be an uncanny decade in more ways than one. The current obsession with the troubled interface between history and memory, narrating the past and commemorating it, is one indication of how concerned we are with the way the past makes cultural demands on us that we have difficulty fulfilling. The explosion of recent debates over alleged repressed memory, often of trauma and abuse, shows that the same uncertainty exists on the level of individual psychology. Another example of the same trend is the postmodernist disruption of modernist dreams of integral purity by the mocking restoration of all those messy impurities it had hoped to leave behind; the positive reevaluation of Surrealism against the high modernist orthodoxy identified with Clement Greenberg is indicative of the change.

Unlike earlier generations, however, we seem less hopeful that a process of working through or mourning will move us resolutely into the future, our ghosts finally laid to rest. Lacking any faith in redemptive narratives or the possibility of a fully worked through relation to the past, we seem now reconciled to repeating what a more naive age thought it had surpassed, inviting in the spooks, suppressing our shudders, and pretending we find their company a delight. If Derrida is right, even Marx, who once was enlisted on the side of the materialist ghost-busters, may turn out to be the biggest revenant of them all. The specter of communism has become a communism of specters, but no one, these days, seems really spooked. Perhaps we have learned a bit too easily to enjoy our symptoms rather than to fight them, gaining whatever modest thrills come with watching horror movies, while becoming increasingly numb to the real horrors on the far side of the screen.

15

Modernism and the Specter
of Psychologism

＊

No genealogist of the complex and heterogeneous cultural field we have
come to call aesthetic modernism can fail to acknowledge its multiple
intersections with that other richly articulated field known as modern psychology. In both cases, an unprecedented preoccupation with the interior
landscape of the subject, a no-longer self-confident self functioning with
increased difficulty in the larger world outside its threatened and vulnerable boundaries, led to voyages of scientific and artistic discovery whose
endpoints have not yet been reached. Whether it be the empiricist tradition
of Ernst Mach, Franz Brentano, and William James recently foregrounded
by Judith Ryan in The Vanishing Subject,[1] Jean Martin Charcot's investigations
of hysteria inspirational for such modernist movements as Surrealism, or
Freudian psychoanalysis, whose importance for modernism is evident in
such accounts as Carl Schorske's Fin-de-siècle Vienna,[2] the story of aesthetic
innovation has seemed impossible to narrate without reference to the no-
less radical developments in psychology happening at virtually the same
time. What Ryan calls the "complex intertextuality"[3] between modernism
and psychology has perhaps reached its zenith in Louis Sass's recent Madness and Modernism, which boldly seeks to understand such familiar aspects
of the modernist temper as perspectivism, dehumanization, alienation,
ironic detachment, hyperreflexivity, and spatialized form precisely by finding affinities with the workings of the schizophrenic mind, which was
itself first labeled in the 1890s and quickly became, Sass tells us, "the
quintessential form of madness in our time."[4]

Cultural fields, however, not only intersect and parallel each other, pro-

ducing reinforcements, homologies, and elective affinities, but also sometimes interact through repulsions and negations, achieving their fragile
definitions by means of abjecting the other. In the case of modernism and
psychology, I want to argue, such a progress of negative exclusion did, in
fact, occur, a process that overlapped and sometimes interfered with the
more positive interaction that has been explored by other scholars. In
particular, I want to show that what the philosophers of this period called
"psychologism" and what many sought mightily to banish from their
search for truth also emerged as a source of anxiety at certain key moments
in the genesis of aesthetic modernism, as well.[5] My evidence will come
from both literary and visual instances of this anxiety.[6] Although I do not
want to be understood as saying modernism was essentially a repudiation
of psychologism, let alone unrelated to developments in the psychological
sciences per se, no understanding of its emergence can afford to ignore the
haunting presence of this stigmatized "ism" as a specter that refused to be
effortlessly exorcised.

The philosophical critique of psychologism can be traced at least as far
back as Kant's claim that "in logic we do not want to know how understanding is and thinks and how it hitherto has proceeded in thinking, but
how it ought to proceed in thinking. Logic must teach us the correct use of
the understanding, i.e., that in which it is in agreement with itself."[7] Kant's
transcendental deduction was thus explicitly distinguished between the
questio facti of the "physiological derivation" of a priori ideas and the questio
juris of their validity. The most elaborate and influential development of the
critique, however, appeared after a period in which psychologism gained
ground among philosophers and the upstart discipline of experimental
psychology had emerged to challenge philosophy as the royal road to
unlocking the mysteries of the mind.[8] Although there were rumblings
throughout the nineteenth century, only at its end did psychologism
emerge as a primary target of a philosophical counterattack. In 1884, Gottlob Frege published The Foundations of Arithmetic, which vigorously criticized
attempts by philosophers such as Friedrich Beneke, Jakob Fries, John
Stuart Mill, and Franz Brentano to reduce the mind, in particular its logical
function, to the psyche.[9] More radical psychologizers like Nietzsche were
beneath Frege's consideration.[10]

Husserl, although himself initially indebted to Brentano, was putatively

won over to Frege's position by a devastating review the latter wrote of
Husserl's early work The Foundations of Arithmetic in 1894.[11] By his Logical
Investigations of 1900, Husserl had come to see that the empirical science of
psychology with its inductive laws of association could not provide a basis
for a pure, deductive logic, which goes beyond mere probabilistic knowledge. In the 1890s, other philosophers, such as the neo-positivist Alexius
Meinong and the neo-Kantians Rudolf Hermann Lotze and Hermann Cohen, also vigorously turned against psychologism, moving away from epis-
temological questions to logical and ontological ones.[12] In physics as well,
a challenge to the radical associationism of Ernst Mach and the "energeticism" of Wilhelm Ostwald was launched by defenders of the reality of
discrete atoms like Ludwig Boltzmann.[13] At the same time, sociologists
like Emile Durkheim and Max Weber sought to avoid reducing social facts
to their alleged psychological substratum, and historians like Wilhelm
Dilthey gave up their search for underlying psychological types in favor of a
hermeneutics of objective meaning.[14]

This is not the place to attempt a full-scale history of anti-psychologism,
a task admirably carried out by Martin Kusch in a recent study in the
sociology of knowledge.[15] Suffice it to say that shortly after Husserl's conversion, it became a fundamental principle of many influential twentieth-
century philosophers in different camps, including such otherwise dispa-
rate figures as Heidegger, Cassirer, Russell, Moore, Carnap, Lukács, and
Goldmann.[16] Even the early Wittgenstein, as Cora Diamond has recently
shown, sought to banish psychology and follow the Kantian dictum that
logic was in agreement only with itself, however much he may have ultimately come to question Frege's belief that logic might be freed of ordinary
language as well and expressed in a pure, unequivocal "concept-script."[17]

There were, of course, many variations in the alternatives to psychologism provided by these critics, and indeed their target was not always
understood in precisely the same way, but the general complaint was as
follows.[18] Reducing the mind to the psyche was problematic for logic and
mathematics because it opened the door to relativism in which truth was
merely a function of the specific thinking mind in which it appeared or of
its cumulative experience over time. Even the concepts of a species-wide
transcendental consciousness or innate biological capacities (of the kind
later defended by Noam Chomsky) were insufficient to ward off the threat

of psychological relativism. As Frege put it, "neither logic nor mathematics has the task of investigating minds and contents of consciousness owned by individual men."[19] The philosophy of Mind, in other words, was not reducible to the philosophy of actual human minds; the apodictic or a priori character of certain universal truths was not the same as the empirical and a posteriori character of contingent knowledge. "2+2=4" and the law of contradiction were entirely independent of the minds that held them. The truth content of propositions had to be rigorously separated from the judgments made about them, judgments that would be better understood as correct or incorrect.[20] The sense of a proposition, to put it slightly differently, had to be distinguished from its presentation or representation; confirmation and refutation were not the same as persuasion. Moreover, whereas psychological laws could never be more than vague and probabilistic, based as they were on inductive generalizations, the laws of logic and mathematics were valid, timeless, and pure; the latter could not therefore be derived from the former.

Husserl, to be sure, ultimately paid more attention than did Frege to the links between disembodied, timeless Mind and the actual cognition of real human beings; the ideal realm of logic and mathematics could, after all, manifest itself in the finite, but rational, consciousness of fallible mortals. If not, Husserl reasoned, we could have no access to it. There is thus a possibility of eidetic intuition, he claimed, which provided the immediate evidence of essential objects.[21] Achieving such intuitions was, in fact, the point of his phenomenological rather than strictly logical method with its continuing debt to Brentano's notion of intentionality. He thus returned to a variant of the transcendentalism that Frege scorned. Nonetheless, both he and Frege resisted the reduction of objective to subjective ideas, understood either as generalizations from empirical experience or as the product of mere introspection into the individual self.

They also shared a strong hostility to what they claimed was the psychologistic confusion of cause and justification, the genetic fallacy that understood validity in terms of origin. Whereas psychologism was determined to reduce logic and mathematics to a prior psychological disposition or the cumulative weight of successive experiences, they wanted to disentangle one from the other. As Frege admonished his readers, "never let us take a description of the origin of an idea for a definition, or an account of the

mental and physical conditions on which we become conscious of a proposition for a proof of it. A proposition may be thought, and again it may be
true; let us never confuse these two things."[22] Logic and mathematics had
timeless validity, which meant their origins or causes were irrelevant to
their intrinsic truth content.

How ultimately compelling these criticisms of psychologism may be
cannot be decided here. There are, in fact, still heated disputes among
philosophers, and defenses have been mounted by positing alternative
versions of psychology that allegedly escape its pitfalls.[23] What is important for our purposes is the remarkable extent of the critique's success in
the very decades when aesthetic modernism was itself emerging, from the
1890s through the First World War.[24] Indeed, its power remained strong
well into the era after the Second World War. Its echo can, for example, still
be clearly heard in one of the most powerful theoretical defenses of modernism made in the 1960s, Theodor W. Adorno's *Aesthetic Theory*. Speaking
of the psychoanalysis of works of art in particular, Adorno writes, "it
neglects to consider their real objectivity, their inner consistency, the level
of form, their critical impulses, their relation to non-psychic reality and,
last but not least, their truth content."[25]

For certain modernist artists as well, the threat to the integrity of the
work of art and its timeless truth value posed by psychologism was also a
palpable reality.[26] There was a modernist "mystique of purity," which, as
Renato Poggioli noted many years ago, "aspires to abolish the discursive
and syntactic element, to liberate art from any connection with psychological and empirical reality, to reduce every work to the intimate laws of its
own expressive essence or to the given absolutes of its own genre or
means."[27] A displaced variant of the time-honored struggle to maintain a
boundary between the sacred and the profane, this aspiration can also be
understood as yet another instance of what sociologists have seen as the
uneven process of differentiating value spheres characteristic of modernization as a whole. At certain times, the dislocations produced by that
process seem to have been especially acute, resulting in a struggle over
boundary maintenance or reconfiguration that was particularly fierce. The
late nineteenth century in Europe was by all accounts a period in which the
cards, cultural as well as social, were being rapidly shuffled in new and
threatening ways.[28]

The threats that resulted in the generalization of anti-psychologism beyond the confines of philosophy were multifarious: for example, the expansion of confidence in natural science produced a scientistic hubris that threatened the value of other approaches to reality; the extension of new forms of popular commodified culture appealing to the desires and fantasies of the masses menaced the allegedly disinterested realm of high art; and the challenge to traditional gender roles in the fin-de-siècle created anxieties about the domination of masculine conceptions of cultural value. Modernism, as Andreas Huyssen has shown, often defined itself against a feminized version of mass culture, which it stigmatized as debased kitsch.[29] Not surprisingly, one weapon in its battle with these demons was the exorcism of psychologism in the name of a universalism that would, however, be based on nonscientific values.

Perhaps the most explicit manifestation of the struggle against psychologism appeared in the development of modernist literature in Britain around the time of the First World War. In virtually all accounts of the evolution of Anglo-American poetry from Yeats to Pound, Ford, and Eliot, the search for something called "impersonality" and the suppression of subjective expressivity has been duly recognized.[30] Although the tangled web of attitudes toward subjective expression and objective presentation in the history of British modernism has prevented the story from being a straightforward narrative of one-dimensional anti-psychologism, it is nonetheless clear that the anxieties we have traced in Frege, Husserl, and the neo-Kantians were given aesthetic voice in the work and theory of the major figures in that story.

In fact, the explicit importance of Husserl's critique of psychologism for the poetry and criticism of the influential critic and poet T. E. Hulme has been widely acknowledged. Although it took some time to disentangle Hulme's initial enthusiasm for Bergson's philosophy of flux and immediate experience from his later, very different position—an entanglement abetted by the ensemble publication of essays from his entire career in the collection entitled *Speculations*, posthumously appearing in 1924—there seems to be a consensus now that he had shifted his opinion in the years directly before the war.[31] Partly due to the relentless critique of Bergsonism as hopelessly romantic and simplistically democratic made by Pierre Lasserre, Charles Maurras, and other neoclassicist stalwarts of the right-wing

Action Française, Hulme's change of heart also reflected a reading of Husserl's attack on psychologism in the *Logical Investigations*, which allowed him to understand for the first time the implications of the anti-idealist realism he had encountered in the analytical philosophy of G. E. Moore and Bertrand Russell.[32] Liberally citing the German philosopher in the essay that opened *Speculations*, "Humanism and the Religious Attitude," a version of which had been already published in 1915, Hulme decried the entire trend of modern thought from the Renaissance on as distressingly anthropomorphic, based on the mistaken reduction of objective ideas to a merely human source, the confusion of pure philosophy with *Weltanschauung*.[33]

But Hulme went beyond Frege and Husserl's critique of psychologism in a crucial way: he applied their argument outside of the realm of logic per se. Citing Moore's *Principia Ethica* of 1903, with its celebrated critique of the naturalist fallacy, Hulme argued that ethical values as well should be understood as irreducible to human construction.[34] It was also possible, he contended (without bothering to demonstrate how), to arrange them in an objective hierarchy. A parallel argument loosely derived from Wilhelm Worringer's 1908 *Abstraction and Empathy* allowed Hulme to denounce aesthetic styles based on intersubjective empathy (or more precisely, on a subject's pantheistic empathy with a beautiful object in the world) as inherently inferior to those, such as Egyptian or Byzantine, which resisted naturalistic organicism in the name of impersonal, geometrical, nonvitalist abstraction.[35] Modern art, exemplified by the sculpture of Jacob Epstein and the paintings of Cézanne and Wyndham Lewis, Hulme argued, promised a return to precision, austerity, and bareness, the anti-humanist values he so admired.[36] It would help clean up the mess produced by transgressing boundaries, that "pot of treacle over the dinner table" Hulme famously identified with the "spilt religion" that was romanticism.[37]

This is not the place and I am not the scholar to present a detailed and nuanced account of the complicated resonances of Hulme's ideas among the English modernists, especially the Imagist poets.[38] Nor can we pause to consider related developments in the modernist novel from Flaubert to Virginia Woolf, in which stylistic innovations like the *style indirect libre* helped create the effect of nonegocentric impersonality in ways that paralleled developments in the poetry of the modern era.[39] And we cannot open

up once again the debate about spatial form in modern poetry and the
novel launched by Joseph Frank, who acknowledged an explicit debt to
Hulme and Worringer.[40] What, however, needs to be at least briefly under-
lined is the pivotal role of a figure of inestimable importance who acknowledged an explicit debt to Hulme and through him to Frege and Husserl:
T. S. Eliot.

In his new journal, The Criterion, and elsewhere, Eliot energetically promulgated many of Hulme's ideas, aesthetic as well as political. In such
celebrated essays as "Tradition and the Individual Talent" of 1919, he presented many of the same anti-psychologistic arguments we have already
encountered. "Poetry," he contended in lines that quickly became canonical, "is not a turning loose of emotion but an escape from emotion; it is not
the expression of personality but an escape from personality."[41] His influential notion of an "objective correlative" seems likely, in fact, to have been
taken directly from Husserl, whom Eliot read when he studied philosophy
at Harvard in 1914.[42] Although his obvious debt to F. H. Bradley, on whom
he wrote his dissertation, has been widely acknowledged, Eliot also drew
on the work of Meinong, Russell, and Moore and other so-called new
realists of the period.[43] According to Sanford Schwartz, "in his thesis he
undermines the assumptions of the psychologist by reducing consciousness to its objects, and later used the same strategy in his critique of
nineteenth-century poetry."[44] Eliot, Schwartz also shows, went on to criticize an equally abstract objectivism, which reified objects as a simple
inverse of the romantic reification of the integral subject; he was clearly no
naturalist seeing art as a passive reflection of an external world.[45] The
poet's ability to fashion words from his immediate experience somehow
overcame the very dichotomy between subject and object, challenging as
well the infamous "dissociation of sensibility" that Eliot claimed had
plagued the modern world ever since the English Revolution placed feeling
above wit.

Through the dissemination of Eliot's ideas by the New Critics of the
1930s and 1940s, impersonality became a new dogma and the isolation of
the poem from its contexts of production and reception, an article of faith.
Like the logic Frege had hoped to rescue from its psychologistic reduction
and the ethical imperatives Hulme had sought to distinguish from the

humans who followed or transgressed them, aesthetic value, often equated
entirely with formal self-referentiality, became an end entirely in itself. The
New Critics' dreaded genetic and affective fallacies and the fallacy of expressive form were all little more than redescriptions in poetic terms of the
warnings against psychologism made by late-nineteenth-century philosophy. Even when later champions of modernism like Charles Altieri sought
to reintroduce a notion of agency, they were careful to distinguish the
structuring activity of the artist from the emotional interiority of the empir-
cal, suffering subject lurking beneath its surface.[46]

All of this is by now well known and needs no belaboring. But what
perhaps warrants some attention is the parallel process that can be discerned in the visual arts during this period. Not surprisingly, the value of
hard-edged visual distinctness, which Hulme and the Imagists defended as
a metaphoric antidote to the sloppy pantheistic continuities they saw in
romanticism, could easily be adopted in literal terms by painters anxious
to experiment with geometric abstractions and fields of color.[47] Despite
the powerful subjectivist impulse in certain visual modernisms, most obviously German Expressionism, others manifested the same suspicion of
psychological expression that we have noted in literary modernists like
Eliot.

The nineteenth century, to be sure, can be said to have been, by and
large, a period of the increasing psychologization of the visual, the abandonment of a geometric optics of representation based on the eye's ability
faithfully to mirror the world outside. The story of how, beginning in the
second decade of the nineteenth century, scientists of perception undermined the classical observer modeled on the automatic functioning of a
camera obscura has been masterfully reconstructed by Jonathan Crary in
his recent *Techniques of the Observer*.[48] No longer a monological, punctual,
mechanical eye coolly recording a world outside itself, the new spectator
was embodied, binocular, and influenced by internal psycho-physiological
processes such as afterimages, the presence of sensations without any simultaneous external stimulus. The psychologization of vision, the loss of
confidence in the veracity of the eye and such systems of representation as
Renaissance perspective, affected art h story and criticism as well as practice. Thus, in his influential *Principles of Art History* of 1915, Heinrich Wölf-

flin would write of the oscillating pattern of classical and baroque styles he saw as a constant of visual representation: "There is no denying it—the development of the process is psychologically intelligible."[49]

The delayed artistic repercussions of the changes Crary details in the early part of the century can be found most readily in the "glancing," embodied, and dynamic—as opposed to "gazing," disembodied, static— eye of Impressionism, to borrow Norman Bryson's well-known distinction.[50] It has thus been easy for commentators on the literary offshoots of psychological empiricism, such as Judith Ryan, to find compelling parallels between them and Impressionism.[51] Both suggest a withdrawal from the world of stable objects and a new preoccupation with the perceiving subject, a subject in crisis, absorbed by its own dissolution, fascinated and sometimes bewildered by the flux of sensations flooding in from without.

It is, however, with the loose and amorphous body of work that has become known as post-Impressionism, and with the painting of Cézanne in particular, that these parallels begin to break down. Indeed, it might be said that the famous "doubt" that Merleau-Ponty detected in Cézanne was directed not only toward the traditional perspectival order of the Renaissance frozen gaze, but also toward the adequacy of the Impressionists' glancing eye.[52] His attempt to return to objects and paint "nature," was not however, a restoration of earlier representational realism; instead, it sought the real entirely on the surface of the canvas, where subject and object, perception and the perceived, were not yet distinct and separate.[53] Here a world of pure monstrance, of visual presence rather than representation, began to supplant the sensationalist psychologism of the Impressionists. Although Merleau-Ponty thought Cézanne had anticipated what later psychologists, such as the Gestaltists, were to realize in their laboratories, his description of the painter's achievement suggests a less psychologistic interpretation: "The lived object is not rediscovered or constructed on the basis of the contributions of the senses; rather it presents itself to us from the start as the center from which these contributions radiate."[54]

Cézanne's project to capture viewer and viewed together on the flat surface of the canvas and thus realize unmediated visual presence may have been utopian, but it provided a challenge to the psychologism that had come to dominate nineteenth-century spectatorship (a challenge, as Altieri has argued, that had an impact on modernist poetry as well).[55] Thierry de Duve describes that challenge in terms of a difficult choice:

> Modernity picked up Cézanne's heritage in the form of an alternative: either I actively destroy the object, the figure, and all the realism that goes along with it, in order to preserve that which remains of my subjective integrity—here I have no other choice than to destroy the represented real, but at least in destroying it I make myself master of it—or I agree to sacrifice my subjective unity and allow the plural significance of my self-image to appear, but to the benefit of an unalterable pseudo-object, the self-sufficient epiphany of a world that excludes me.[56]

At different times, different movements and figures opted for one or the other of these alternatives (and some, to be sure, sought to overcome them by somehow including a dispersed notion of subjectivity in the epiphany itself).[57] But it is perhaps legitimate to say that in the long run most modernist painting, at least as it became canonically described in the criticism of Roger Fry, Clive Bell, Clement Greenberg, and Michael Fried, took the second course. That is, it sought to purge painting of anything allegedly superfluous to it, any expression of the painter's interiority, any representational reference, decorative functionality, or theatrical appeal to the beholder. Instead, painting came increasingly to be understood as a quest to realize only the essential and immanent laws of painting themselves, a quest for an authentic, truth-telling art that would be ontologically "absolute." Even when that absolute was understood in spiritual terms, as it was by Kandinsky, it meant the extirpation of the psychological subject.[58] Very much in the spirit of Kant's defense of logic as understanding "in agreement with itself," high modernism became a game of purification and reduction in which formal pictorial qualities were their own ends.[59] Indeed, for Greenberg, Kant himself was "the first real Modernist" because he "used logic to establish the limits of logic, and while he withdrew much from its old jurisdiction, logic was left in all the more secure possession of what remained to it."[60]

Not surprisingly, the aesthetic variant of this strategy of *reculer pour mieux sauter*, most explicitly realized in the writing of Greenberg after his break with Marxism, often earned a comparison with the New Criticism that was the scholarly handmaiden of literary modernism at this time.[61] Greenberg's explicit embrace of Eliot's banishment of personality from aesthetic judgment was also remarked, as was the similarity between his position and that of Adorno.[62] Although Eliot's later ruminations on culture and tradition suggest a more hermeneutic, contextual perspective, both he and Greenberg could be seen as championing self-reflexivity and self-absorption, in which the aesthetic object is rigidly segregated from anything outside its apparent boundaries.[63]

The anti-psychologistic impulse in the Greenbergian version of high modernism is thus not difficult to discern. More surprising is that something similar can be detected in the work of a modernist figure, who fell entirely outside of the canon established by Greenberg and the other champions of optical purity and self-sufficiency: Marcel Duchamp. What has been called his "pictorial nominalism," which perhaps became most explicit when Duchamp began fashioning his celebrated "readymades," meant foregrounding the constitutive power of the artist, who named an object an artwork through an act of enunciation ultimately valorized by the institutions of art rather than by his own genius or skill.[64] Eschewing the search for optical purity, indeed truculently indifferent to any optical values, and hostile to the search for the "absolute" essence of the medium of painting, Duchamp was in many respects the antithesis of the artist who hopes for the epiphanous revelation of a self-sufficient world on the flat surface of his canvas.[65] Instead, he promoted the invasion of the realm of the visual by the textual and discursive, allowed the real world literally to appear through the surface of the "canvas" (the *Large Glass* was a transparent "window" mocking both the old metaphor of the canvas as window and the new celebration of its two-dimensional opacity), and foregrounded the constructed persona of the artist, whose unstable identity registered the crisis of the genius model of creativity.

And yet, despite his radical problematizing of the mainstream modernist quest for pure visual presence and his deliberate mockery of its ontological pretensions, Duchamp was, I want to argue, equally suspicious of certain versions of psychologism in art. His famous dismissal of "retinal painting" was aimed at the positing of the painter's or beholder's eye, whether gazing or glancing, as the foundation of aesthetic value. His nominalism extended, we might say, to the perception of the artist, whose sensitively recorded act of ephemeral seeing was no less a questionable standard of veracity than the idealized representation of objects allegedly present in the visual field of a disembodied, camera obscura gaze.

Duchamp was even more antagonistic to an aesthetic of expressivity, arguing instead for an anti-romantic art of dehumanization. As Werner Hofmann has noted, "his act of choice consciously opposed the glorification of subjective creation and the principle which holds that the lowly object is ennobled by artistic 'expression.' "[66] Not surprisingly, in the 1950s Duchamp took to quoting T. S. Eliot's "Tradition and the Individual Talent" with its famous distinction between 'the man who suffers" and "the mind who creates," and told one critic in 1961 that "Eliot's essay presents his own feelings as well or better than he himself has ever done in writing."[67] In short, even so maverick a figure in the pantheon of modernism as Marcel Duchamp felt obliged to distance himself from the lure of psychologism.

Duchamp and Eliot, to be sure, are certainly an odd couple and can only remain together in a tense constellation for a short while before they begin to drift apart. Duchamp, in fact, has emerged in the past few decades as the quintessential critic of modernist pretensions to formalist purity, optical essentialism, and the integrity of the medium. Although he may have called into question expressive notions of genius and disparaged the empirical perception of the artist, his own role in dismantling the Greenbergian consensus has been increasingly written in heroic terms.[68] So too the personal, often erotic traces in his work have come to the fore, in ways that invite the charge of a renewed psychologism.[69]

The postmodernist appropriation of Duchamp, in fact, would not feel offended by this charge, for one of the most explicit dividing lines between modernism and its putative successor is precisely their differing attitudes toward psychologism. Indeed, in one sense, postmodernism can be said to be a "second psychologism."[70] Its return seems to have been prepared by the widespread recognition that the modernist project of ruthless purification had reached a dead end, as there was little interesting left to write or paint about once all contaminations were banished. The indifference to human suffering that seemed too often to accompany the modernist differentiation of value spheres also made many uneasy, as the troubling extent of the modernist entanglement with fascism became clearer. Sim-

ilarly, the modernist pretensions to disinterestedness have seemed increasingly hollow in the face of multiculturalist and feminist critiques of soi-
disant universalism, as well as the sociological claim that aesthetic value is
really just another name for "cultural capital."[71] And finally, the threat of a
scientistic version of psychology seemed less pressing once the literary and
hermeneutic dimensions of psychoanalysis came to the fore.

The recent return to some form of psychologism is, in fact, evident in
philosophy itself, where a reaction against the privileging of self-identical
logic has taken many forms, among them a new sensitivity to the impact of
the institutional context of the discipline on its subject matter.[72] The neopragmatism of Richard Rorty is a salient example of a renewed distrust of
the fallacy that defenders of psychologism had once mockingly dubbed
"logicism."[73] In *Philosophy and the Mirror of Nature*, he notes with satisfac-
tion that

> seventy years after Husserl's "Philosophy as Rigorous Science" and
> Russell's "Logic as the Essence of Philosophy," we are back with the
> same putative dangers which faced the authors of these manifestoes:
> if philosophy becomes too naturalistic, hard-nosed positive disci-
> plines will nudge it aside; if it becomes too historicist, then intellec-
> tual history, literary criticism, and similar soft spots in "the human-
> ities" will swallow it up.[74]

Rorty's plea is to stop worrying in the face of these putative dangers and
accept the inevitable blurring of the lines between philosophy and its scientific and historicist neighbors. Heeding his message, some followers of
Rorty have reread the modernist tradition itself in the hope of resituating
its figures in the new context; one has gone so far as to try to rescue even
T. S. Eliot by turning him into a closet pragmatist, who ultimately came to
believe in the virtues of historical tradition and practical wisdom over
logical (or aesthetic) truth.[75]

Deconstruction has likewise taken aim at Husserl's attempt to use eidetic intuition to provide an avenue of entry into the timeless world of
logical truth. Derrida's *Speech and Phenomena* begins with an attack on the
confusions of a transcendental psychologism that seeks to exclude precisely those intrusions from without that any psychologism necessitates.[76]
Gleefully extolling the very contamination and pollution that so troubled

critics of psychologism, celebrating the temporal deferral and traces of
the past that the fetish of spatial form in modernism hoped to keep at
bay, restoring modified respect for the representation and mimesis that
modernist self-reflexivity had banished, deconstruction transgresses many
of the same boundaries that nineteenth-century psychologism had also
violated.

Its effects on literary critical attitudes toward psychologism have been
evident. Although eschewing any strong notion of the expressive subject
and no less suspicious of humanist pieties than Hulme and Eliot were,
deconstruction has reversed the New Critics' disdain for romanticism and
reintroduced complicated notions of intentionality.[77] One need only mention New Historicism, reception aesthetics, the pervasive influence of
Nietzsche, and the proliferation of psychoanalytically informed approaches
to reinforce the same point: the taboo against psychologism now seems
firmly laid to rest among literary critics. Or more precisely, many have come
to feel at home in a gray area between the absolute alternatives of a maximalist psychologistic reductionism, in which all mental activity and all
cultural artifacts are merely an expression of emotional states, and an anti-
psychologistic purism, in which everything of value must be protected
against any pollution from without.[78]

Indeed, one of the reasons it may be meaningful to distinguish between
modernism and postmodernism, however volatile that distinction may be,
is the recent undermining of the taboo, which operated so powerfully
during the modernist era. As I hope is now evident, "psychologism," with
all of its connotations of reductionism, contamination, and relativism,
became one of the main anxieties of that era, a veritable "specter," as one
recent commentator has called it, haunting the modernist mind.[79] Postmodernists, in contrast, seem more relaxed and untroubled by these dangers, having learned to live with the ghosts of the past rather than trying to
exorcise them. Although they hold no brief for the notion of an integrated
subject, whose individual psychology can be the genesis of art, they feel
comfortable with a dispersed and decentered subjectivity whose impulses,
desires, fetishes, and fantasies disturb the smooth workings of any cultural
sublimation.[80]

But to give the screw one final turn, postmodernism may itself be
haunted by a specter of its own, which refuses to die: the ghost of modern-

ist anti-psychologism. Some contemporary philosophers of mind still struggle, after all, to produce a transcendental account of consciousness that will establish the autonomy of at least mathematics and logic.[81] Certain ethical theorists continue to balk at the "emotivist" reduction of moral imperatives to personal preferences.[82] And what Adorno liked to call the "truth content of art" stubbornly refuses to lose its fascination for those unwilling to level all aesthetic distinctions and reduce all judgments to matters of individual taste.

If Derrida is right in claiming that the specter of Marx still haunts our apparently post-Marxist world, the same might well be the case for the anti-psychologism that flourished during the heyday of modernism.[83] As the continuing wars over multiculturalism and the canon testify, it would be premature to believe that the pressures that produced the fear of psychologism have entirely subsided, or that the search for aesthetic value is entirely a thing of the past. Whatever the future of the debate, one thing is clear: it would be a serious mistake to ignore the creative energies unleashed by the effort to fend off psychologism during the previous era. For even if it now seems a losing battle, or its outcome at best a stalemate, the struggle was an indisputable ingredient in the making of that remarkable phenomenon we call modern art.

16

Modern and Postmodern Paganism:

Peter Gay and Jean-François Lyotard

✳

The history of that odd hybrid we have come to call "Judeo-Christian" civilization has been haunted by what its defenders have so mightily sought to suppress and forget: the dogged persistence of the cultures and religions that came before.[1] Although widely divergent, these have been collectively defined by a term that none ever in fact chose as a self-description, but which has served their enemies well as a blanket term of opprobrium. That term is, of course, paganism. Derived from *pagus*, the Latin for "from the country" and drawing on the Roman soldiers' use of *paganus* to stigmatize civilians, it was initially employed by the early Christians to refer to all those non-Jews who were not militants in Christ's army.[2] Although more neutral uses were occasionally adopted, the term's negative connotation was only intensified when the Church Fathers launched their polemics against classical philosophy and culture.

In fact, for well over a millennium, "pagan" served Christendom—as well as Judaism and the newer monotheistic culture of Islam—as a potent label to stigmatize those who departed from the dominant cultural norm. Clustered with its close neighbors "heathen," "idolater," and "infidel," it came to separate those who were saved from those who were damned. When paired with "savage" or "barbarian," it divided those who were civilized from those who were not. Linked with "diabolical" and identified with witchcraft and black magic,[3] it suggested an even more radical distinction between the truly human who possessed a dignity that must be honored and those who fell outside the pale of humanity and could be crushed with impunity. As demonstrated by the vicious persecution of the gypsies, who first wandered into Europe from India in the fourteenth century, "pagan" could become an epithet with very fateful consequences indeed.[4]

No binary opposition can, however, retain its boundaries for very long without some erosion, and that between "pagan" and its various others proved no exception.[5] Indeed, the pollution (or invigoration) of Jewish, Christian, and Islamic culture by paganism is so fundamental a theme of our history that no justice can be done to it in the short compass of an essay. But certain salient features of that story, especially its Christian chapters, must be quickly highlighted before we turn to the true focus of our enterprise, the comparison between modern and postmodern revivals of the pagan legacy as represented respectively by Peter Gay and Jean-François Lyotard.

Although Tertullian had contemptuously remarked "What has Athens to do with Jerusalem?" many others continued to ask the same question in a less dismissive manner, ultimately helping to blur the distinction. One early way in which the opposition between the monotheistic religions and the pagan past started to erode was, in fact, through the allegorical reading of the ancient myths as prefigurations of Christian moral teachings. This practice began with the neo-Platonists in the Church, who were themselves borrowing a tactic from the Stoics, and reached a crescendo with the Jesuits during the Counter-Reformation.[6] Another was the tacit recognition and grudging acceptance of the tenacity of pre-Christian survivals in Christian practices. Thus, it was possible to discern in the medieval cult of local saints and their relics a residue of an earlier worship of local deities, in the same way that holy sites could be understood as reminiscent of Roman *loca sacra*. So too the mobilization of images in Christian worship, although a periodic source of iconoclastic anxiety,[7] could be understood as continuous with the pagan celebration of theophanous divinities.

The risk of such a recognition was, of course, the damage it might do to orthodox Christian belief. In the hands of such seventeenth-century skeptics as Pierre Bayle or such deists as John Toland, the similarities between pagan myth and Christian gospel were, in fact, deliberately brought to the fore to discredit the latter.[8] Catholicism in particular could be reviled as a polytheistic superstition only pretending to believe in one God. By the time folklore and ethnography began to emerge as scholarly disciplines in the nineteenth century, even the central story of the Crucifixion and Resurrection could be situated in the context of a universal pagan belief in a dying and reborn God of nature, as Sir James Frazer famously argued in *The Golden Bough*.

If one way of calling into question the absolute distinction between Christian and pagan was by showing how much of the latter had remained transfigured in the former, another was by reversing the order and finding in what had been stigmatized much to admire. Here perhaps the first sustained rehabilitation came with the renewed respect for classical learning in the Renaissance, when humanist naturalism sought inspiration in Greek and Roman philosophy, architecture, and the visual arts.[9] What one of our protagonists, Peter Gay, was to call "the era of pagan Christianity"[10] from 1300 to 1700 somehow found a way to combine orthodox faith and a new interest in antiquity. Many of the hermetic traditions of astrology, necromancy, and alchemy were combined in a heady way with a Christian spirituality that seemed to need their energizing power. But the equilibrium proved in the long run hard to maintain and by the time of the neoclassical Enlightenment, paganism and free-thinking began inexorably to gravitate toward each other, turning revealed religion into a target.[11]

Neoclassicism, to be sure, had a highly selective reading of the pagan past, which identified it largely with its most elevated and ennobling achievements, an attitude that spawned a tradition—increasingly privileging Greece over Rome—whose best known exponents were Johann Joachim Winckelmann in Germany and Matthew Arnold in England. Deliberately aimed at the Lutheran and Puritan attempt to reinforce the boundary between an uncorrupted Christianity and its allegedly idolatrous predecessors, a boundary that had been apparently weakened during the late Middle Ages and Renaissance, it sought to free itself from what it construed as the moralizing, life-denying rigorism derived from an exaggerated fidelity to the competing tradition it called "Nazarene" or "Hebraic."[12] The pagan Greece that "tyrannized" not only Germany, to borrow E. M. Butler's celebrated verb, but also much of English and French thought from the mid-eighteenth century on, found an aesthetic wholeness and reconciliation between nature and culture in the Hellenic world, which helped legitimate that nonanthropocentric respect for nature whose rise Keith Thomas has identified in the early modern world.[13] It could also paradoxically provide

both a retreat from vulgar politics into inward-looking individual cultivation (Bildung) and a utopian model for the modern state.[14] Inspiration for
the latter was readily found in the classical traditions of civic virtue and
public rhetoric, which were revived by thinkers like Giambattista Vico,
whose New Science also did much to urge belief in the truth-telling function
of mythopoeic fantasy before Christian gospel and modern science.[15]

The new appreciation for the indigenous folk cultures of Europe, which
began in the eighteenth century with Herder and intensified with the romantic fascination with diversity and particularity, provided, however, a
very different model of paganism, which helped it survive the decline in the
actual reading of classical and humanist texts during the late Enlightenment.[16] What can be called the desublimated alternative to neoclassical
Hellenism found much to admire in the simplicity, vitality, and authenticity
of supposedly "primitive" cultures. Celtic, Teutonic, Baltic, Slavic, and
Magyar myths, rituals, and holy sites were rediscovered and incorporated
into the developing national consciousness of various modern communities. Druidism, to take a salient example, was actively studied and even
revived in eighteenth-century Britain, often for the purposes of inventing
usable, if somewhat fanciful, cultural traditions.[17] In France, a positive
reevaluation of nos ancêtres les gaulois went along with the revolution's attempt to discredit the aristocracy, which was identified instead with those
allegedly foreign pagans known as the Franks.[18]

A similar desublimating reassessment of classical paganism itself began
as early as the mid-eighteenth century, when the buried Roman cities of
Herculaneum and Pompeii were uncovered.[19] A new taste for the more
"primitive" poetry of Homer went along with a fascination for the locales
described in his epics.[20] Although it took until the era of romanticism for
the full effect to be felt, these sites revealed an antiquity that was more than
the highest examples of timeless beauty; instead, they showed a whole way
of life, including the most mundane details of quotidian existence. The
archaeological discoveries of Heinrich Schliemann, who unearthed Troy in
1873 and Mycenae in 1874, and Arthur Evans, who uncovered even earlier
Minoan sites on Crete after 1900, further excited the imaginations of those,
like Sigmund Freud, who were anxious to dig beneath the surface of
Winckelmann's idealized aesthetic of "noble simplicity and serene great-
ness"[21] to find an earlier, "archaic" period. By the late nineteenth century,

the so-called Cambridge School of anthropology, led by Jane Ellen Harrison and Francis Cornford, sought to show the roots of classical Greece in the esoteric cults of primitive religion.

A frank admiration for the fleshly delights of pagan sensuality, sometimes understood as a model of naïve innocence, sometimes as a symptom of overripe decay often accompanied this excitement. Present in increasingly desublimated ways from the Pre-Raphaelites (who were themselves sometimes called neo-Pagans) and Walter Pater to Oscar Wilde and Edward Carpenter in Britain, this enthusiasm was also evident among the French Decadents and Austrian Aesthetes. The struggle to give dignity to homosexual practices in particular explicitly borrowed from their honored role in Greek life. So too an appreciation of archaic Greece often resulted in a celebration of an allegedly benign matriarchal civilization ruthlessly suppressed by its patriarchal successor as was argued by Johann Jakob Bachofen, Otto Gross, and their followers.[22]

The emergence of a less idealized image of Greek culture—ripping off the fig leaves, we might say, that had been added in the period of pagan Christianity—was, in fact, a Europeanwide phenomenon. In Germany, for example, its beginnings in the visual arts can be traced to the campaign to restore the vivid colors that had faded from the blanched image of neoclassical art with its marmoreal coldness, a cause championed, among others, by the great architect Gottfried Semper in the 1820s and 1830s.[23] In literature, the same impulse has often been discerned in Heinrich Heine's debunking poem "The Gods of Greece," which registered Heine's disillusionment with Goethe's Olympian Hellenism and anticipated Nietzsche's *The Birth of Tragedy*. The latter celebrated the mythic community reflected in the integration of Apollonian and Dionysian impulses in Attic tragedy, a community whose return Nietzsche saw foreshadowed in Wagner's operas. Although he abandoned the quest when he lost faith in Wagner's mission, attempts to realize it in the years before World War I were made by such militantly anti-Christian publicists as the brothers August and Ernst Horneffer, who promoted an explicitly "pagan life course" based on the values of heroic nationalism.[24]

Whether such a revival had any meaningful influence on the fuzzy embrace of a Teutonic pseudo-religion on the part of the Nazis a generation later remains in dispute.[25] But it is clear that the self-proclaimed paganism of such Weimar figures as Ludwig Klages and Alfred Schuler could easily be given not only an anti-Christian, but also an explicitly anti-Semitic flavor, abetted by the demeaning identification of Judaism with "soulless" patriarchal intellectuality and alienation from nature. The ground had already been prepared by nineteenth-century classicists, who, if Martin Bernal's controversial argument is to be believed, had sought to find an "aryan" lineage from antiquity to the modern age, thus repressing the African roots of Hellenic civilization.[26] In fact, even the most respectable exponents of philhellenism, such as Werner Jaeger, could turn their love for pagan Greece into an implied apologia for the Third Reich.[27]

However one construes such episodes, it is clear that by the end of the nineteenth century and the beginning of the twentieth, the term "pagan" was available widely again for positive identification in many other, less sinister contexts. In Britain, for example, novelists like Thomas Hardy and D. H. Lawrence sought to draw on its power as an antidote to the repressive dreariness of modern life. In 1908, a group of young nature-worshiping, friendship-extolling, anti-Victorians at Cambridge gathered around the poet Rupert Brooke could self-consciously choose to call themselves "neo-pagans" in order to signal their desire to inhabit groves that were once again sacred.[28] Although the First World War put paid to the mobilization of Homeric images of heroic valor for patriotic purposes and hastened the decline of classical studies,[29] other variants of the tradition were still available for later revival. Whether optimistically vitalist or pessimistically entropic—the Decadent imagination, as noted, was often fueled by languid images of a pagan world in delicious, indolent decay—paganism had shown itself to be an especially buoyant floating signifier with remarkable staying power, but no settled meaning.

In our own day, it has, as we know, been reappropriated by a wide variety of nature-venerating, anti-technological groups, whose New Age spirituality is an eclectic amalgam of many different beliefs, customs, and rites. Repudiating the heroic masculinist readings of some earlier revivals, these often take on an explicitly feminist coloration. As in the period of Bachofen and Gross, such goddesses as Isis, Artemis, and Astarte, whose closeness to the earth is extolled as an antidote to the transcendent striving of typically patriarchal religions such as Judaism or Christianity, are put at the center of the pagan pantheon. Although it is difficult to assess the literalness of their belief, many New Age devotees seem determined to reverse the secularization of pagan religion, which allowed it to survive only in aesthetic form in Renaissance and neoclassical Europe, and hope instead to reenchant the world. Even the diabolic variant of paganism, however apocryphal the connection between early modern witchcraft and ancient practices may actually be, has found its adherents, at least so it would seem from the popular press's fascination with Satanism today. More secular celebrants of pop culture's profitable mixture of sex and violence, such as Camille Paglia in her widely discussed *Sexual Personae*, equally exult in the claim that "the latent paganism of western culture has burst forth again in all its daemonic vitality."[30]

To complicate the picture still further, the term has also retained its aura for those who stubbornly hold on to an ennobling notion of Hellenic culture. The right-wing British moral philosopher John Casey, for example, has recently sought to make a case for paganism not on aesthetic or religious, but on ethical grounds. Casey defends the worldly virtues of pride, courage, magnanimity, temperance, fame, and practical wisdom against the world-denying ones of Christian and Kantian humility, self-abnegation and fairness.[31] Paganism in this usage becomes a weapon in the struggle against the leveling egalitarianism of the modern age, a justification for accepting the privileges provided by fortune as instances of what Bernard Williams has called "moral luck."[32] Right-wing German hermeneuticians such as Odo Marquard have also found in pagan polytheism and "polymyths," at least in their disenchanted form as histories and stories, an alternative to "philosophy as an orthological mono-logos,"[33] which is shorthand for Habermasian Critical Theory. And French radical right-wingers such as Jacques Marlaud have sought to concoct a pagan pedigree for Alain de Benoist and the "nouvelle Droite" by tracing the defense of myth in Henri de Montherlant, Jean Cau, Louis Pauwels, Pierre Gripari, and their ilk.[34] Countering this usage is the persistent evocation of the democratic polis of Periclean Athens as a radical antidote to the authoritarian implications of Platonic politics, a case that has been perhaps most vigorously made by Hannah Arendt and her followers.

With all of this as a prelude, it may well seem that nothing much can be gained from trying to slow down the whirl of denotations and connotations that have surrounded the history of this vexed term and assign it a single, coherent meaning. I would, in fact, agree that no benefit would accrue from attempting to privilege one variant of the term over another, for what has made it so powerful a semantic resource is precisely its polysemic indeterminacy. What, however, may be worth attempting is a more modest comparison of the use made of it by two of its most respected recent advocates, who are too clever to hope for the magical reenchantment of the world and thus successfully avoid the New Age *Schwärmerei* that often surrounds the term. By comparing the modern paganism of Peter Gay with its postmodern counterpart in Jean-François Lyotard, we may be able to appreciate how at least some of its lessons still have something to teach us as the second millennium of the Christian era draws to a close.

✳

Writing in defiance of the attempt, most vigorously made by Carl Becker,[35] to reduce the Enlightenment to a secularized variant of medieval Christian thought, Peter Gay provocatively subtitled the first volume of his magisterial work of 1966 (*The Enlightenment: An Interpretation*), "The Rise of Modern Paganism." Explicitly drawing on Heine's distinction between "Hebrews" and "Hellenes," he sought to situate the "party of humanity" squarely in the latter camp. The greatest figures of the Enlightenment—Montesquieu, Fontenelle, Gibbon, Lessing, Rousseau, Diderot, Winckelmann—were virtually all in the thrall of the classical world, moving beyond mere identification with its heroes to an active pagan identity of their own. "The philosophes," Gay claimed, "did not merely quote antiquity, they earned it, and they experienced it."[36] The battle between the Ancients and the Moderns turned out in a way to be a victory for both.

That of the Enlightenment was, however, a distinctly "Mediterranean paganism," which ought not to be confused with the "Teutonic paganism" that Gay described as a "strange mixture of Roman Catholic, primitive Greek and folkish Germanic notions." Nor, despite their frequent resort to sensualist rhetoric, should they be thought of as particularly licentious: "these preachers of libertinism," he insisted, "were far less self-indulgent, far more restrained in their habits, then their pronouncements would lead us to believe." Instead, their paganism meant first and foremost an extension of the slow replacement of myth and superstition by reason that had characterized antiquity (Vico, let it be noted, was entirely absent from Gay's account). The philosophes, he claimed, primarily admired the ancients "for their realism, their impatience with obfuscation and mystery."[37]

They were, to be sure, explicitly "modern" pagans, by which Gay meant that they spurned a pedantic study of antiquity for its own sake, casting off what Diderot had called "the spectacles of anticomania."[38] Resistant to any nostalgia, cautiously upholding the ideal of progress, but not naively utopian, the philosophes went beyond the "first Enlightenment" that had taken place in Greece and Rome. Anti-Platonic, they rejected all variants of metaphysics, including the speculative Rationalism that had prevailed in the century before them, as a compromise with religion. Their focus instead was on epistemology and psychology, which allowed them to probe the underlying sources of humankind's need for false consolations.[39] "What made the pagans modern and gave them hope for the future," Gay argued in the second volume of The Enlightenment, "was that they could use science to control their classicism by establishing the superiority of their own, second age of criticism over the first, and thus keep their respect for their ancestors within proper bounds."[40]

Endorsing Ernst Cassirer's celebrated defense of the eighteenth century as an age of analytical critique rather than synthetic system-building,[41] Gay nonetheless placed David Hume rather than Cassirer's hero Kant as the culminating figure in his narrative. The more militantly anti-religious Hume, successfully liberated from the shackles of his Scottish Presbyterian upbringing, was, Gay contended, "the complete modern pagan" who "makes plain that since God is silent, man is his own master: he must live in a disenchanted world, submit everything to criticism, and make his own way."[42]

Reading the Enlightenment in this light meant that Gay had clearly chosen to pursue the second of the two ways through which paganism lost its stigma described above: being elevated over its religious opponents through a reversal of the initial hierarchy. Although he admitted that the philosophes had exaggerated in their contempt for Christian learning, which had in fact acted as a "transmission belt"[43] of the classical legacy, Gay endorsed their larger point: that the Middle Ages had undermined the pagan world's healthy progress from myth to reason. For Gay, not only was there little genuinely pagan left in Christianity, but paganism itself was also purged of its original religious substance. The polytheism of antiquity, as

Montesquieu and Hume had noted, may have been superior to monotheism to the extent that it promoted the toleration of difference, but its religious content as such was nugatory.

Not surprisingly, Gay's attempt to keep the boundary between paganism and Christianity firmly in place met with some skepticism. Students of the specifically German *Aukflärung*, such as Peter Hanns Reill, argued that at least its adherents would have been shocked to find themselves called pagans and would have rejected the model of classical learning derived from the Renaissance as overly intellectual and lacking in moral fervor.[44] Defenders of the specifically British contribution to the Enlightenment, such as Hans Kohn, argued for the importance of religious dissenters, most notably John Milton, in preparing the ground.[45] Historians of medieval and early modern culture, such as Amos Funkenstein, agreed that Gay had had the better of the argument with Becker, but claimed nonetheless that "the Enlightenment inherited from Christianity not its apocalypticism, but rather its social and pedagogical drive. . . . From Christianity the Enlightenment inherited its missionary zeal—not from any pagan religion of classical Antiquity, for none of them possessed it."[46] According to Funkenstein, the similarities between the Freemasons and traditional churches also demonstrate the Enlightenment's dependence on an ecclesiastical surrogate with its own counterrituals and countersacraments.[47] And from a very different perspective, that of a self-proclaimed contemporary pagan immoralist, Camille Paglia chided Gay for reducing paganism to its Apollonian guise, thus shortchanging its more transgressive Dionysian counterpart, which she followed Nietzsche in insisting must be revived to reenchant culture.[48]

Whatever the justice of these complaints, the abiding power in Gay's argument can perhaps be appreciated if we now turn to our second major figure, Jean-François Lyotard. For there turns out to be a surprising convergence between his postmodernist use of the pagan tradition and that of the resolutely modernist Gay. There are, to be sure, obvious differences between the two; no one, after all, would charge Lyotard with being a worshipper of Apollonian moderation or the scientific spirit. Nor does he share Gay's taste for an elegant and lucid style as the best means of presenting his ideas.[49] The Freud he uses to justify a "libidinal politics" of desire often seems more transgressive than Gay's embattled liberal humanist.[50] And there is symptomatically only a marginal role for the "sublime," that privileged Lyotardian concept, in Gay's consideration of the eighteenth century.[51] But in certain unexpected ways, Lyotard's "lessons in paganism" reinforce those taught in Gay's study of the Enlightenment.

Lyotard's embrace of the pagan ideal, it must first be understood, came in the wake of his "drift" (dérive) away from the phenomenological Marxism of his Socialisme ou Barbarie period.[52] Although he had been an outspoken critic of French control of Algeria and supported the "events" of 1968,[53] by the 1970s, Lyotard was rapidly modulating his politics of resistance in a new key. In 1977, he collected his essays of the past few years under the title Rudiments païens and published a short dialogue with an imaginary interlocutor called Instructions païennes. Two years later, the record of his actual conversation with Jean-Loup Thébaud appeared under the title Au Juste (Just Gaming in its punning English translation).[54]

In these works, Lyotard proposed a pagan politics and philosophy that defined itself in opposition to the redemptive utopianism of the Marxist tradition, which he now detected in Socialisme ou Barbarie's call for worker self-management. Indeed, he challenged any strong hope, Kantian as well as Marxist, for absolute human autonomy.[55] Such grandiose expectations, Lyotard now contended, were only a secularized version of an essentially religious desire for absolute redemption, which paganism had explicitly denied. "When I say 'pagan'," Lyotard made clear, "I mean godless."[56] Like Peter Gay's, his paganism was thus deliberately impious, "without Olympus and without pantheon, without prudentia, without fear, without grace, without debt and hopeless."[57] If it drew any inspiration from classical polytheism, it was to deny the single master narrative that accompanied a potentially totalitarian monotheism (an argument that was to be repeated with great effect in Lyotard's celebrated description of postmodernism a few years later).[58] Instead, it favored many local narratives, whose fallible narrators knew they were not omniscient.

Although lacking hope in redemption, paganism was not a denial of the possibility of justice. But it was a justice that operated case by case and judged according to no fixed rules or a priori principles. "When I speak of paganism," Lyotard insisted, "I am not using a concept. It is a name, neither better nor worse than any other, for the denomination of a situation in which one judges without criteria."[59] Very much in the spirit of Gay's skeptical "party of humanity," even if he was anxious to avoid the taint of humanism,[60] Lyotard rejected the certainties of Platonic idealism as well as the speculative rationalism of the seventeenth century in favor of moral and political realism.[61] If his position had any relation to Kant, it was only to the *Critique of Justice,* "not the Kant of the concepts and the moral law, but the Kant of the imagination, the one who recovered from the sickness of knowledge and rules and converted to the paganism of art and nature."[62]

If paganism meant a certain return to nature from the Olympian realm of transcendence, it did not, however, mean what many of its critics have claimed it did: a pantheistic worship of the world as an immanent totality.[63] Although there is no privileged vantage point outside the world, no single God's eye view of the whole, no metalevel or metanarrative, self-sufficient immanence was also a mistaken fantasy of full presence. The word "pagus," Lyotard insisted, is the opposite of the village or "home" (here he introduced the highly charged German word *Heim*).[64] Instead, it meant the borderlands, a place of endless negotiation between peoples, all in a kind of exile, a porous boundary through which different intensities clashed without resolution. "The paganism I have in mind," he wrote, "could not be that of instituted ancient religions, even Dionysian ones. Rather, this paganism resides in an infiltration of the social body—at the surface of the social body—of areas left open to imaginations and to so-called disordered, useless, dangerous, and singular concrete enterprises: areas left open to the instincts."[65]

It was thus very much in tension with the French Revolution's version of dechristianization, which merely put another exclusive cult, that of a unified Reason, in the place of the dethroned Church. The Revolution's pseudo-Roman republic—a neoclassicism of masculine heroic virtue which led to the Terror—was not the paganism Lyotard favored. His instead meant the parodic laughter and the subversive theatricality of the women who were repressed by Rousseauist austerity and authoritarianism, "the wild, nocturnal, 'unchained' woman whom the powers that be (and Jacobins first of all) try to eradicate."[66]

Lyotard would ultimately come to question the unconstrained libidinal politics informing his work of the 1970s and with it a fully desublimated version of paganism as themselves a variant of romantic enthusiasm. But in *The Differend,* originally published in 1983, he would still positively contrast the *pagus*, the borderland between heterogeneous genres of discourse, with the *Heim*, a zone of internal consensus and self-identity. "The *Volk*," he wrote, "shuts itself up in the *Heim*, and it identifies itself through narratives attached to names, narratives that fail before the occurrence and before the differends born from the occurrence. Joyce, Schönberg, Cézanne: *pagini* waging war among the genres of discourse."[67]

In his transference of the metaphor of the *pagus* from a libidinal to a discursive context, Lyotard, however, began to introduce a new component in his thought, which relativized his identification with paganism, especially in its more Dionysian moods. Judaism, he argued in *Just Gaming*, complements paganism in its hostility to that absolute autonomy and mastery of the modern subject exemplified by the Kantian tradition.[68] Both Judaism and paganism represent the repressed and abjected "other" of a Christian civilization that culminated in humanist hubris and self-assertion. In the case of the Greeks, "their gods are not masters of the word in the sense in which the Christian God is a master of the word, that is, their word is not performative as the word of the Christian God is. It does not create the world. . . . these gods, even when they have the position of the first speaker, are themselves narrated in narratives that tell what they are telling."[69]

Although the Jewish God is also normally understood as a single creator God,[70] Lyotard chose to follow Emmanuel Levinas in stressing the importance of the ethical obligation in Judaism to defer to the other rather than any ontological description of the created world. There was, he argued, a fundamental incommensurability—in his terminology, a "differend"— between a prescriptive language game and a descriptive one, a linguistic variant, as we have seen, of pagan polytheism. In the former, the focus was on the addressee of the obligation, the subject who was "hostage" to the ethical demands of the other, not the one who actually did the addressing. It did not matter if the one imposing the obligation was God or the finite other, a simple human being; what did matter was the sense of quasi-heteronomous, asymmetrical dependence of the one called to duty, a call that came in the form of a command, not a conceptual justification.

This is not the place to probe the full implications of Lyotard's complicated appropriation of Levinas's thought.[71] Suffice it to say that it did not mean a replacement of paganism by a new religious piety or a seamless amalgam of religious and pagan ideals. What it did do was allow Lyotard some distance from another amalgam, that between Christianity and paganism,[72] which he was to locate in Heidegger, whose anti-Semitism he probed in the aftermath of the scandal in France over the philosopher's Nazi past. In a book of 1988 entitled *Heidegger and "the jews,"* Lyotard cautioned that "Heidegger's god is merely pagan-Christian, the god of bread, wine, earth and blood. He is not the god of the unreadable book, which only demands respect and does not tolerate that one liberate oneself from respect and disrespect (of good and evil) through the sublation of the sacrifice, the old mainstay of the dialectic."[73] Judaism, like paganism, was thus figured for Lyotard as a kind of resistance to the imperative to return home, an uncanny (*unheimlich*) remembrance of the wandering and dispersion that comes before the alleged original unity and will remain after any realized sublation of alterity and difference.

Introducing the notion of "pagan-Christianity" returns us to Peter Gay, whose account of the Enlightenment, it will be recalled, stressed a repudiation of the Renaissance attempt to integrate the classical past with Christian faith. There are, in fact, other surprising similarities between our two protagonists' impious use of the pagan legacy. Both are anti-nationalists resolutely hostile to any nostalgia for an alleged world of cultural wholeness before the fall into modern, diasporic alienation. Both insist on a strictly disenchanted reading of the pagan legacy, which they contrast with revealed religion and its secular equivalents, such as the cults of Reason and the People. Both are impatient with romantic notions of full reconciliation with a benign nature, such as those that fuel certain New Age, goddess-worshipping understandings of paganism. Both decry dialectical sublations, whether idealist or materialist, of the alleged contradictions of existence, sublations that do the work of mythic reconciliation. And both are moral realists, who resist a utopian notion of perfect justice or naive faith in the perfectibility of the species.[74]

"I believe that modernity is pagan,"[75] Lyotard would, in fact, write in 1978, echoing without acknowledgment the argument of Gay's volumes on the Enlightenment. Although he would emend that formula a year later to say that the variant of modernity that was most pagan was best called "postmodern" because it jettisoned the problematic notion of a collective addressee called "the people" and ost its regulative ideal, he was careful to deny that postmodernity was a period concept meant to indicate an era after the end of modernity. Instead, Lyotard, claimed, it was an intermittent impulse within the modern period itself. One might even say that the postmodern modern was haunted—benignly haunted, to be sure—by the *unheimlich* return of what it thought it had left behind, the pagan past, an argument that was not so far from Gay's reading of the Enlightenment as a whole.

Lyotard has, to be sure, often lashed out against the universalism of the Enlightenment, decried its alleged metanarrative of progress, and attacked the totalizing intellectuals who claim to speak in its name.[76] As a result he is routinely pitted in contemporary discussions against Jürgen Habermas as the champion of the postmodernist counter-Enlightenment.[77] But when the philosophes are seen through the lenses of a Peter Gay rather than those of, say, a Carl Becker, it is no longer so obvious that his target merits such scorn. For the Enlightenment that Lyotard and so many other postmodernist thinkers attack may have been far less of a secularized heavenly city than an impious pagan borderland, where critique rather than certainty rules and where the boundaries between language games resist becoming completely porous.[78]

Nor, to turn the argument around, is it clear that for all his stress on incommensurable local narratives and a plurality of language games, Lyotard has entirely escaped the cosmopolitan impulse of the Enlightenment, which Gay frankly applauds. Even though he has often written an epitaph for the intellectual, distancing himself from the practice of speaking in the name of voiceless victims Lyotard's own penchant for giving lessons and prescribing cures—even, tongue only half in cheek, explaining postmodernism "to children"[79]—seems suspiciously familiar.[80] What two of his sympathetic commentators have called "Lyotard's hesitance to dissociate himself entirely from the project of the Enlightenment"[81] is evident in his desire to "perform" philosophy as an intervention in the world, including the world of politics.

In short, if we acknowledge the unlikely alliance of our two impious pagans, Peter Gay and Jean-François Lyotard, it becomes difficult to accept without reservation the conventional contrast between modern and postmodern, which seems so widely assumed in contemporary discourse. For although there have been paganisms that have sought to reverse secularization, reenchant the world, and restore mythos over logos, theirs is a very different brand indeed. It shows us that even the most iconoclastic and critical impulses can find surprising sustenance in the return of the repressed.

17

The Manacles of Gavrilo Princip

✳

The trip by bus northwest from Prague to Terezín—better known to the world by its German name, Theresienstadt—takes about an hour and traverses some of the prettiest countryside in Bohemia. Arriving late at the bus station, the little group with whom I traveled one morning in April 1994 was forced to stand for the entire trip, a somehow fitting reminder that this was to be anything but a pleasure outing. When we descended at the bus stop next to the town square, the grim and blustery weather further deepened the sense of bleak uneasiness that would accompany any visit to such a place, even under the sunniest of skies. No less forbidding was the virtual emptiness of the square itself, once the passengers disgorged by the bus scattered their separate ways. Only a few children played in the park in its center, a park surrounded by nondescript buildings betraying nothing of their sinister past.

One, a former school and children's home, has been turned, we soon discovered, into a museum of sorts, which is in the process of mounting a permanent exhibition recording the events in Theresienstadt during its most troubled years. Now that the Communist rulers of Czechoslovakia have departed, that story can be told without the anti-Semitic inflection they had imposed on it (an inflection perhaps best expressed by the petty gesture of erasing the names of Holocaust victims painstakingly written on the walls of one of the synagogues in Prague's ghetto as a "protest" against Israeli politics in the mid-1980s). The story it tells is of a showcase concentration camp, planned by Reinhard Heydrich shortly before his assassination, a model ghetto given over from June 1942 to May 1945 almost entirely to Jewish detainees, who were supposedly allowed to continue their lives with only minor inconvenience. It was designed especially for those Jews whose prominence abroad might have meant that their disappearance would have been noticed; among the most eminent was Leo Baeck, the chief rabbi of Berlin. Others "lucky" enough to be assigned there were decorated or disabled Jewish veterans of the First World War, and those deemed too old or too young for labor service.

In late 1943, early 1944, a cynical "beautification" of the camp, whose name was changed to a "Jewish Settlement," was carried out with the intention of hoodwinking world opinion. Represented by Danish and Swiss delegates, the Red Cross, to its everlasting shame, was fooled into believing—or deliberately chose not to expose—the Nazis' sham, giving the camp its seal of approval in June 1944, by which time transports of prisoners were already making their way east to considerably less hospitable conditions in Auschwitz-Birkenau. As part of the Nazi deception, some were forced to send postcards back to their relatives assuring them of their well-being. Of the 140,000 Jews who passed through Theresienstadt, only from 17,000 to 29,000—the estimates in the literature differ—remained alive when the Red Army liberated it in 1945.

The new museum has on its ground floor several rooms filled with the art produced by Theresienstadt's inmates, many of them young children, which was miraculously hidden before the camp was dismantled. Although I had seen examples in Berkeley where a traveling exhibition came a few years before, the cumulative effect of encountering them in the place where they were made was shattering. Daily life in a concentration camp seen through the innocent eyes of a child produces images that are unbearably poignant, especially those that try to preserve the individual faces of the people around them. Upstairs, the exhibition contained a mixture of documents from the camp, including programs for concerts, cabarets, and theatrical performances, as well as photographs and other reproduced evidence of the melancholy history endured by Hitler's "protected Jews," the term cynically used in the propaganda film about Theresienstadt made by the Nazis to mask their actual intentions.

It is, of course, a cliché that stories of mass horror move us most when we can identify with one or a few of the victims on an individual basis. In my case, it is most often a young man at the stage of life when he is poised on the threshold of self-definition through the choice of a career and a mate. Somehow, I remember the promise and uncertainty of those years with a heightened sense of their significance and pathos and thus inevitably find their abrupt termination especially disturbing. Among the victims of Theresienstadt fitting this description was a playwright, poet, and painter named Petr Kien, whose confident, open face is preserved in one of the individual photographs on display, a photograph that has the air of a graduation picture or publicity still. In an adjoining cabinet is a stunning puppet of a rabbi fashioned by Kien for one of his productions, a marionette in the great tradition of imaginative Czech puppetry. I have no idea of his theatrical talents or whether any of his work endures, but so skilled a puppet-maker surely deserved a better chance to realize his promise.

Leaving the museum, our small party walked the fifteen minutes out of the center of town it takes to get to the business end of Theresienstadt, the so-called Small Fortress. First constructed in the late eighteenth century at the confluence of the rivers Eger and Elbe as part of the northern defense perimeter of the Habsburg empire—Theresienstadt was, in fact, named by Emperor Joseph II in honor of his mother, Maria Theresa—the complex of barracks and cells that make up the fortress was used during the Holocaust to punish Jews who were having trouble adjusting to the comforts of life in the center of town, as well as to house other victims of Nazi terror. Some 32,000 inmates in all spent part of World War II in the Small Fortress of Theresienstadt. Although most were ultimately deported to their deaths elsewhere, a gallows and a platform for public executions at the end of a large courtyard testify to the fate many suffered there as well.

Before actually passing through the gate of the Small Fortress, inscribed, as were other such gates in other such places, with the infamous words "Arbeit macht frei," we paused for lunch at the only place to eat within sight. The dreary café turned out to be the former canteen for the SS men who were charged with guarding the camp. With only a kind of a gallows humor to protect us against the profound sense of discomfort that accompanied this wretched meal, we soon began a serious discussion of our responses to the visit. Three of us were American Jewish men (the two others both psychoanalysts and experts in continental philosophy, myself a student of European intellectual history), who had been preoccupied by post-Holocaust questions for as long as we could remember. Like that of the "imaginary Jew" sensitively dissected by the French writer Alain Finkielkraut, our Jewish identity was in significant measure a product of identification with the victims rather than a positive embrace of the tenets of Judaism or adherence to the preassimilated culture of Yiddishkeit. With Finkielkraut, we could all easily have said "I was born too close to the Holocaust to be able to keep it from view, and at the same time I was protected by all the horror of this event from a renewal of anti-Semitism, at least in its organized and violent form. In a sense I was *overjoyed*: the war's proximity at once magnified and preserved me; it invited me to identify with the victims while giving the all but certain assurance that I would never be one."[1]

Although there was not much joy, let alone "overjoy," evident on that day, it was nonetheless true that our relation to the Holocaust was clearly different from that of our companions, two women from Ireland, both professors of philosophy, and a man from Denmark, who taught political and social theory. For not only could we more viscerally identify with the victims, we were also far more intimate with what might be called the many tropes of Holocaust response than they. That is, having been so long immersed in both learned and popular accounts, depictions and reenactments of the Holocaust, having been drawn professionally as well as personally to many of the survivors teaching in America, we had come to Theresienstadt with our expectations of what we were to see and how we were to respond—or at least the range of permissible responses—already firmly in place (in my own case, I had made earlier melancholy pilgrimages to Dachau and the Warsaw Ghetto, so that even being on an actual site of horror was not entirely unprecedented).

We were thus supremely aware of the mediated quality of our reactions in a way that our companions perhaps were not. For to be an American intellectual and particularly a Jewish one the past few years is to be especially alert to the ways in which modes of narration and memorialization give the Holocaust an inevitable inflection, even in cases far less heavy-handed than the Communist white-washing of the Prague synagogue walls. Recent books like James Young's *Writing and Rewriting the Holocaust: Narrative and the Consequences of Interpretation*, Saul Friedlander's collection *Probing the Limits of Representation: Nazism and the "Final Solution,"* Berel Lang's collection *Writing and the Holocaust*, and Dominick LaCapra's *Repre-*

senting the Holocaust: History, Theory Trauma have made it increasingly difficult to ignore the constructive moment in our reconstruction of the events,
no matter how dry and factual the account. The impassioned public response to the Holocaust Memorial Museum in Washington and the Simon
Wiesenthal Center for Holocaust Studies and Museum of Tolerance in Los
Angeles, the burgeoning field of "Holocaust studies" in American universities, shadowed by the alarming upsurge of so-called Holocaust revision-
ists who question its very existence, heated polemics over the right-wing
Zionist manipulation of the "lessons" of the Holocaust and the German
historians' attempt to "normalize" the past, all these have combined to
make second- or even third-order reflection on the meaning of it all impossible to avoid. What the German magazine *Der Spiegel* in a particularly
distasteful article of 1993 entitled ' Das Shoah-Business" called America's
"Holocaust intoxication"[2] has at least meant that no visit by people like me
to an actual concentration camp can hope to escape its already scripted
quality, its filtration through a myriad of prior reflections and feelings.
Even the sound of those maudlin and lachrymose violins playing incessantly in a minor key throughout *Schindler's List* could not be kept from the
mind's ear as we plodded through the silent streets of Theresienstadt.

✳

Or rather everything conformed to a certain tropic prefiguration until one
remarkable and completely unexpected moment in our trip. In one of the
small cells used for holding prisoners in solitary confinement in the Small
Fortress, we came upon a pair of iron manacles chained to the far wall,
rusted but still formidable in their weighty horror. I don't recall if there was
a small sign identifying them or if our guidebook gave us the information,
but much to our astonishment they turned out to be the manacles not of a
Holocaust victim, but rather of no less a historical figure than Gavrilo
Princip, the man—or rather nineteen-year-old boy—whose assassination
of Archduke Franz Ferdinand and his wife, Sophie, in Sarajevo on June 28,
1914, precipitated the crisis that led to World War I.

As soon after the trip as I was able to get to a library, I tried to find out
how he had come to this miserable destination. Princip had taken cyanide
after he fired his shots, but somehow survived. Too young to be executed by
the law of the Dual Monarchy, he and two other members of the so-called

Black Hand, the conspiratorial group of Serbian nationalist fanatics who had plotted and almost bungled the assassination, were imprisoned instead in Theresienstadt, which had housed other celebrated political prisoners in the past, such as the Greek freedom fighter Alexander Ypsilanti, Jr. Already suffering from tuberculosis of the bones, Princip literally rotted away in his solitary confinement, his body covered with sores, his left arm ultimately amputated. He died in agony on April 28, 1918, only a few months before the war he helped unleash finally itself expired. He was buried anonymously by the Austrians, who wanted to avoid creating another Slav martyr by acknowledging his grave. But one of the soldiers in the burial party was an anti-Habsburg Czech who remembered the spot, allowing the Serbs to exhume and bury the body with honors in Sarajevo in 1920.

What made the surprising discovery of the manacles of Gavrilo Princip so remarkable was its effect on my experience of Theresienstadt as a site of the Holocaust, or rather on the script that I was following in doing so. Initially, the manacles seemed an annoying intrusion from another, totally different narrative, which somehow had gotten mixed up with the one I was so intensely following. It was as if suddenly in the pages of *Middlemarch*, someone had surreptitiously inserted a chapter, say, from *The Charterhouse of Parma*. What was a Serb nationalist martyr, whose desperate act had precipitated one world war, doing in a concentration camp created in another? Why, I wondered, was my identification with one young man whose premature death had so moved me a short time before suddenly being disrupted by the appearance of a second, and one to boot with whom I had no real ability to empathize? How could I reconcile my admiring revery for the gifted hands of an innocent young puppeteer with the shock I felt in the "presence" of the manacled hands of an infamous assassin?

No less insistent were thoughts of the ironic undercutting of the heroism attributed to Princip by those who mourned him as a martyr, an undercutting produced not only by the horrible slaughter of the war he helped unleash, but also by events in the Balkans eighty years later. Serb nationalism, after all, has shown a face today far darker than its defenders before World War I would have thought possible. The people who reburied Princip with honors in 1920 seemed not so far removed, I couldn't help thinking, from the people who were trying to bury Sarajevo and Gorazde in 1994. The imagined sound of Spielberg's violins began to fade as I held Princip's rusted manacles in my hands, and that of the guns bombarding those unhappy cities filled their place.

But perhaps of all the effects produced by the unexpected intrusion, the most profound had to do with the challenge it presented to the self-contained and incommensurable quality of the events that posterity has chosen to call the Holocaust or the Shoah. There has, of course, been a problematic attempt to diminish their importance by comparing the gen-ocidal "war against the Jews," as Lucy Dawidovicz famously called it, with other such campaigns, such as the Soviet extermination of the Kulaks or the Nazis' decimation of the Poles. When such "relativization" of the Holo-caust is done with the purpose of minimizing Jewish suffering or playing the treacherous game of victim one-up-manship, it is rightly decried.

But perhaps no less problematic is the utter isolation of the Holocaust from the larger historical context, its elevation into a metahistorical phe-nomenon so unlike anything before and since that its meaningful relation to any other event in history is severed. Its radical incommensurability can then become an excuse to attribute to it a no less absolute incomprehen-sibility, which, as my colleague Amos Funkenstein has warned, gives the Nazis the posthumous victory of robbing the victims of whatever narrative meanings their lives may have had.[3]

The rude intrusion of Princip's miserable story into that of Hitler's Potemkin Village is a reminder of the tangled web of violence and its ideological justifications that allowed the Holocaust to happen and that permits new atrocities today. For even though we are wisely told not to attribute great and overdetermined events to the acts of individuals—a warning made as far back as Pascal's famous gloss on the putative effects of Cleopatra's nose—it is nonetheless true that seemingly minor acts can have extraordinary consequences. The war triggered by Princip's fatal bul-let was an indispensable precondition of the discontent that spawned a second global war and the opportunity for Theresienstadt to become a reality. The lessons in "ethnic cleansing" taught so well by the Nazis have not been forgotten by the descendants of those who applauded Princip's bold deed.

Only in Hollywood movies can the Holocaust be contained within the boundaries of an aesthetic frame; in real life, it spills out and mingles with the countless other narratives of our century. Its real horror, we might say, is not confined to the actual genocidal acts it has come to signify. Historicizing the Holocaust need not mean reducing it to the level of the "normal" massacres of the innocents that punctuate all of recorded history, but rather remembering those quickly forgotten and implicitly forgiven events with the same intransigent refusal to normalize that is the only justifiable response to the Holocaust itself.

No wonder that when I held the rusting manacles of Gavrilo Princip in my hands, the impulse that overwhelmed me was to shake them as furiously as I could, while impotently hurling at the ghost of the boy who once filled them the earthy epithet that the inmates of Theresienstadt would have understood all too well: "Schmuck!!!"

Introduction

1   Honoré de Balzac, *Louis Lambert*, trans. Katharine Prescott Wormeley (Boston, 1892), 4.

2   Derek Attridge, "Language as History/History as Language: Saussure and the Romance of Etymology," in *Post-structuralism and the Question of History*, ed. Derek Attridge, Geoff Bennington, and Robert Young (Cambridge, 1987).

3   Maurice Olender, *The Languages of Paradise*, trans. Arthur Goldhammer (Cambridge, Mass., 1992).

4   In *The Genealogy of Morals*, Nietzsche insisted that "there is no set of maxims more important for an historian than this: that the actual cause of a thing's origins and its eventual uses, the manner of its incorporation into a system of purposes, are worlds apart; that everything that exists, no matter what its origin, is periodically reinterpreted by those in power in terms of fresh intentions; that all processes in the organic world are processes of outstripping and overcoming, and that, in turn, all outstripping and overcoming means reinterpretation, rearrangement, in the course of which the earlier meaning and purpose are necessarily either obscured or lost" (*The Birth of Tragedy and The Genealogy of Morals*, trans. Francis Golffing [Garden City, N.Y., 1956], 209).

5   Raymond Williams, *Keywords: A Vocabulary of Culture and Society* (New York, 1976), 13.

6   Raymond Williams, *Culture and Society: 1780–1950* (New York, 1960).

7   Quentin Skinner, "Language and Social Change," in *Meaning and Context: Quentin Skinner and His Critics*, ed. James Tully (Oxford, 1988).

8   Attridge, "Language as History/History as Language," 202.

9   There are, to be sure, other historians who have also been aware of these issues, for example the social historian Joan Wallach Scott. See her *Gender and the Politics of History* (New York, 1988).

10 On this theme, see my essay "Should Intellectual History Take a Linguistic Turn? Reflections on the Habermas-Gadamer Debate,' in *Fin-de-siècle Socialism and Other Essays* (New York, 1988), and "The Textual Approach to Intellectual History," in *Force Fields: Between Intellectual History and Cultural Critique* (New York, 1993). The latter contains a bibliography of the relevant literature.

11   George Boas, *The History of Ideas: An Introduction* (New York, 1969), 11.

12   Martin Jay, *Marxism and Totality: The Adventures of a Concept from Lukács to Habermas* (Berkeley, 1984). The inspiration was, of course, Merleau-Ponty's *The Adventures of the Dialectic.*

13   Martin Jay, "The Reassertion of Sovereignty in a Time of Crisis: Carl Schmitt and Georges Bataille" and "The Textual Approach to Intellectual History," *Force Fields.*

14   Theodor W. Adorno, "Words from Abroad," in *Notes to Literature,* ed. Rolf Tiedemann, trans. Shierry Weber Nicholsen (New York, 1991), 2 vols., 1:189. Adorno mistakenly accuses Germans of being particularly insistent on linguistic integrity, claiming that "in the French language, where the Gallic and the Roman elements interpenetrated so early and so thoroughly, there seems to be no consciousness of foreign borrowings at all" (187). The current language police in Paris anxious to root out any corruption by "franglais" suggest otherwise.

15   It appeared as part of the proceedings called "Theory and Theoreticians" alongside essays by Janet Gouldner, Michael D. Kennedy, Karen Fields, and Jerome Karabel, in *Theory and Society* 25.2 (April 1996).

16   Bill Readings, *Introducing Lyotard: Art and Politics* (London, 1991), xxviii. Readings then identified theory as "an order of discourse that acts to establish the exclusive rule of a network of oppositions between concepts and signifiers," which is only one of the meanings developed in "For Theory."

17   Martin Jay, "Hierarchy and the Humanities: The Radical Implications of a Conservative Idea," *Fin-de-siècle Socialism and Other Essays.*

18   *Leviathan* 13 (Athens 1993); *New Formations* 20 (Summer 1993); *Rediscovering History: Culture, Politics and the Psyche,* ed. Michael Roth (Stanford, 1994).

19   Denis Hollier, *Georges Bataille après tout* (Paris, 1995); *Constellations* 2.2 (1995).

20   See, for example, David Ames Curtis's attack on the column in his introduction to Cornelius Castoriadis, *Political and Social Writings,* vol. 3 (Minneapolis, 1993), xxiii.

21   A partial exception can be found in John S. Sitton, "Hannah Arendt's Argument for Council Democracy," in *Hannah Arendt: Critical Essays,* ed. Lewis P. Hinchman and Sandra K. Hinchman (Albany, 1994).

22   Elliot Neaman, "Fascism and Postmodernism: A Reply to Martin Jay," *Tikkun* 8.6 (November/December 1993); and Anjana Shrivastava, "German Neo-Fascism and the Politics of Meaning," *Tikkun* 9.4 (July/August 1994).

23   Gertrud Koch, *Auge und Affekt: Wahrnehmung und Interaktion* (Frankfurt, 1995); in English in *The Semblance of Subjectivity: Essays in Adorno's Aesthetic Theory,* ed. Lambert Zuidervaart and Thomas Huhn (Cambridge, Mass., 1997).

24   Martin Jay, "Unsympathetic Magic: Michael Taussig's *Nervous System* and *Mimesis and Alterity,*" *Visual Anthropology Review* 9.2 (Fall 1993); Taussig and Paul Stoller reply in *Visual Anthropology Review* 10.1 (Spring 1994), which also contains my counterrebuttal.

25   In addition to the references in the text, see Hal Foster, *The Return of the Real: The Avant-Garde at the End of the Century* (Cambridge, Mass., 1996), 153–68; and Foster, "Obscene, Abject, Traumatic," and Rosalind Krauss, "Informe without Conclusion," *October* 78 (Fall 1996).

26 Modernism/Modernity 3.2 (May 1996).

27 Forthcoming in Mark Micale and Robert Dietle, eds., *Enlightenment, Culture, and Passion: Essays in Honor of Peter Gay* (Stanford, 1998).

1   For Theory

1 Alvin W. Gouldner, *For Sociology: Renewal and Critique in Sociology Today* (New York, 1973), 120.

2 It is perhaps most extensively developed in Alvin W. Gouldner, *The Future of Intellectuals and the Rise of the New Class* (New York, 1979), 28f.

3 The momentum of theory, to be sure, is by no means entirely spent, if the proliferation of titles in all fields is any indication. But there is a sense that theoretical creation is less ebullient now than it was in the previous decades; instead, most works seem to be consolidations and summations. See, for example, Anthony Giddens and Jonathan Turner, eds., *Social Theory Today* (Stanford, 1987); Peter Beilharz, ed., *Social Theory: A Guide to Central Thinkers* (North Sydney, Australia, 1991); Richard Münch, *Sociological Theory: From the 1850's to the Present* (Chicago, 1994).

4 Louis Althusser, *Essays in Self-Criticism*, trans. Grahame Lock (London, 1976).

5 See, for example, Raymond Geuss, *The Idea of a Critical Theory: Habermas and the Frankfurt School* (Cambridge, 1981). By the 1990s, Habermas was defensively claiming "I don't force everything into one theoretical frame, and I don't assimilate everything into the basic concepts of a holistic master theory" (*The Past as Future*, interviews with Michael Haller, ed. and trans., Max Pensky (Lincoln, Neb., 1994), 114.

6 See, for example, Mieke Bal, who explained the disillusionment of hopes, her own included, in semiotics in a 1990 essay entitled "Visual Poetics: Reading with the Other Art," in *Theory between the Disciplines: Authority, Vision, Politics*, ed. Martin Kreiswirth and Mark A. Cheetham (Ann Arbor, 1990): "model building has been marginalized, as most scholars abandoned the belief in the use and the tenability of scientific rigor. The very notion of a master theory stopped being appealing" (135).

7 J. Hillis Miller, "Presidential Address 1986. The Triumph of Theory, the Resistance to Reading, and the Question of the Material Base," PMLA 102 (1987). How the term "theory" came to be appropriated by deconstruction in the mid-1980s would be an interesting question to answer. Only a few years before Miller's address, Jonathan Arac could write that "the Yale Critics support old-fashioned American aversion to theory. For after Heidegger and Derrida, the philosophical tradition of 'theory,' as the systematic enclosure of being within the gaze of knowledge, has lost its authority for them." "Afterword" to *The Yale Critics: Deconstruction in America*, ed. Jonathan Arac, Wlad Godzich, and Wallace Martin (Minneapolis, 1983), 188.

8 Stanley Fish, "Consequences" (1985) reprinted in *Doing What Comes Naturally* (Oxford, 1989), 340–42.

9 David Carroll, "Introduction: The States of 'Theory' and the Future of History and Art," *The States of "Theory": History, Art, and Critical Discourse* (New York, 1990), 1.

10 Michael Haller, "What Theories Can Accomplish—and What They Can't," in Habermas

interviewed by Michael Haller, *The Past as Future*, 99. Habermas, it should be noted, immediately disputed this diagnosis, arguing instead for an analysis of why certain theories appeal to people at this historical moment, while others do not.

11   Paul de Man, *The Resistance to Theory* (Minneapolis, 1986).

12   W. J. T. Mitchell, ed., *Against Theory* (Chicago, 1985).

13   For an extended discussion of this issue, see Bill Readings, "Why Is Theory Foreign?" in Kreiswirth and Cheetham, *Theory between the Disciplines*.

14   David F. Gruber, "Foucault and Theory: Genealogical Critiques of the Subject," in *The Question of the Other: Essays in Continental Philosophy*, ed. Arleen B. Dallery and Charles E. Scott (Albany, 1989), 189. The same point is made in the collection's next essay, Ladelle McWhorter's "Foucault's Move beyond the Theoretical."

15   Gruber, "Foucault and Theory," 195.

16   Max Horkheimer, "Traditional and Critical Theory," in *Critical Theory: Selected Essays*, trans. Matthew J. O'Connell et al. (New York, 1972), 188, 227.

17   De Man, *The Resistance to Theory*, 17.

18   Michaels and Knapp, "Against Theory," 12.

19   Ibid., 30.

20   See note 9.

21   Martin Jay, "Scopic Regimes of Modernity," in *Force Fields: Between Intellectual History and Cultural Critique* (New York, 1993).

22   Michel Serres, "Panoptic Theory," in *The Limits of Theory*, ed. Thomas M. Kavanagh (Stanford, 1989).

23   Martin Jay, *Downcast Eyes: The Denigration of Vision in Twentieth-century French Thought* (Berkeley, 1993).

24   Hans-Georg Gadamer, *Truth and Method* (New York, 1975), 111.

25   Wlad Godzich, *The Culture of Literacy* (Cambridge, Mass., 1994), 20–21.

26   Ibid., 21.

27   Immanuel Kant, *Critique of Pure Reason* (London, 1929), 93.

28   For a reading of Adorno's prose in these terms, see Fredric Jameson, *Late Marxism: Adorno, or, The Persistence of the Dialectic* (New York, 1990), 68.

29   See, for example, Clément Rosset, "Reality and the Untheorizable," in Kavanagh, *The Limits of Theory*.

30   Hannah Arendt, *The Human Condition* (Chicago, 1958).

31   For an overview, see Nicholas Lobkowicz, *Theory and Practice: History of a Concept from Aristotle to Marx* (Notre Dame, 1967).

32   It was a typical reproach against Western Marxism that its adherents were elite theorists removed from the masses. Thus, for example, Perry Anderson could chastisingly remark in *Considerations on Western Marxism* (London, 1976), "the language in which [the works of the Western Marxists] were written came to acquire an increasingly specialized and inaccessible cast. Theory became, for a whole historical period, an esoteric discipline whose highly technical idiom measured its distance from politics" (53).

33 Martin Heidegger, "The Self-Assertion of the German University," in *The Heidegger Controversy: A Critical Reader*, ed. Richard Wolin (New York, 1991), 31–32.

34 I have tried to unpack some of its meanings in "Experience without a Subject: Walter Benjamin and the Novel" and "The Limits of Limit-Experience: Bataille and Foucault," reprinted below.

35 Readings, "Why is Theory Foreign?" 34. At times, to be sure the notion of "reading" has been used by deconstructionists to imply a kind of anti-immanentist relation to texts, which at other times, is suggested by the word "theory." See, for example, J. Hillis Miller, *The Ethics of Reading* (New York, 1987), where he claims that "the value of a reading, against all reason, lies in its difference and deviation from the text it purports to read" (118).

36 Seyla Benhabib, "Hannah Arendt and the Redemptive Power of Narrative," *Social Research* 57.1 (Spring 1990).

37 Jürgen Habermas, *Knowledge and Human Interests*, trans. Jeremy J. Shapiro (Boston, 1971), 306f.

38 Daniel Herwitz, *Making Theory/Constructing Art: On the Authority of the Avant-Garde* (Chicago, 1993).

39 For a critique of Stanley Fish that elaborates this point, see Fred Botting, "Whither Theory," *Oxford Literary Review* 15.1–2 (1993): 215f.

40 For a critique of this assumption, see Vivek Dhareshwar, "The Predicament of Theory," in Kreiswirth and Cheetham, *Theory between the Disciplines*.

41 Botting, "Whither Theory," 202.

2   European Intellectual History and the Specter of Multiculturalism

1 H. Stuart Hughes, *Gentleman Rebel: The Memoirs of H. Stuart Hughes* (New York, 1990).

2 John Murray Cuddihy, *The Ordeal of Civility: Freud, Marx, Lévi-Strauss, and the Jewish Struggle with Modernity* (New York, 1974).

3   Songs of Experience

1 The debate has come to be called the "Historikerstreit." The principle advocates of some sort of normalization are Ernst Nolte, Andreas Hillgruber, and Michael Stürmer. The major interventions are contained in "Historikerstreit": Die Dokumentation der Kontroverse um die Einzigartigkeit der nationalsozialistischen Judenverrichtung (Munich, 1987).

2 These are the rough translations of Habermas's intervention, *Eine Art Schadensabwicklung* (Frankfurt, 1987), and Wehler's, *Entsorgung der deutschen Vergangenheit? Eine polemischer Essay zum "Historikerstreit"* (Munich, 1988).

3 The phrase "unmastered past" has been used by critics of the Germans' unwillingness to work through their trauma, perhaps most notably by Theodor W. Adorno in a celebrated essay of the 1960s, "Was bedeutet 'Aufarbeitung der Vergangenheit'" now available in English in *Bitburg in Moral and Political Perspective*, ed. Geoffrey H. Hartman (Bloomington, Ind., 1986).

4   See Charles Maier, *The Unmasterable Past: History, Holocaust, and German National Identity* (Cambridge, Mass., 1988) and Richard Evans, "The New Nationalism and the Old History: Perspectives on the West German *Historikerstreit*," *Journal of Modern History* 59.4 (December 1987): 761–97.

5   For a recent collection of examples in English, see Richard Bessel, ed., *Life in the Third Reich* (Oxford, 1987).

6   Evans, "The New Nationalism," 763.

7   See the record of the colloquium on the subject at the *Institut für Zeitgeschichte* in Munich in 1983: Martin Broszat et al., *Alltagsgeschichte der NS-Zeit. Neue Perspektive oder Trivilisierung?* (Munich, 1984).

8   Kenneth D. Barkin, "Modern Germany: A Twisted Vision," *Dissent* (Spring 1987), 225.

9   Mack Walker, *German Home Towns: Community, State, and General Estate 1648–1871* (Ithaca, 1971).

10   Gertrude Himmelfarb, *The New History and the Old: Critical Essays and Reappraisals* (Cambridge, Mass., 1987).

11   Michel de Certeau, *The Practice of Everyday Life*, trans. Steven F. Rendall (Berkeley, 1984); Agnes Heller, *Everyday Life*, trans. G. L. Campbell (London, 1984).

12   de Certeau, *The Practice of Everyday Life*, xv.

13   Detlev J. K. Peukert, "Alltag und Barberei: Zur Normalität des Dritten Reiches," in *Ist der Nationalsozialismus Geschichte? Zu Historisierung und Historikerstreit*, ed. Dan Diner (Frankfurt, 1987).

14   Detlev J. K. Peukert, *Inside Nazi Germany: Conformity, Opposition, and Racism in Everyday Life*, trans. Richard Deveson (New Haven, 1987), 79.

15   David Schoenbaum, *Hitler's Social Revolution: Class and Status in Nazi Germany, 1933–1939* (Garden City, N.Y., 1967), 174.

16   Dan Diner, "Zwischen Aporie und Apologie: Über die Grenzen der Historisierbarkeit des Nationalsozialismus," in Diner, *Ist der Nationalsozialismus Geschichte?* 71.

17   Claudia Koonz, *Mothers in the Fatherland: Women, the Family, and Nazi Politics* (New York, 1987).

18   Anton Kaes, *Deutschlandbilder: Die Wiederkehr der Geschichte als Film* (Munich, 1987), 183.

19   See Hans-Ulrich Wehler, "Neoromantik und Pseudorealismus in der neuen 'Alltagsgeschichte'," in *Preussen ist wieder chic* (Frankfurt, 1983), and Kocka's remarks in *Alltagsgeschichte der NS-Zeit*, 51. Wehler links the movement of "barefoot" historians with the anti-modernism of the Greens at their neo-romantic worst.

20   R. G. Collingwood, *The Idea of History* (New York, 1956).

21   E. P. Thompson, *The Poverty of Theory and Other Essays* (New York, 1978), and Perry Anderson, *Arguments within English Marxism* (London, 1980).

22   See the debate between Joyce, Gates, and Baker in *New Literary History* 18.2 (Winter 1987) and Barbara Christian, "The Race for Theory," *Cultural Critique* 6 (Spring 1987).

23   Michael Oakeshott, *Experience and Its Modes* (Cambridge, 1933), 9.

24   For Gadamer's discussion of this usage, which he sees originating with Hegel, see *Truth and Method* (New York, 1986), 316f.

25 Dilthey's mediation on the varieties of experience took place throughout his works. For a helpful summary of the results, see Michael Ermarth, *Wilhelm Dilthey: The Critique of Historical Reason* (Chicago, 1978), 225f. Benjamin's thoughts on the subject are also scattered throughout his oeuvre. For a fine account of their significance, see Richard Wolin, *Walter Benjamin: An Aesthetic of Redemption* (New York, 1982), chap. 7.

26 Peter Bürger, *Theory of the Avant-Garde*, trans. Michael Snow, foreword Jochen Schulte-Sasse (Minneapolis, 1984), 33.

27 One of the few participants in the debate who has acknowledged the problematic status of the concept of experience is Klaus Tenfelde. See his "Schwierigkeiten mit dem Alltag," in *Geschichte und Gesellschaft* 10 (1984): 387.

4   Experience without a Subject

1   Hans-Georg Gadamer, *Truth and Method* (New York, 1986), 310.

2   Michael Oakeshott, *Experience and Its Modes* (Cambridge, 1933), 9.

3   Philip Rahv, "The Cult of Experience in American Writing," in Rahv, *Literature and the Sixth Sense* (New York, 1969), and Joan W. Scott, "The Evidence of Experience," *Critical Inquiry* 17.4 (Summer 1991).

4   Gary Smith, "Thinking through Benjamin: An Introductory Essay," in *Benjamin: Philosophy, Aesthetics, History*, ed. Smith (Chicago, 1983), xii.

5   Richard Wolin, *Walter Benjamin: An Aesthetic of Redemption* (New York, 1982); Marleen Stoessel, *Aura: Das vergessene Menschliche* (Munich, 1983); Torsten Meiffert, *Die enteignete Erfahrung: Zu Walter Benjamins Konzept einer "Dialektik im Stillstand"* (Bielefeld, 1986); Michael Jennings, *Dialectical Images: Walter Benjamin's Theory of Literary Criticism* (Ithaca, 1987); Miriam Hansen, "Benjamin, Cinema and Experience: 'The Blue Flower in the Land of Technology,' " *New German Critique* 40 (Winter 1987); Michael Makropolous, *Modernität als ontologischer Ausnahmezustand? Walter Benjamins Theorie der Moderne* (Munich, 1989).

6   Walter Benjamin, *One-Way Street and Other Writings*, trans. Edmund Jephcott and Kingsley Shorter (London, 1979); "Erfahrung und Armut," in Benjamin, *Gesammelte Schriften*, 7 vols., ed. Rolf Tiedemann and Hermann Schweppenhäuser (Frankfurt, 1977), 2:1; "The Storyteller" and "On Some Motifs in Baudelaire," in Benjamin, *Illuminations*, ed. Hannah Arendt, trans. Harry Zohn (New York, 1968).

7   See Wilhelm Dilthey, *Das Erlebnis und Dichtung: Lessing, Goethe, Novalis, Hölderlin*, 13th ed. (Göttingen, 1957). For a discussion of Dilthey's usage, see Michael Ermarth, *Wilhelm Dilthey: The Critique of Historical Reason* (Chicago, 1978), 97f.

8   Edmund Husserl, *Experience and Judgment* ed. Ludwig Landgrebe, trans. J. S. Churchill and K. Ameriko (Evanston, 1973).

9   Ernst Jünger, *Der Kampf als innere Erlebnis* [1922], *Werke* 5 (Stuttgart, n.d.).

10 Gadamer, *Truth and Method*, 317, where he credits Hegel for a dialectical concept of experience as "skepticism in action."

11 Yosef Hayim Yerushalmi, *Zakhor: Jewish History and Jewish Memory* (New York, 1989). Curiously, Benjamin is never mentioned in this remarkable book. For a discussion of the relevance of Yerushalmi to Benjamin, see Susan A. Handelman, *Fragments of Redemption:*

Jewish Thought and Literary Theory in Benjamin, Scholem, and Levinas (Bloomington, Ind., 1991), 164. It would be fruitful to compare Benjamin's distinction between two types of memory, *Gedächtnis* (the memory of the many) and *Erinnerung* (the interiorization of the past) or *Eingedenken* (the memory of the one) with Yerushalmi's distinction between memory and history. For a helpful account of Benjamin's ideas on this issue, see Irving Wohlfahrt, "On the Messianic Structure of Walter Benjamin's Last Reflections," *Glyph* 3 (1978).

12   A similar argument is suggested by Reinhart Koselleck in " 'Space of Experience' and 'Horizon of Expectation': Two Historical Categories," in Koselleck, *Futures Past: On the Semantics of Historical Time*, trans. Keith Tribe (Cambridge, Mass., 1985). Koselleck argues that modernity is defined by the growing gap between experience, which he defines as "present past, whose events have been incorporated and can be remembered, . . ." (272) and an expectational horizon which distances itself radically from the status quo. He links this transformation with the notions of "history in general" and "progress," both of which were anathema to Benjamin.

13   For a discussion of the implications of this word, see Makropoulos, *Modernität als ontologischer Ausnahmezustand*, chap. 3.

14   Benjamin, "On Some Motifs in Baudelaire," 165. Benjamin's ambivalence about the ability of the masses to recover *Erfahrung* is discussed in Hansen, "Benjamin, Cinema and Experience." She stresses the links between his concept of aura and experience, and argues that "with the denigration of the auratic image in favor of reproduction, Benjamin implicitly denies the masses the possibility of aesthetic experience" (186).

15   For an analysis of it in these terms, see Wolin, *Walter Benjamin*, chap. 7; and "Experience and Materialism in Benjamin's *Passagenwerk*," in Smith, *Benjamin: Philosophy, Aesthetics, History*.

16   Gershom Scholem, *Walter Benjamin: The Story of a Friendship*, trans. Harry Zohn (New York, 1981), 60. Here Scholem describes the lengthy discussions he had with Benjamin in Muri, Switzerland, in 1918 over the issue of experience in the work of Hermann Cohen.

17   Walter Benjamin, "On the Program of the Coming Philosophy," in Smith, *Benjamin: Philosophy, Aesthetics, History*. For discussions of the importance of this essay, see Smith's introduction and Jennings, *Dialectical Images*, chap. 3. Prior to this piece, when he was in the Youth Movement, Benjamin published a short essay in 1912 entitled "*Erfahrung*," in which he attacked the concept as an excuse for adults to lord it over the young. See Benjamin, *Gesammelte Schriften* 2:1.

18   Benjamin, "On the Program of the Coming Philosophy," 10.

19   Ibid., 11.

20   Ibid., 5.

21   For an example, see Peter Bürger, "Art and Rationality: On the Dialectic of Symbolic and Allegorical Form," in *Philosophical Interventions in the Unfinished Project of Enlightenment*, ed. Axel Honneth et al., trans. William Rehg (Cambridge, Mass., 1992), where an *Erfahrung* "deserving of the name" is defined as something that "does not happen to us but rather is *made* by us" (234).

22 Benjamin, "On the Program of the Coming Philosophy," 9.

23 Winfried Menninghaus, "Walter Benjamin's Theory of Myth," in *On Walter Benjamin: Critical Essays and Reflections*, ed. Gary Smith (Cambridge, Mass., 1988), 321–22. Benjamin, to be sure, was skeptical of certain types of mythic thinking, even attacking *Lebensphilosophie* as proto-fascist for its interest in myth. See "On Some Motifs in Baudelaire," 158. But Menninghaus shows the extent to which he distrusted the simple myth/enlightenment dichotomy.

24 Theodor W. Adorno, *Prisms*, trans. Samuel and Shierry Weber (London, 1967), 235.

25 See, for example, Heidegger's critique of *Erlebnis* as too dependent on the Cartesianism it purports to transcend in *Grundfragen der Philosophie: Ausgewählte "Probleme" der "Logik,"* *Gesamtausgabe* 45, ed. Friedrich-Wilhelm von Herrmann (Frankfurt, 1984), 149.

26 For an attempt to do so, see Rainer Nägele, "Benjamin's Ground," in *Benjamin's Ground: New Readings of Walter Benjamin*, ed. Nägele (Detroit, 1988).

27 Walter Benjamin, "Surrealism: The Last Snapshot of the European Intelligentsia," in Benjamin, *Reflections: Essays, Aphorisms Autobiographical Writings*, ed. Peter Demetz, trans. Edmond Jephcott (New York, 1978), 179.

28 Georg Lukács, *The Theory of the Novel*, trans. Anna Bostock (Cambridge, Mass., 1971), 41, cited by Benjamin, "The Storyteller," 99.

29 Benjamin, "The Storyteller," 87.

30 According to Benjamin, "the important thing for the remembering author is not what he experienced, but the weaving of his memory, the Penelope work of recollection" ("The Image of Proust," in *Illuminations*, 205).

31 Roland Barthes, "To Write: An Intransitive Verb?" in Barthes, *The Rustle of Language*, trans. Richard Howard (Berkeley, 1989).

32 Walter Benjamin, "Theses on the Philosophy of History," in *Illuminations*, 257. In a letter to the author of Aug. 23, 1992, Richard Wolin contends that Benjamin would not have accepted the formalist distrust of plenitudinous meaning evident in critics like Barthes; for him, the stylistic moments of absolute experience demanded an experiential fulfillment that such critics thought impossible.

33 Charles Bally, "Le style indirect libre en français moderne I et II," *Germanisch-Romanische Monatsschrift* (Heidelberg, 1912). There were some prior discussions in the work of the linguists A. Tobler and Th. Kaplevsky, but it was not until Bally, who was one of the two students of Saussure who published the notes of the *Cours de linguistique générale* in 1916, that a sustained analysis was made. "Libre" means syntactically independent.

34 Marcel Proust, "About Flaubert's Style," in *Marcel Proust: A Selection from His Miscellaneous Writings*, trans. Gerard Hopkins (London, 1948).

35 Étienne Lorck, *Die "Erlebte Rede": Ein sprachliche Untersuchung* (Heidelberg, 1921); Otto Jespersen, *The Philosophy of Grammar* (London, 1924).

36 V. S. Vološinov, *Marxism and the Philosophy of Language* [1930] trans. Ladislav Metejka and I. R. Titunik (New York, 1973); Stephen Ullmann, *Style in the French Novel* (New York, 1964); Dorrit Cohn, *Transparent Minds: Narrative Modes for Presenting Consciousness in Fiction* (Princeton, 1978); Roy Pascal, *The Dual Voice: Free Indirect Speech and Its Functioning in the*

Nineteenth-Century European Novel (Manchester, 1977); Hans Robert Jauss, "Literary History as a Challenge to Literary Theory," in Jauss, *Toward an Aesthetic of Reception*, trans. Timothy Bahti (Minneapolis, 1982); and Ann Banfield, *Unspeakable Sentences* (Boston, 1982).

37 Dominick LaCapra, *"Madame Bovary" on Trial* (Ithaca, 1982).

38 For an account of Vossler and the Vosslerites, see Vološinov, *Marxism*, 32.

39 LaCapra, *"Madame Bovary,"* 138.

40 Cited ibid., 57–58.

41 It also might be conjectured that anxiety about another confusion was also reinforced by the *style indirect libre*, that between character and reader. In the eighteenth century, the moral implications of the novel were contested precisely because of the dangerously fluid boundaries between amoral characters and sympathetic (often female) readers. *Madame Bovary* itself, of course, draws on the fear that impressionable readers will confuse their lives with those of romantic heroines.

42 Interestingly, one of the other Vosslerites who worked on *erlebte Rede*, Gertraud Lerch, used the Diltheyan notion of *Einfühlung* (empathy) as the key to the style. See the discussion in Vološinov, *Marxism*, 150.

43 Pascal, *Dual Voice*, 25.

44 Vološinov, *Marxism*, 155.

45 Ann Banfield, "Where Epistemology, Style, and Grammar Meet Literary History: The Development of Represented Speech and Thought," *New Literary History* 9.3 (1978): 449.

46 Emile Benveniste, *Problems in General Linguistics*, trans. Mary Elizabeth Meek (Coral Gables, Fla., 1971), chap. 14.

47 Jacques Derrida, "Différance," in Derrida, *Margins of Philosophy*, trans. Alan Bass (Chicago, 1982), 9.

48 Barthes, "To Write," 19.

49 For an analysis of *écriture* in terms of intransitive writing, the middle voice, and the *style indirect libre*, see Ann Banfield, "Écriture, Narration and the Grammar of French," in *Narrative: From Malory to Motion Pictures*, ed. Jeremy Hawthorn (London, 1985). She makes the point that the impersonal grammatical function of writing was lost in America when the pragmatists substituted "The Experience Curriculum" in the 1930s (17–18). In the Benjaminian terms we have been using, the "absolute experience" of *écriture* was replaced by mere *Erlebnis*.

50 Ann Banfield, "Describing the Unobserved: Events Grouped Around an Empty Center," in *The Linguistics of Writing: Arguments between Language and Literature*, ed. Nigel Fabb et al. (Manchester, 1987); and "L'Imparfait de l'Objectif: The Imperfect of the Object Glass," *Camera Obscura* 24 (Fall 1991).

51 Banfield, "L'Imparfait de l'Objectif," 77.

52 Walter Benjamin, "A Short History of Photography," *Screen* 13.1 (Spring 1972). For a discussion of the links between Benjamin's visual concerns and the issue of experience, see Hansen, "Benjamin, Cinema and Experience."

53 Berel Lang, *Act and Idea in the Nazi Genocide* (Chicago, 1990) and Hayden White, "Historical Emplotment and the Problem of Truth," in *Probing the Limits of Representation: Nazism and*

the "Final Solution," ed. Saul Friedländer (Cambridge, Mass., 1992). White has explored these issues in "Writing in the Middle Voice," *Stanford Literature Review* 9.2 (Fall 1992).

54   White, "Historical Emplotment," 49.

55   Ibid., 52.

56   Martin Jay, "Of Plots, Witnesses and Judgments," in Friedländer, *Probing the Limits of Representation.* The distinction between active agent and passive victim seems to be nowhere as important to maintain as in accounts of the Holocaust; otherwise, we risk the travesty of evenhanded remembrance evident at Bitburg and in the work of certain historians during the *Historikerstreit.*

57   Banfield, "Where Epistemology, Style, and Grammar Meet Literary History," 415.

58   Vincent Pecora, "Ethics, Politics and the Middle Voice," *Yale French Studies* 79 (1991): 203–30.

59   Ibid., 212.

60   See the discussion in Katerina Clark and Michael Holquist, *Mikhail Bakhtin* (Cambridge, Mass., 1984), chap. 6; and the translators' introduction to Vološinov, *Marxism.*

61   LaCapra, "*Madame Bovary,*" 149.

62   Terry Eagleton, *Walter Benjamin: Or Towards a Revolutionary Criticism* (London, 1981), where he claimed that in Bakhtin exists a "Judeo-Christian mysticism in some ways akin to Benjamin's—that Marxism and the Philosophy of Language [which he takes to be written by Bakhtin] contains as its secret code a theological devotion to the incarnational unity of word and being similar to that which marks Benjamin's own meditations" (153–54).

63   Jürgen Habermas, "Consciousness-Raising or Redemptive Criticism: The Contemporaneity of Walter Benjamin," *New German Critique* 17 (Spring, 1979): 45–46.

64   Leo Bersani, *The Culture of Redemption* (Cambridge, Mass., 1990), 60. Bersani's own anti-redemptive concept of experience derives in large measure from Georges Bataille, *Inner Experience,* trans. Leslie Anne Boldt (Albany, N.Y., 1988).

5   The Limits of Limit-Experience

1   Julia Kristeva, "Bataille, l'expérience et la pratique," in *Bataille,* ed. Philippe Sollers (Paris, 1973), 272.

2   Hans-Georg Gadamer, *Truth and Method* (New York, 1986), 310. For a brief treatment on the debate in relation to the controversy over the history of everyday life, see Chapter 3, "Songs of Experience: Reflections on the Debate over *Alltagsgeschichte.*" Included are references to other recent debates in which experience played a key role, e.g., between Marxist historians E. P. Thompson and Perry Anderson and African American literary critics Joyce A. Joyce, Barbara Christian, Henry Louis Gates, Jr., and Houston Baker. For another analysis, which discusses the work of the Marxist art critic John Berger, see Bruce Robbins, "Feeling Global: John Berger and Experience," in *Postmodernism and Politics,* ed. Jonathan Arac (Minneapolis, 1986). The anthropological debate about experience is discussed in James Clifford, *The Predicament of Culture: Twentieth-Century Ethnography, Literature, and Art* (Cambridge, Mass., 1988), chap. 1.

3 For another, see the chapter "The Demise of Experience: Fiction as Stranger than Truth?" in Alice A. Jardine, *Gynesis: Configurations of Woman and Modernity* (Ithaca, 1985).

4 Joan W. Scott, "The Evidence of Experience," *Critical Inquiry* 17.4 (Summer 1991): 797.

5 Elizabeth J. Bellamy and Artemis Leontis, "A Genealogy of Experience: From Epistemology to Politics," *Yale Journal of Criticism* 6.1 (Spring 1993). In the 1960s, the antipsychiatrist R. D. Laing coined the term "politics of experience" as a key concept for a radical "social phenomenology." See his *The Politics of Experience and The Bird of Paradise* (London, 1968).

6 Bellamy and Leontis, "A Genealogy of Experience," 171.

7 Ibid., 180.

8 Jacques Derrida, *Of Grammatology*, trans. Gayatri Chakravorty Spivak (Baltimore, 1976), 60.

9 Louis Althusser, *Lenin and Philosophy and Other Essays*, ed. Ben Brewster (New York, 1971), 223.

10 Jean-François Lyotard, *The Differend: Phrases in Dispute*, trans. Georges Van Den Abbeele (Minneapolis, 1988), 45 and 88. Lyotard's undeveloped reference to the Hegelian reading of experience implicitly invokes Martin Heidegger's *Hegel's Concept of Experience* (New York, 1970), in which the centrality of experience to the entire project of dialectical phenomenology is carefully spelled out. Many of the poststructuralist objections against experience—e.g., its reliance on a strong notion of subjectivity, a subject present to itself after a process of apparent alienation, and its pivotal role in mediating between consciousness and science—are anticipated in Heidegger's gloss on Hegel.

11 For an account of Buber's *Erlebnismystik*, see Paul Mendes-Flohr, *From Mysticism to Dialogue: Martin Buber's Transformation of German Social Thought* (Detroit, 1989), chap. 3. In his vocabulary, *Erfahrung* meant the cognitive knowledge of the world produced by sense data or what Kant had called synthetic a priori judgments of the world, whereas *Erlebnis* had a more affective and holistic implication. The literature on Benjamin's very different discussion of the two notions of experience is vast; for my own attempt to deal with it, see Chapter 4, "Experience without a Subject: Walter Benjamin and the Novel."

12 See, for example, the critique of Benjamin's celebration of *Erfahrung* in Bellamy and Leontis, "A Genealogy of Experience," 169. A similar complaint is voiced by Leo Bersani in *The Culture of Redemption* (Cambridge, Mass., 1990), where he writes of Benjamin, "very little of what he said makes any sense—and this is especially true of his elaboration of such distinctions as *Erlebnis* and *Erfahrung*—unless we place it within the logical assumptions behind all his thought: assumptions of lost wholeness, of fallen being" (53).

13 Another candidate for such an analysis might be Philippe Lacoue-Labarthe, whose study of the poet Paul Celan, *La poésie comme expérience* (Paris, 1986), uses the term in the sense of *Erfahrung* as opposed to *Erlebnis* (or *le vécu*) in a positive way. He does so by emphasizing its etymological origins in the Latin *experiri*, which contains the same root as the word for peril, *periculum*. "Experience," he concludes, "is from the beginning and fundamentally without doubt, a placing oneself in danger" (31). Another candidate would be Maurice Blanchot, whose *Thomas l'obscur* of 1943 has sometimes been called the fictional double of

Bataille's *Inner Experience*. See, for example, Michel Surya, *Georges Bataille: La Mort à l'œuvre* (Paris, 1987), 315. Still another possibility would be Philippe Sollers, whose *Writing and the Experience of Limits*, ed., David Hayman, trans. Philip Barnard and David Hayman (New York, 1983) owes a great deal to Bataille. Even Jacques Lacan might be cited as a poststructuralist whose attitude toward a certain notion of experience was positive. See François Regnault, "Lacan and Experience," in *Lacan and the Human Sciences*, ed. Alexandre Leupin (Lincoln, Neb., 1991).

14 For another recent attempt to break through the impasse, based on a reading of Deweyan pragmatism, see Timothy V. Kaufman-Osborne, "Teasing Feminist Sense from Experience," *Hypatia* 8.2 (Spring 1993).

15 Michael Foucault, *The Archaeology of Knowledge and the Discourse on Language*, trans. A. M. Sheridan Smith (New York, 1972), 16. Smith translates *"expérience"* as "experiment," which is one of its French meanings, but "experience" would be better because Foucault was referring to the primal, inarticulate state of consciousness labeled as madness, which the book hoped to redeem. See the preface to *Madness and Civilization: A History of Insanity in the Age of Reason*, trans. Richard Howard (New York, 1965), where Foucault calls madness "an undifferentiated experience, a not yet divided experience of division itself" (ix). Foucault's apparent abandonment of the concept allowed one commentator to claim that after 1963, "one is struck by the total disappearance of the concept 'experience' " (Allan Megill, *Prophets of Extremity: Nietzsche, Heidegger, Foucault, Derrida* [Berkeley, 1985], 202), and another to remark that Foucault's major achievement was "the conversion of phenomenology to epistemology. . . . Everything is knowledge, and this is the first reason why there is no 'savage experience': there is nothing beneath or prior to knowledge" (Gilles Deleuze, *Foucault*, trans. Seán Hand [Minneapolis, 1986], 109). One source of this reading of Foucault is his debt to the French philosophy of science represented by Gaston Bachelard and Georges Canguilhem. For an account of their critique of experience in the empiricist tradition and its impact on Foucault, see Dominique Lecourt, *Marxism and Epistemology: Bachelard, Canguilhem and Foucault*, trans. Ben Brewster (London, 1975). However, for a different interpretation of the meaning of experience in the early Foucault, see David Carroll, *Paraesthetics: Foucault, Lyotard, Derrida* (New York, 1987). Carroll conjectures that "it would even be possible to argue in Foucault's own terms that the 'raw being of order' and the 'being of madness' point to the limitations of experience and cannot be experienced as such. Foucault's enigmatic notion of 'experience' is really, therefore, a non-experience, or what I would call a paraexperience" (195). Or in other words, he never had a naive, phenomenological notion of experience.

16 Michel Foucault, "How an 'Experience-Book' is Born," in *Remarks on Marx: Conversations with Duccio Trombadori*, trans. R. James Goldstein and James Cascaito (New York, 1991), 27.

17 Ibid., 31.

18 Ibid.

19 Ibid., 36.

20 Ibid., 8.

21 Ibid., 40.

22 I am borrowing Freud's term, *sekundäre Bearbeitung,* sometimes translated as "secondary revision," for that part of the dream-work that turns the incoherence of the dream's raw material into a meaningful narrative, often at the moment of awakening.

23 James Miller, *The Passion of Michel Foucault* (New York, 1993). See also Miller's essay "Foucault's Politics in Biographical Perspective" and the essays that followed by Lynn Hunt, Richard Rorty, Alasdair MacIntyre and David M. Halperin in *Salmagundi* 97 (Winter 1993).

24 Miller, "Foucault's Politics in Biographical Perspective," 42.

25 Alexander Nehamas, *Nietzsche: Life as Literature* (Cambridge, Mass., 1985). According to Nehamas, Nietzsche was "engaged in a constantly continuing and continually broadening process of appropriation of one's experiences and actions, of enlarging the capacity for assuming responsibility for oneself which Nietzsche calls 'freedom'" (190–91). Another model for Miller is Jean Starobinski, who also treats texts and life as a coherent project, following the phenomenological method developed by the Geneva School. For an account of its procedures and assumptions about experience, see Sarah Lawall, *Critics of Consciousness: The Existential Structures of Literature* (Cambridge, Mass., 1968), who writes its members see "literature as the verbal transcription of a coherent human experience" (viii).

26 Miller, *The Passion of Michel Foucault,* 30.

27 Ibid., 87. As Alasdair MacIntyre remarks, "the cult of extreme experiences, with its roots in nineteenth-century romanticism, is not obviously at home within Nietzsche's project . . . [it is not] clear how the extreme experiences are put to Nietzschean uses, except by a retrospective assignment of a significance to those experiences which is very different from that which they could have had prospectively. Zarathustra after all does not seem to summon us in the direction of sadomasochism" ("Miller's Foucault, Foucault's Foucault," *Salmagundi* 97 [Winter 1993]: 56).

28 Miller, *The Passion of Michel Foucault,* 88, where he cites a passage from Bataille, *Erotism: Death and Sensuality,* trans. Mary Dalwood (San Francisco, 1986), 23, and 116, where he cites a passage from Foucault, *Les Mots et les choses* (Paris, 1966), 395.

29 The main difference, to be sure, is that the Hegelian version stresses the rational dimension of *Erfahrung,* whereas Miller's does not.

30 Miller, *The Passion of Michel Foucault,* 7.

31 Ibid., 156. Here Miller, trying hard to be as tolerant as possible, seeks to go beyond conventionally negative stereotypes of sadomasochism, but in so doing makes it almost as untransgressive as stamp collecting.

32 Ibid., 265.

33 One commentator, Francis Marmande, calls it a "fundamental rupture" in his work. See his *Georges Bataille Politique* (Lyon, 1985), 8.

34 Bataille, *Inner Experience,* trans., Leslie Anne Boldt (Albany, N.Y., 1988). The other two volumes were *Le Coupable* (Paris, 1944), and *Sur Nietzsche* (Paris, 1945). According to Pierre Prévost, Bataille's own first "inner experience" took place shortly after the war began,

while he walked in his neighborhood in Paris at night, an umbrella open despite the ending of the rain: "At a certain moment, he began to laugh, an intense laugh and let the umbrella drop. It covered his head. He immediately fell into a state of unique entrancement, like none he had ever known. . . . It was that night that he discovered what he called 'inner experience' " (Prévost, *Rencontre Georges Bataille* [Paris, 1987], 74).

35   Allan Stoekl, *Agonies of the Intellectual Commitment, Subjectivity, and the Performative in the 20th-Century French Tradition* (Lincoln, Neb., 1992), 268. Such a reading is given credence by later evocations of "subjective" and "experience" in such texts as *Erotism*, for example, on pp. 32–35. But even here, Bataille writes that "man achieves his inner experience at the instant when bursting out of the chrysalis he feels that he is tearing himself, not tearing something outside that resists him" (39).

36   Denis Hollier, *Against Architecture: The Writings of Georges Bataille*, trans. Betsy Wing (Cambridge, Mass., 1989), 45.

37   Bataille, *Inner Experience*, 3–9. But see his remarks on p. 169: "Can one not free from its religious antecedents the possibility for mystical experience—this possibility having remained open to the non-believer, in whatever way it appears? Free it from the ascesis of dogma and from the atmosphere of religions? Free it, in a word, from mysticism—to the point of linking it to the nudity of ignorance?" It should, however, be acknowledged that in later texts Bataille seems to forget this reservation, for example in his examination of Emily Brontë in *Literature and Evil*, trans. Alastair Hamilton (New York, 1973), 14–15, or in *Erotism*, 23.

38   Jacques Derrida, *Writing and Difference*, trans. Alan Bass (Chicago, 1978), 272.

39   Rebecca Comay notes a number of passages in which Bataille falls back on a nostalgic rhetoric of paradise lost. See her "Gifts without Presents: Economics of 'Experience' in Bataille and Heidegger," *Yale French Studies* 78 (1990): 78.

40   According to Prévost, Bataille sought—not, from Prévost's point of view, with complete success—to clarify the relationship between inner experience and ecstasy. Bataille's major complaint against the simple equation of the two terms was that religious ecstasy sought a union with God, which inner experience denied. See Prévost, *Rencontre Georges Bataille*, 78. For the same reason, Prévost recalls, he felt uncomfortable with the label of mystic (153).

41   Bataille, *Inner Experience*, xxxii. He also endorses Blanchot's version of the spiritual life, which has "its principle and its end in the absence of salvation, in the renunciation of all hope" (102).

42   Ibid., 8. In *Erotism*, Bataille argued that Hegel's system "assembles ideas, but at the same time cuts those assembled ideas off from experience. That no doubt was his ambition, for in Hegel's mind the immediate is bad, and Hegel would certainly have identified what I call experience with the immediate" (255).

43   Bataille even goes so far as to say that "inner experience is led by discursive reason. Reason alone has the power to undo its work, to hurl down what it has built up. . . . Without the support of reason, we don't reach 'dark incandescence' " (*Inner Experience*, 46–47).

44   Bataille, *Erotism*, 260.

45   Ibid., 22.

46   For an account of the idiosyncratic use of the term sovereignty in Bataille, see my "The Reassertion of Sovereignty in a Time of Crisis: Carl Schmitt and Georges Bataille" in *Force Fields: Between Intellectual History and Cultural Critique* (New York, 1993).

47   Jean-Michel Heimonet, *Négativité et communication* (Paris, 1990), 95.

48   Bataille, *Inner Experience*, 46

49   Not surprisingly, Sartre in his celebrated critique of *Inner Experience* would find this argument particularly troubling, because it implied an impossible external point of view on the subject, underestimated the power of intentionality, tacitly valorized the inauthenticity of what Heidegger had called "Das Man," and failed to acknowledge the temporal future-oriented flow of inner experience. See Jean-Paul Sartre, "Un Nouveau Mystique," *Cahiers de Sud* (Paris, 1947). For a sustained analysis of the Sartre/Bataille dispute, see Michele H. Richman, *Reading Georges Bataille: Beyond the Gift* (Baltimore, 1982), chap. 5. For a general account of the reception of the book, see Surya, *Georges Bataille*, 332–39.

50   Jünger's book was translated into French as *La guerre notre mère* in 1934, and may have played a role in Bataille's thoughts on the army. See Denis Hollier's introduction to Bataille's 1938 lecture "The Structure and Function of the Army" in *The College of Sociology*, ed. Hollier, trans. Betsy Wing (Minneapolis, 1988), 138. Hollier includes notes written by Bataille in 1941 in which he distances himself from the positive identification with war apparent in such earlier texts as "The Practice of Joy before Death" of 1939, reprinted in *Visions of Excess: Selected Writings, 1927–1939*, ed. Allan Stoekl (Minneapolis, 1985). Comay correctly notes the distance between Bataille's position and any notion of *Erlebnis*, including Jünger's. Cf. "Gifts without Presents," 84.

51   Bataille, "Formless," in *Visions of Excess*, 31. A parallel argument informs his critique of Jean Genet (and Sartre's attempt to turn Genet into a saint) in *Literature and Evil*, where he attacks the novelist for his vain attempt to achieve a positive, self-sufficient sovereignty, a mode of pure being, which does not allow itself to communicate with others.

52   Bataille, *Inner Experience*, 13.

53   Ibid., 7.

54   Ibid.

55   Foucault, "A Preface to Transgression," in *Language, Counter-Memory, Practice: Selected Essays and Interviews*, ed. Donald F. Bouchard (Ithaca, 1977), 36.

56   Kristeva, "Bataille, l'expérience et la pratique," 290. This essay of 1972 is written from an essentially Althusserian point of view, which tries to enlist Bataille's anti-Hegelian notion of experience for Maoist politics. For more on the relationship between Lacan and Bataille, see Carolyn J. Dean, *The Self and Its Pleasures: Bataille, Lacan, and the History of the Decentered Subject* (Ithaca, 1992). For an analysis of the visual concerns of both thinkers, see Martin Jay, *Downcast Eyes: The Denigration of Vision in Twentieth-Century French Thought* (Berkeley, 1993).

57   Kristeva also notes that "because it is the place of the contestation of power, a place

where a subject is constituted that is not the subject of power (as society, and especially Western society, has always thought and lived), but a contestatory, free subject, that experience has effects that largely exceed 'the interior' " ["Bataille, l'expérience et la pratique," 287).

58 Bataille, *Inner Experience*, 27

59 As Bataille told Prévost, "experience is thus posed first of all independently of the subject who lives it and the object it discovers: it is the putting of subject and object into question. But it is clear that is not a question of the experience of a being that I am. Experience is thus first of all putting into question the limits of being, essentially of the isolation in which the particular being finds itself" (*Rencontre Georges Bataille*, 104).

60 Bataille, *Literature and Evil*, 170.

61 Comay, "Gifts without Presents," 85.

62 Lacoue-Labarthe, *La poésie comme expérience*, 30. See also Jean-Luc Nancy, *The Experience of Freedom*, trans. Bridget McDonald (Stanford, 1993), 20, for more on the link between peril and experience, which involves being "exposed like the pirate (*peirates*) who freely tries his luck on the high seas."

63 Jean-Luc Nancy, *The Inoperative Community*, ed. Peter Connor, trans. Peter Connor, Lisa Garbus, Michael Holland, and Simona Sawhney (Minneapolis, 1991). For ruminations on Nancy's work, see The Miami Theory Collective, eds., *Community at Loose Ends* (Minneapolis, 1991).

64 Nancy, *The Inoperative Community*, 21.

65 Ann Smock, translator's footnote to Maurice Blanchot, *The Writing of the Disaster*, trans. Ann Smock (Lincoln, Neb., 1986), 148. She also notes its association with idleness and inertia.

66 Nancy, *The Inoperative Community*, 19.

67 Ibid., 15. By ego, Nancy means a strong sense of a subject at one with its substance in an eternal unity, in short, a Hegelian subject.

68 "I employ the term 'communication' in the manner of Bataille," Nancy writes, "that is to say, following the pattern of a permanent violence done to the word's meaning, both because it implies subjectivity or intersubjectivity and because it denotes the transmission of a message and a meaning. Rigorously, this word is untenable. I retain it because it resonates with 'community,' but I would superimpose upon it (which sometimes means substitute for it) the word 'sharing'" (157). For an extensive comparison of Habermas and Bataille on communication, see Heimonet, *Negativité et communication*.

69 It will be recalled that Freud's term was *sekundäre Bearbeitung*, which invokes the very concept of working that the *communauté désoeuvrée* denies.

70 Nancy, *The Inoperative Community*, 21.

71 Nancy, *The Experience of Freedom*, 87.

72 Ibid., 95.

73 Jürgen Habermas, *The Philosophical Discourse of Modernity: Twelve Lectures*, trans. Frederick Lawrence (Cambridge, Mass., 1987), 236.

74   Barbara Herrnstein Smith, *Contingencies of Value: Alternative Perspectives for Critical Theory* (Cambridge, Mass., 1988), 137f. For a consideration of Bataille's strategies for dealing with this potential, see Steven Connor, *Theory and Cultural Value* (Oxford, 1992), 71–80.

75   Richard Wolin, *The Terms of Cultural Criticism: The Frankfurt School, Existentialism, Poststructuralism* (New York, 1992), 14.

6   No Power to the Soviets

1   Lenin, to be sure, had himself defined the "dictatorship of the proletariat" in terms of councils in *The State and Revolution* in 1917, in which the experience of the Paris Commune was adduced as the model for replacing the bourgeois, parliamentary state. But he was careful to stress that they would be centrally, not federally, organized, which opened the door for a very different version of the dictatorship once he assumed power.

2   For useful historical accounts of the councils in these different contexts, see Oskar Anweiler, *Die Rätebewegung in Russland, 1905–1921* (Leiden, 1958), and "Die Räte in der ungarischen Revolution," in *Osteuropa* 8 (1958); Branko Pribicevic, *The Shop Stewards' Movement and Workers' Control* (Oxford, 1959); and F. L. Carsten, *Revolution in Central Europe, 1918–1919* (Berkeley, 1972).

3   For a recent examination of this impulse in relation to messianic Jewish thought, see Michael Löwy, *Rédemption at Utopia: Le judaïsme libertaire en Europe centrale* (Paris, 1988).

4   Russell Jacoby, *Dialectic of Defeat: Contours of Western Marxism* (Cambridge, 1981), 77.

5   See, for example, the discussions in George Konrád and Ivan Szelényi, *The Intellectuals on the Road to Class Power: A Sociological Study of the Role of the Intelligentsia in Socialism*, trans. Andrew Arato and Richard E. Allen (New York, 1979), 175; and Ferenc Fehér and Agnes Heller, *Eastern Left, Western Left: Totalitarianism, Freedom and Democracy* (Oxford, 1987), 224.

6   See, for example, Arendt's panegyric to them in *On Revolution* (New York, 1963).

7   Perhaps the most explicit attempt to harness the desire for community for leftist purposes was made by the anarchist Gustav Landauer. See Eugene Lunn, *Prophet of Community: The Romantic Socialism of Gustav Landauer* (Berkeley, 1973). His idea of the Bund differed from the workers council per se in its openness to all social groups and anti-urban, anti-industrial bias.

8   Not all council communists, however, abandoned the idea of dual power between Soviets and party. Hermann Gorter, for example, defended the role of the party against those like Otto Rühle, who argued for its absorption into the councils. See the discussion in Mark Shipway, "Council Communism," in *Non-Market Socialism in the Nineteenth and Twentieth Centuries*, ed. Maximilien Rubel and John Crump (London, 1987), 120f.

9   When Solidarity first emerged in Gdansk a decade ago, it did include what it called "employees' councils" among its demands. See the account by Stanislaw Starski (pseudonym for Slawomir Magala), *Class Struggle in Classless Poland* (Boston, 1982), 146f. But the more drastic economic measures of the recent era seem to leave no place for strong workers' self-management.

10   For a useful summary of the recent debates, see David Held, *Models of Democracy* (Stanford, 1987).

11   Norberto Bobbio, *Which Socialism? Marxism, Socialism, Democracy*, ed. Richard Bellamy, trans. Roger Griffen (Minneapolis, 1987), 36f. Bobbio points out, among other problems, the continued importance of the nternational state system, which necessitates the continuation of some centralized state function.

12   See, for example, Isaac D. Balbus, *Marxsm and Domination: A Neo-Hegelian, Feminist, Psychoanalytic Theory of Sexual, Political, and Technological Liberation* (Princeton, 1982), 122f.

13   See Mark Poster, *The Mode of Information: Poststructuralism and Social Context* (Chicago, 1990).

14   For a suggestive exploration of this issue, see Paul Smith, *Discerning the Subject* (Minneapolis, 1988).

15   Ernesto Laclau and Chantal Mouffe, *Hegemony and Socialist Strategy: Towards a Radical Democratic Politics*, trans. Winston Moore and Paul Cammack (London, 1985); for a typical orthodox Marxist response, see Ellen Meiksins Wood, *The Retreat from Class: A New "True" Socialism* (London, 1986).

7   Who's Afraid of Christa Wolf?

1   Günter Grass, "Nötige Kritik oder Hinrichtung?" interview with *Der Spiegel*, no. 29 (1990): 143.

2   Cited in Ulrich Greiner, "Dumm & dümmlich," *Die Zeit*, July 20, 1990.

3   Christa Wolf, "Stell dir vor, es ist Sozialismus, und keiner geht weg," November 4, 1989, printed in *Die Taz* (Berlin), November 11, 1989.

4   Cited in Nigel Hamilton, *The Brothers Mann: The Lives of Heinrich and Thomas Mann, 1871–1950 and 1875–1955* (New Haven, 1978), 335.

5   Wolf, "Der Schatten eines Traumes," foreword to Karoline von Günderrode, *Der Schatten eines Traumes*, ed. Christa Wolf (Berlin, 1979); "Nun ja! Das nächste Leben geht aber heute an. Ein Brief über Bettina," afterword to Bettina von Arnim, *Die Günderrode* (Leipzig, 1980). Not only feminist documents, these essays were also challenges to the official GDR literary policy concerning romanticism.

6   Wolf, "Culture Is What You Experience—An Interview with Christa Wolf," *New German Critique* 27 (Fall 1982): 94.

7   Ulrich Greiner, "Keiner is frei von Schuld," *Die Zeit*, August 3, 1990, 1.

8   See, for example, Paul Piccone, "The Changing Function of Critical Theory," *New German Critique* 12 (Fall 1977): 29–37; Tim Luke, "Culture and Politics in the Age of Artificial Negativity," *Telos* 35 (Spring 1978): 55–72.

9   Gerald Graff, "Co-optation," in *The New Historicism*, ed. H. Aram Veeser (New York, 1989), 173.

8   Postmodern Fascism?

1   Ernst Nolte, *Martin Heidegger: Politik und Geschichte im Leben und Denken* (Berlin, 1992).

2   Ernst Nolte, *Three Faces of Fascism*, trans. Leila Vennewiz (New York, 1965).

3   See the review essay by Klaus Epstein, "A New Study of Fascism," in *Reappraisals of Fascism*, ed. Henry A Turner, Jr. (New York, 1975).

4 George Lichtheim, "The European Civil War," *New York Review of Books*, February 3, 1966; reprinted in *The Concept of Ideology and Other Essays* (New York, 1967), 237.

5 Saul Friedländer, "From Anti-Semitism to Extermination," in *Unanswered Questions: Nazi Germany and the Genocide of the Jews*, ed. François Furet (New York, 1989), 7.

6 Nolte, *Three Faces of Fascism*, 40.

7 Ibid., 38.

8 Ibid., 537.

9 Ibid., 537.

10 Wolfgang Sauer, "National Socialism: Fascism or Totalitarianism," in Turner, *Reappraisals of Fascism*, 103.

11 Nolte, *Three Faces of Fascism*, 567.

12 Fredric Jameson, *Postmodernism: Or, the Cultural Logic of Late Capitalism* (Durham, N.C., 1991). For an extended consideration of its argument, see my review in *History and Theory* 32.3 (1992).

13 Fredric Jameson, *Fables of Aggression: Wyndham Lewis, the Modernist as Fascist* (Berkeley, 1979), 14.

9 Educating the Educators

1 Kurt Tucholsky, "Wir Negativen," *Die Weltbühne* 15 (March 13, 1919), reprinted in *Manifeste und Dokumente zur deutschen Literatur 1918–1933*, ed. Anton Kaes (Stuttgart, 1983), 36.

2 J. P. Nettl, "Ideas, Intellectuals, and Structures of Dissent," in *On Intellectuals*, ed. Philip Rieff (New York, 1969).

3 Andrew Ross, *No Respect: Intellectuals and Popular Culture* (New York, 1989), 213.

4 Peter Sloterdijk, *Critique of Cynical Reason*, trans. Michael Eldred (Minneapolis, 1987), 546.

5 Greil Marcus, *Lipstick Traces: A Secret History of the Twentieth Century* (Cambridge, Mass.), 1989).

10 The Aesthetic Alibi

1 Richard Serra, "Art and Censorship," *Critical Inquiry* 17.3 (Spring 1991). See also, Barbara Hoffman, "Law for Art's Sake in the Public Realm," in the same issue.

2 Serra, "Art and Censorship," 575.

3 Ibid., 576. This phrase refers to a bill submitted by Senator Edward Kennedy protecting the artist's "moral rights" supported by Serra. It was passed in October 1990 as the "Visual Artists Rights Act." For its details and implications, see Hoffman, "Law for Art's Sake," 568f.

4 That this is not entirely a fantasy is demonstrated by the controversy over David Nelson's portrait of the late Chicago mayor Harold Washington in women's underwear in May 1988. It was seized by officials of the city government from the student exhibition where it was being shown, and returned only after it was slashed.

5 Jean-François Lyotard, *The Differend: Phrases in Dispute*, trans. Georges Van Den Abbeele (Minneapolis, 1988).

6 M. H. Abrams, "Art-as-Such: The Sociology of Modern Aesthetics," in *Doing Things with Texts: Essays in Criticism and Critical Theory*, ed. Michael Fischer (New York, 1989).

7   Wilde as quoted in Ernest Raynaud, *Souvenirs sur le symbolisme* (Paris, 1895), 397.

8   In addition to the Abrams essay cited above, see Terry Eagleton, *The Ideology of the Aesthetic* (Cambridge, Mass., 1990); Luc Ferry, *Homo Aestheticus: L'Invention du goût a l'âge démocratique* (Paris, 1990); Howard Caygill, *Art of Judgment* (Cambridge, Mass., 1989).

9   Pierre Bourdieu, *Distinction: A Social Critique of the Judgment of Taste*, trans. Richard Nice (Cambridge, Mass., 1984).

10   Peter Bürger, *Theory of the Avant-Garde*, trans. Michael Shaw (Minneapolis, 1984).

11   Jacques Derrida, *The Truth in Painting*, trans. Geoff Bennington and Ian McLeod (Chicago, 1987); Philippe Lacoue-Labarthe and Jean-Luc Nancy, *The Literary Absolute: The Theory of Literature in German Romanticism*, trans. Philip Barnard and Cheryl Lester (Albany, 1988); Paul de Man, *The Rhetoric of Romanticism* (New York, 1984) and *The Resistance to Theory* (Minneapolis, 1986).

12   This issue was at the center of the celebrated debate between Derrida and the speech-act philosopher John Searle in *Glyph* in the late 1970s.

13   Elsewhere, I have sought to grapple with the implications of this critique. See my " 'The Aesthetic Ideology' as Ideology: Or What Does It Mean to Aestheticize Politics?" in *Force Fields: Between Intellectual History and Cultural Critique* (New York, 1993).

14   For accounts, see Maurice Nadeau, *The History of Surrealism*, trans. Richard Howard with intro. by Roger Shattuck (London, 1987), chap. 14; and Helena Lewis, *The Politics of Surrealism* (New York, 1988), chap. 6.

15   André Breton, "The Poverty of Poetry: The Aragon Affair and Public Opinion," in *Selected Writings*, ed. Franklin Rosemont (London, 1989), 77.

16   Gayatri Chakravorty Spivak, "Criticism, Feminism, and the Institution," in *Intellectuals: Aesthetics, Politics, Academics*, ed. Bruce Robbins (Minneapolis, 1990); Rosi Braidotti, "The Politics of Ontological Difference," in *Between Feminism and Psychoanalysis*, ed. Teresa Brennan (London, 1989).

11   Mimesis and Mimetology

1   Roland Barthes, *S/Z* (Paris, 1970), 145.

2   Jacques Derrida, "The Double Session,' in *Dissemination*, trans. Barbara Johnson (Chicago, 1981), 245.

3   Gilles Deleuze and Félix Guattari, *Mille plateaux* (Paris, 1980), 144.

4   Jean-François Lyotard, "On the Strength of the Weak," in Lyotard, *Toward the Postmodern*, ed. Robert Harvey and Mark S. Roberts (Atlantic Highlands, N.J., 1993), 68.

5   Paul de Man, *The Resistance to Theory* (Minneapolis, 1986), 11.

6   For a useful comparison of the Platonic with the poststructuralist complaints against mimesis, see Christopher Prendergast, *The Order of Mimesis: Balzac, Stendhal, Nerval, Flaubert* (New York, 1986), chap. 1.

7   Walter Benjamin, "On the Mimetic Faculty," in *Reflections: Essays, Aphorisms, Autobiographical Writings*, ed. Peter Demetz, trans. Edmund Jephcott (New York, 1978); "Doctrine of the Similar," *New German Critique* 17 (Spring 1979): 65–69.

8   Roger Caillois, *Le mythe et l'homme* (Paris, 1938); see also his "Mimicry and Legendary Psychasthenia," *October* 31 (Winter 1984): 17–32.

9   Max Horkheimer and Theodor W. Adorno, *Dialectic of Enlightenment*, trans. John Cumming (New York, 1972), for example, 180–81, 227.

10 In *Dialectic of Enlightenment*, however, the ambiguities of mimesis are perhaps more explicitly stressed than in later works like *Aesthetic Theory*. For a discussion that contends that Adorno understands the impossibility of disentangling the reductive from the emancipatory moments in mimesis, see Alexander García Düttmann, *Das Gedächtnis des Denkens: Versuch über Heidegger und Adorno* (Frankfurt, 1991).

11 Theodor W. Adorno, *Aesthetic Theory*, ed. Gretel Adorno and Rolf Tiedemann, trans. C. Lenhardt (London, 1984), 453, 465. Herbert Marcuse, however, was less convinced. In *The Aesthetic Dimension: Toward a Critique of Marxist Aesthetics* (Boston, 1978), he writes, "the realm of freedom lies beyond mimesis. . . . Mimesis remains re-presentation of reality. This bondage resists the utopian quality of art" (47). But he also acknowledges the role of aesthetic mimesis in preserving the memory of past happiness (67). In the later Critical Theory of Jürgen Habermas, mimesis plays a much more marginal role, and when it appears, it is usually assimilated into his communicative notion of intersubjective rationality. See, for example, his remark in "Questions and Counter-Questions," in *Habermas and Modernity*, ed. Richard J. Bernstein (Cambridge, Mass., 1985), that "modern art harbors a utopia that becomes a reality to the degree that the mimetic powers sublimated in the work of art find resonance in the mimetic relations of a balanced and undistorted intersubjectivity of everyday life" (202).

12 Michael Taussig, *Mimesis and Alterity: A Particular History of the Senses* (New York, 1993), 45; Fredric Jameson, *Late Marxism: Adorno or the Persistence of the Dialectic* (New York, 1990), 64; for other discussions, see Martin Lüdke, *Anmerkungen zu einer "Logik des Zerfalls": Adorno—Beckett* (Frankfurt, 1981), chap. 5; Michael Cahn, "Subversive Mimesis: Theodor W. Adorno and the Modern Impasse of Critique," in *Mimesis in Contemporary Theory: An Interdisciplinary Approach*, ed. Mihai Spariosu (Philadelphia, 1984); Karla L. Schultz, *Mimesis on the Move: Theodor W. Adorno's Concept of Imitation* (New York, 1990); and most notably, Josef Früchtl, *Mimesis: Konstellation eines Zentralbegriffs bei Adorno* (Würzberg, 1986).

13 A partial exception is Früchtl, who devotes some interesting pages to Julia Kristeva's relation to Adorno. See his *Mimesis*, 181.

14 See, for example, David Carroll, *Paraesthetics: Foucault, Lyotard, Derrida* (New York, 1987), 101–5.

15 Philippe Lacoue-Labarthe, *Typography: Mimesis, Philosophy, Politics*, ed. Christopher Fynsk, introduction by Jacques Derrida (Cambridge, Mass., 1989). The texts, translated by various hands, were chosen from his collections, *Le suject de la philosophie: Typographies I* (Paris, 1979) and *L'imitation des modernes: Typographies II* (Paris, 1986); and from *Mimesis: Des articulations* (Paris, 1975).

16 This second tradition is Kantian. See the critical discussion in Derrida, "Economimesis," *Diacritics* 11 (June 1981): 9.

17 Adorno, *Aesthetic Theory*, 162.

18 It is for this reason that Adorno explicitly repudiates the *verum-factum* principle adopted by Hegelian Marxists like Lukács. For a discussion, see my "Vico and Western Marxism,"

Fin-de-siècle Socialism and Other Essays (New York, 1988). W. Martin Lüdke points out that, for Adorno, a more primitive adaptation to nature, which can be called mimicry, becomes true mimesis only when it turns into a conscious and intentional doubling of nature (Anmerkungen zu einer "Logik des Zerfall," 58). This is true it seems to me, only if the constructive impulse of this doubling is not understood to outweigh the assimilative.

19 For a discussion, see Cahn, "Subversive Mimesis," 6, n. 44.

20 W. Tatarkiewicz, "Mimesis," Dictionary of the History of Ideas, vol. 3 (New York: Scribner, 1973), 226.

21 For example, by David Roberts, who claims that "Adorno's utopia of reconciliation in turn may be seen as the rational veneer for a profoundly arational mysticism of redemptive mimesis beyond and behind all civilization" (Art and Enlightenment: Aesthetic Theory after Adorno [Lincoln, Neb., 1991], 70).

22 Jürgen Habermas, The Theory of Communicative Action, vol. 1, trans. Thomas McCarthy (Boston, 1984), 382. His attempt, like that of Albrecht Wellmer, in Zur Dialektik von Moderne und Postmoderne: Vernunftkritik nach Adorno (Frankfurt, 1985), to relocate mimesis within an intersubjective, communicative sphere has been criticized by Früchtl, Mimesis, 290. Interestingly, it was conservative theorists like David Hume and Edmund Burke who first pointed to the positive role of mimesis in sociability. See the discussion in Terry Eagleton, The Ideology of the Aesthetic (Cambridge, Mass., 1990), 53. Imitation was also privileged by Gabriel Tarde and then criticized by Emile Durkheim in his classic study Suicide.

23 Adorno, Aesthetic Theory, 80, 453.

24 Ibid., 453. A major weakness of Taussig's Mimesis and Alterity is its failure to make this distinction. See my review in Visual Anthropology Review 9.2 (Fall 1993).

25 For a helpful comparison of Adorno and Kant on this issue, see J. M. Bernstein, The Fate of Art: Aesthetic Alienation from Kant to Derrida and Adorno (University Park, Pa., 1992), 201–6.

26 García Düttmann argues that in Dialectic of Enlightenment, the name "nature" stands metonymically for the relations with the other (Das Gedächtnis des Denkens, 118). If so, it would be important to recognize that it includes what in French is nicely differentiated as l'autre and l'autrui, the objective and subjective "other."

27 Adorno, Aesthetic Theory, 162. Although the suffering of mute nature is expressed in mimesis, it takes human intervention to enable its appearance (an argument that in some ways parallels Heidegger's description of the relationship between Dasein, the being that cares for Being, and Sein).

28 According to Adorno, "Realism, which does not grasp subjective experience, to say nothing of going beyond it, only mimics reconciliation" ("Trying to Understand Endgame," in Notes to Literature, 2 vols., ed. Rolf Tiedemann, trans. Shierry Weber Nicholsen [New York, 1991], 1: 250).

29 Here the effects of Benjamin's anti-structuralist linguistics on Adorno can be discerned, for Benjamin saw the Saussurean insistence on the absolute arbitrariness of the sign as evidence of the fall of language from its pre-lapsarian state, in which a mimetic relationship between names and things prevailed. For a helpful account of the differences between Benjaminian and structuralist linguistics, see Irving Wohlfarth, "On Some

Jewish Motifs in Benjamin," in *The Problems of Modernity: Adorno and Benjamin*, ed. Andrew Benjamin (New York, 1989). For a suggestive gloss on Adorno's "mimetic" relationship to Benjamin, which goes beyond simple imitation through "influence," see Jameson, *Late Marxism*, 52. Jameson argues, in fact, that on the question of mimesis itself, the two were by no means as unified as is often assumed (256).

30 For a lucid account of Adorno's argument about the dialectic of mimesis and rationality, see Peter Osborne, "Adorno and the Metaphysics of Modernism: The Problem of a 'Postmodern' Art," in A. Benjamin, *The Problems of Modernity*, 29–32.

31 Adorno, *Aesthetic Theory*, 174.

32 Theodor W. Adorno, *Negative Dialectics*, trans. E. B. Ashton (New York, 1973), 14.

33 Adorno, *Aesthetic Theory*, 153.

34 Lambert Zuidervaart, *Adorno's Aesthetic Theory: The Redemption of Illusion* (Cambridge, Mass., 1991), 181.

35 Theodor W. Adorno, *Philosophy of Modern Music*, trans. Anne G. Mitchell and Wesley V. Blomster (New York, 1973), 64.

36 Adorno, *Aesthetic Theory*, 455.

37 Jameson, *Late Marxism*, 68. For another consideration of the relation between mimesis and narrative, see Prendergast, *The Order of Mimesis*, 216–72.

38 Still another possibility would be to follow his discussion of hieroglyphic writing and *écriture* in mass culture and modernist art, as Miriam Hansen has suggested in "Mass Culture as Hieroglyphic Writing: Adorno, Derrida, Kracauer," *New German Critique* 56 (Spring/Summer 1992): 43–73.

39 Adorno, "Parataxis: On Hölderlin's Late Poetry," in Tiedemann, *Notes to Literature*, 2:130.

40 Ibid., 131.

41 Lacoue-Labarthe, *Typography*, 226. The comparison was made in ibid., 133. Lacoue-Labarthe's most extensive discussion of Adorno comes in a later piece, "The Caesura of Religion," in *Opera through Other Eyes*, ed. David J. Levin (Stanford, 1994), 45–77, which is a critique of Adorno's essay on Schoenberg's *Moses und Aron*, "Sakrales Fragment." Here he chastises Adorno for finding a redemptive moment in the music of the opera, which Lacoue-Labarthe claims reflects a failure to recognize the importance of the libretto in producing a sublime rather than redeemed work.

42 Lacoue-Labarthe, *Typography*, 208.

43 Ibid., 214. Unlike Adorno, Lacoue-Labarthe emphasizes the importance of imitating the ancients, as opposed to imitating nature, which emerged into prominence in the Renaissance. As Tartarkiewicz points out, "The watchword of *imitating antiquity* appeared as early as the fifteenth century and by the end of the seventeenth century it supplanted almost completely the idea of *imitating nature*. This was the greatest revolution in the concept of imitation. It changed the classical theory of art into an academic one. A compromise formula was devised for the principle of imitation; nature should be imitated but in the way it was imitated by the Ancients" ("Mimesis," 229).

44 Derrida, like Adorno, generally denies the identity of mimesis and straightforward imitation. See his remarks in "The Double Session," 183. He is, however, far more eager

than Adorno to uncouple mimesis from any notion of truth, defined either as unveiling (*alētheia*) or agreement (*homoiōsis* or *adaequatio*). See "The Double Session," 192, 207.

45   Lacoue-Labarthe, *Typography*, 224.

46   As does Derrida in "The Double Session," 207.

47   Lacoue-Labarthe, *Typography*, 227.

48   Benjamin cites Hölderlin's Sophocles translations as evidence of a belated "baroque" confusion of *Trauerspiel* and Greek tragedy. See *The Origin of German Tragic Drama*, trans. John Osborne (London, 1977), 189. For a useful discussion of the more totalizing and harmonizing version of the baroque against which Benjamin and Lacoue-Labarthe warned, that of Hugo von Hofmannstahl and the Salzburg Festival, see Michael P. Steinberg, *The Meaning of the Salzburg Festival: Austria as Theater and Ideology, 1890–1938* (Ithaca, 1990), 223–41. Steinberg borrows Adorno's distinction between theater and drama from *In Search of Wagner* to set the ideological totalization of Hofmannstahl's baroque against Benjamin's critical version.

49   As Derrida puts it, in his introduction, "Desistance," in *Typography*, "A *Trauerspiel* plays at mourning, it doubles the work of mourning: the speculative, dialectic, opposition, identification, nostalgic interiorization, even the double bind of imitation. But it doesn't avoid it" (42).

50   Lacoue-Labarthe, *Typography*, 258–59.

51   For a helpful account of Adorno's thoughts on semblance, see Zuidervaart, *Adorno's Aesthetic Theory*, chap. 8.

52   Lacoue-Labarthe, *Typography*, 260.

53   Adorno, *Aesthetic Theory*, 193.

54   Ibid.

55   Theodor W. Adorno, *Minima Moralia: Reflections from Damaged Life*, trans. E. F. N. Jephcott (London, 1974), 155.

56   Adorno, *Aesthetic Theory*, 191–92. In his introduction to *Typography*, Derrida introduces the term "desistance" to signify Lacoue-Labarthe's playing with the relationship between mimesis and truth: "Mimesis 'precedes' truth in a certain sense; by destabilizing it in advance, it introduces a desire for *homoiōsis* [adequation, similitude, resemblance], and makes it possible, perhaps, to account for it, as for everything, that might be its effect, up to and including what is called the subject" (27).

57   For another way to approach the allegorical implications of this argument, see Terry Eagleton, who writes of Adorno's appropriation of Benjamin's notion of nonsensuous correspondences: "One might even name this mimesis allegory, that figurative mode which relates through difference, preserving the relative autonomy of a set of signifying units while suggesting an affinity with some other range of signifiers" (*The Ideology of the Aesthetic*, 356).

58   Philippe Lacoue-Labarthe and Jean-Luc Nancy, "The Nazi Myth," *Critical Inquiry* 16.2 (Winter 1990): 291–312.

59   Ibid., 298. For a critical gloss on this claim, see Jean-François Lyotard, *The Differend: Phrases in Dispute*, trans. Georges Van Den Abbeele (Minneapolis, 1988), 152.

60   Lacoue-Labarthe and Nancy, "The Nazi Myth," 312. It is also evident, Lacoue-Labarthe claims in "Transcendence Ends in Politics," *Typography* (297), in Heidegger's pre-*Kehre* work, whose mimetological flaws help explain his political "error." For a critique of this argument, which sees it as a subtle way to exonerate the later Heidegger, see Richard Wolin, "French Heidegger Wars," in *The Heidegger Controversy: A Critical Reader*, ed. Richard Wolin (New York, 1991), 294–304.

61   Horkheimer and Adorno, *Dialectic of Enlightenment*, 180.

62   Lacoue-Labarthe, "Transcendence Ends in Politics," *Typography*, 300.

63   Lacoue-Labarthe, *Heidegger, Art and Politics: The Fiction of the Political*, trans. Chris Turner (Oxford, 1990), 96.

64   Horkheimer and Adorno, *Dialectic of Enlightenment*, 186.

65   Lacoue-Labarthe and Nancy, "The Nazi Myth," 311.

66   Lacoue-Labarthe's critique of ocularcentrism is typical of many other recent French thinkers, as I have tried to demonstrate in *Downcast Eyes: The Denigration of Vision in Twentieth-Century French Thought* (Berkeley, 1993). See the similar discussion of sight in Derrida, "Economimesis," where the privileging of vision is related directly to the symbolic recuperation he identifies with mourning, because vision is less directly affected by the unsublatable object than other senses are (19). He claims that the disgust associated with vomit resists such a mourning process, because it produces objects that cannot be reabsorbed or symbolically represented. Derrida, to be sure, also strongly attacks hearing when it is a matter of hearing oneself speak, which implies autoaffection.

67   Lacoue-Labarthe, *Typography*, 179.

68   Ibid., 199.

69   Derrida, introduction to ibid., 33.

70   In fact, in *Dialectic of Enlightenment*, he and Horkheimer include the prohibition on images among the ways in which rulers prevented the subjugated masses from reverting to mimetic behavior (180–81). They do, to be sure, claim in that text that the sense of smell is superior in terms of the ability to assimilate to the other—"when we see we remain what we are; but when we smell we are taken over by otherness" (184)—but visuality plays a more critical role as the source of mimetic resistance to conceptuality in *Aesthetic Theory*.

71   Gertrud Koch, "Mimesis and *Bilderverbot*," *Screen* 34.3 (Autumn 1993): 211–22; Hansen, "Mass Culture as Hieroglyphic Writing."

72   Adorno, *Aesthetic Theory*, 141. For a discussion of the value of visuality in Adorno and its relation to Benjamin's notion of "dialectical images," see Susan Buck-Morss, *The Origin of Negative Dialectics: Theodor W. Adorno, Walter Benjamin, and the Frankfurt Institute* (New York, 1977), 102–10.

73   Adorno, *Aesthetic Theory*, 141–42.

74   Adorno, *Philosophy of Modern Music*, 155.

75   Früchtl, *Mimesis*, 260.

76   See, for example, Leo Bersani, *The Freudian Body: Psychoanalysis and Art* (New York, 1986), chap. 3.

77 Theodor W. Adorno, "Looking Back on Surrealism," in *The Idea of the Modern in Literature and the Arts*, ed. Irving Howe (New York, 1967), 223. For a recent account of surrealism that thematizes its debts to the uncanny and the compulsive repetitions of the death drive, see Hal Foster, *Compulsive Beauty* (Cambridge, Mass., 1993).

78 See, in particular, Theodor W. Adorno, "The Position of the Narrator in the Contemporary Novel," *Notes to Literature*, vol. 1.

79 In "Economimesis," Derrida, borrowing Bataille's distinction, argues that it is neither a "restricted economy" of circulation nor a "general economy" of waste but something other (4).

80 Homi Bhabha, "Of Mimicry and Man: The Ambivalence of Colonial Discourse," *October* 28 (1984): 125–33; for a discussion of Sherman and mimicry, see Craig Owens, "Posing," in *Beyond Recognition: Representation, Power, and Culture*, ed. Scott Bryson, Barbara Kruger, Lynn Tillman, and Jane Weinstock (Berkeley, 1992), 83–85. Both are indebted to Lacan's discussion of mimicry in *The Four Fundamental Concepts of Psycho-analysis*, ed. Jacques-Alain Miller, trans. Alan Sheridan (New York, 1978), 97–100.

12   The Academic Woman as Performance Artist

1 Jerome Christensen, "From Rhetoric to Corporate Populism: A Romantic Critique of the Academy in an Age of High Gossip," *Critical Inquiry* 16 (Winter 1990). D. A. Miller's upfront gay persona is more extensively developed in the remarkable companion piece he wrote to Roland Barthes's cruising journals, *Incidents*, trans. Richard Howard (Berkeley, 1992). Originally destined as an introduction to the Barthes, Miller's *Bringing Out Roland Barthes* (Berkeley, 1992) was published separately, but packaged as a dual production wrapped in a band showing the eyes of each author. The result is the textual equivalent of safe-sex "buddy booths" now featured in gay porno houses.

2 Avital Ronell, *Telephone Book: Technology—Schizophrenia—Electric Speech* (Lincoln, Neb., 1989); *Crack Wars: Literature Addiction Mania* (Lincoln, Neb., 1992).

3 Jane Gallop, *Thinking through the Body* (New York, 1988). In her introduction, Gallop muses about the suitability of using the picture, but coyly chooses not to identify the mother and child in it. The photo credit is given, however, to Dick Blau, so certain conclusions can be drawn.

4 Alvin W. Gouldner, *The Future of Intellectuals and the Rise of the New Class* (New York, 1979). Gouldner claimed that the CCD, as he called it, was the discursive ideology of a "new class" of intellectuals on the rise. Like other such ideologies, however, it has shown itself to be fractured by the stubborn persistence of identities that refuse to be subsumed under the rubric of class.

5 Martin Jay, "Name-Dropping or Dropping Names? Modes of Legitimation in the Humanities," in *Force Fields: Between Intellectual History and Cultural Critique* (New York, 1993).

6 Nancy K. Miller, *Getting Personal: Feminist Occasions and Other Autobiographical Acts* (New York, 1991). Significantly, the cover claims the book is "organized around a number of academic scenes in which Miller analyzes the states of feminist critical performances . . . the mini-dramas of institutional politics."

7 The general consequences of deconstruction for pedagogy are spelled out by Gregory Ulmer in *Applied Grammatology* (Baltimore, 1985). French feminist theorists also influenced by deconstruction, like Hélène Cixous, were among the pioneers of the performance artist style. For an insightful discussion of the links between French theory, gender politics, and performance artistry, see Craig Owens, "Posing," in *Beyond Recognition: Representation, Power, and Culture*, ed. Scott Bryson, Barbara Kruger, Lynne Tillman, and Jane Weinstock (Berkeley, 1992).

8 Gallop, *Thinking through the Body*, 92.

9 For a discussion of this correlation, see Andreas Huyssen, *After the Great Divide: Modernism, Mass Culture, Postmodernism* (Bloomington, Ind., 1986).

10 It is not surprising to discover that Paglia has become the darling of a new right-wing rag called *Heterodoxy*, edited by Peter Collier and David Horowitz.

13   Abjection Overruled

1 Eduardo Cadava, Peter Connor, and Jean-Luc Nancy, eds., *Who Comes after the Subject?* (New York, 1991).

2 David Carroll, *The Subject in Question: The Languages and the Strategies of Fiction* (Chicago, 1982).

3 J. M. Bernstein, *The Fate of Art: Aesthetic Alienation from Kant to Derrida and Adorno* (University Park, Pa., 1992). An interesting gloss on the crisis of the "we" is provided by Michel Foucault, who, when challenged by Richard Rorty to situate himself in a collective context, replied: "But the problem is, precisely, to decide if it is actually suitable to place oneself within a 'we' in order to assert the principles one recognizes and the values one accepts; or if it is not, rather, necessary to make the future formation of a 'we' possible, by elaborating the question. Because it seems to me that the 'we' must not be previous to the question; it can only be the result—and the necessarily temporary result—of the question as it is posed in the new terms in which one formulates it" (*The Foucault Reader*, ed. Paul Rabinow [New York, 1984], 385). The implication of this—very Sartrean—response is that "we" are not determined by our past solidarities, but always choose new ones instead, which perhaps too easily attributes a constructive power ex nihilo to those who pose and try to answer questions.

4 David Hollinger, "How Wide the Circle of the We?" *American Historical Review* 98.2 (April 1993).

5 Michael André Bernstein, *Bitter Carnival: Ressentiment and the Abject Hero* (Princeton, 1992).

6 John Fletcher, "Introduction," to John Fletcher and Andrew Benjamin, eds., *Abjection, Melancholia and Love: The Work of Julia Kristeva* (London, 1990), 4.

7 Catherine Liu, "The Party of Affirmative Abjection," *Lusitania* 1.4 (n.d.). Rather than a conventional article, this is actually a comic strip drawn by Martim and lettered by Phil Felix.

8 Jack Ben-Levi, Craig Houser, Leslie C. Jones, Simon Taylor, "Introduction," *Abject Art: Repulsion and Desire in American Art*, catalogue of Whitney Museum of American Art, June 23–August 29, 1993, p. 7.

9   Julia Kristeva, *Powers of Horror: An Essay on Abjection*, trans. Leon S. Rudiez (New York, 1982).

10 For example, Georges Bataille, "L'Abjection et les formes miserables," in *Essais de sociologie*, in *Oeuvres completes* (Paris, 1970). However, Bataille's editor, Denis Hollier, recently remarked that "all the pages he wrote under the heading of abjection were left unfinished; they were textual failures, published posthumously . . ." ("The Politics of the Signifier II: A Conversation on the *Informe* and the Abject," *October* 67 [Winter 1994]: 4).

11 Kristeva, *Powers of Horror*, 15.

12 Ibid., 206. A similar argument has been applied to T. S. Eliot by Maud Ellman: "Eliot's Abjection," in Fletcher and Benjamin, *Abjection, Melancholy and Love.*

13 Kristeva, *Powers of Horror*, 138.

14 I have tried to explore their implications in "The Apocalyptic Imagination and the Inability to Mourn," in *Force Fields: Between Intellectual History and Cultural Critique* (New York, 1993).

15 For a discussion of *délire*, see Jean-Jacques Lecercle, *Philosophy through the Looking-Glass: Language, Nonsense, Desire* (London, 1985). Kristeva herself speaks of the "avowed delirium" of Celine's anti-Semitic pamphlets. See *Powers of Horror*, 180.

16 Jacques Derrida, "Economimesis," *Diacritics* 11 (June 1981): 25.

17 In the catalogue, however, the curator of the MIT List Visual Arts Center promotes a more conventional agenda of humanist redemption, when she contends that these artists tell us "that our intimate and social bodies are in need of healing. . . . In order to heal, however, we must pay attention, and in order to pay attention we cannot be ashamed to look" (Helaine Posner, "Separation Anxiety," in *Corporal Politics* [Boston, 1992], 30).

18 Allon White, "Prosthetic Gods in Atrocious Places: Gilles Deleuze/Francis Bacon," in *Carnival, Hysteria, and Writing* (Oxford, 1993), 177.

19 Elizabeth Gross, "The Body of Signification" in Fletcher and Benjamin, *Abjection, Melancholia and Love,* 95.

20 Judith Butler, *Bodies That Matter: On the Discursive Limits of "Sex"* (New York, 1993), 3.

21 Craig Houser, "I, Abject," in *Abject Art*, 99.

22 Simon Taylor, "The Phobic Object: Abjection in Contemporary Art," in *Abject Art*, 72.

23 Interestingly, Céline wrote his doctoral dissertation on Ignaz Semmelweis, the doctor who invented obstetric hygiene as a response to the infection, puerperal fever, that attacks women during childbirth. His fascination with the abject links between sexuality, femininity, and death suggests a reversal of the isolating and separating program of Semmelweis. See the discussion in Kristeva, *Powers of Horror*, 159f.

24 Bernstein, *Bitter Carnival*, 29.

25 Kristeva, *Powers of Horror*, 17.

26 Rosalind Krauss in "The Politics of the Signifier II: A Conversation on the *Informe* and the Abject," *October* 67 (Winter 1967): 3.

27 Hollier, in ibid., 20.

28 Kristeva, *Powers of Horror*, 134.

29 Georges Bataille, *Literature and Evil*, trans. Alastair Hamilton (New York, 1973), 150.

30 For a history, see Geoffrey Galt Harpham, *On the Grotesque: Strategies of Contradiction in Art and Literature* (Princeton, 1982). The "Abject Art" catalogue goes only as far back as Duchamp.

31 White, "Prosthetic Gods in Atrocious Places," 172.

32 Bernstein, *Bitter Carnival*, 22.

33 Ibid., 182.

14 The Uncanny Nineties

1 Sigmund Freud, "The 'Uncanny,'" *Standard Edition*, vol. 17, trans. James Strachey (London, 1955), 224.

2 Hélène Cixous, "La fiction et ses fantômes: Une lecture de l'*Unheimliche* de Freud," *Poétique* 3 (1972), in English in *New Literary History* 7 (Spring 1976); Jacques Derrida, "La double séance," *La Dissémination* (Paris, 1972), in English in *Dissemination*, trans. Barbara Johnson (London, 1981).

3 Anthony Vidler, *The Architectural Uncanny: Essays in the Modern Unhomely* (Cambridge, Mass., 1992). Vidler, to be sure, was not the first to employ the concept to explore the implications of modern urban existence. In 1928, the German theologian Paul Tillich published an essay entitled "Die Technische Stadt als Symbol," which investigates the paradoxical implications of technology as both a means to overcome the uncanniness of nature and the creator of a new uncanniness produced by its growing independence from its human origins. It is reprinted in his *Auf der Grenze: Eine Auswahl aus dem Lebenswerk* (Munich, 1987).

4 Hal Foster, *Compulsive Beauty* (Cambridge, Mass., 1993); Margaret Cohen, *Profane Illumination: Walter Benjamin and the Paris of Surrealist Revolutions* (Berkeley, 1993); Rosalind E. Krauss, "Corpus Delecti," in *L'Amour fou: Photography and Surrealism*, ed. Krauss and Jane Livingstone (New York, 1985). It remains a key term in her *The Optical Unconscious* (Cambridge, Mass., 1993).

5 Jean Siegel, "Uncanny Repetition: Sherrie Levine's Multiple Originals," *Art in America* 81 (October 1993).

6 See, for example, James Donald, "The City, the Cinema, Modern Spaces," in *Visual Culture* ed. Chris Jenks (New York, 1995); and Andrew H. Miller, "Prosecuting Arguments: The Uncanny and Cynicism in Cultural History, *Cultural Critique* 29 (Winter 1994–95).

7 Jeffrey Mehlman, *Walter Benjamin for Children: An Essay on His Radio Years* (Chicago, 1993), 59–61.

8 Jeffrey Mehlman, *Revolution and Repetition: Marx/Hugo/Balzac* (Berkeley, 1977). Written before Mehlman's break with deconstruction, this reading draws explicitly on Derrida's analysis of the uncanny in *Dissemination*.

9 Jacques Derrida, *Specters of Marx: The State of the Debt, the Work of Mourning, and the New International*, trans. Peggy Kamuf, intro. Bernd Magnus and Stephen Cullenberg (New York, 1994).

10 Ibid., 37.

11 The link between the two terms is also made clear in Lacoue-Labarthe's discussion of it

in Typographies: Mimesis, Philosophy, Politics, ed. Christopher Fynsk (Cambridge, Mass., 1989), where he writes: "in its undecidability, the Unheimliche has to do not only with castration (this also can be read in Freud), the return of the repressed or infantile anxiety; it is also that which causes the most basic narcissistic assurance (the obsessional 'I am not dead' or 'I will survive') to vacillate, in that the differentiation between the imaginary and the real, the fictive and the non-fictive, comes to be effaced (and mimesis, consequently, 'surfaces')" (195).

12 Georg Lukács, Theory of the Novel, trans. Anna Bostock (Cambridge, Mass., 1971), 41.

13 Derrida, Specters of Marx, 161.

14 See Cecelia Applegate, A Nation of Provincials: The German Idea of Heimat (Berkeley, 1990); and Anton Kaes, From Hitler to Heimat: The Reform of History as Film (Cambridge. Mass. 1989).

15 Mehlman, Revolution and Repetition, 6.

16 Derrida, Specters of Marx, 81.

17 Vidler, The Architectural Uncanny, 13.

18 Foster, Compulsive Beauty, 210.

15   Modernism and the Specter of Psychologism

1 Judith Ryan, The Vanishing Subject: Early Psychology and Literary Modernism (Chicago, 1991).

2 Carl E. Schorske, Fin-de-Siècle Vienna: Politics and Culture (New York, 1980).

3 Ryan, The Vanishing Subject, 224.

4 Louis A. Sass, Madness and Modernism: Insanity in the Light of Modern Art, Literature, and Thought (Cambridge, Mass., 1994), 13.

5 The most recent and complete account of the debate over "psychologism" can be found in Martin Kusch, Psychologism: A Case Study of the Sociology of Philosophical Knowledge (New York, 1995). He notes that the term itself was coined by Johann Eduard Erdmann in his Grundrisse der Geschiche der Philosophie (Berlin, 1866). A Hegelian, Erdmann introduced the term to describe the work of Friedrich Eduard Beneke, but did not actively criticize it (Kusch, Psychologism, 101).

6 It would also be possible to make a case based on musical examples, beginning with Eduard Hanslick's defense of "absolute music," continuing through the post-Wagnerian rejection of romanticism and culminating in Schoenberg's twelve-tone row. If Ortega y Gasset is right in his well-known analysis of the modernist "dehumanization of art," the pivotal figure was Debussy. For a recent discussion of anti-psychological impulses in Stravinsky, see Richard Taruskin, "A Myth of the Twentieth Century: The Rite of Spring, the Tradition of the New, and 'The Music Itself,' " Modernism/Modernity 2.1 (January 1995).

7 Immanuel Kant, Logic, trans. Robert S. Hartman and Wolfgang Schwarz (Indianapolis, 1974), 16. The origins of what was later called psychologism can perhaps be put in the late seventeenth century, with the rise of British empiricism. It had an impact in Germany through such figures as Johann Nicolaus Tetens, whose Philosophische Versuche über die menschliche Natur und ihre Entwicklung, 2 vols (Leipzig, 1777) was a spur to the first Critique. For a discussion of Kant on psychology, see Gary Hatfield, "Empirical, Rational,

and Transcendental Psychology: Psychology as Science and as Philosophy" in *The Cambridge Companion to Kant*, ed. Paul Guyer (Cambridge, 1992). In Germany, psychologism was revived by the post-Kantians Jakob F. Fries and Friedrich E. Beneke in the early nineteenth century. See the discussion in John Fizer, *Psychologism and Psychoaesthetics: A Historical and Critical View of Their Relations* (Amsterdam, 1981), introduction.

8 For a discussion of the growth of experimental psychology and the philosophers' defensive response, see Mitchell G. Ash, *Gestalt Psychology in German Culture, 1890–1967: Holism and the Quest for Objectivity* (Cambridge, 1995), especially chap. 3.

9 Gottlob Frege, *The Foundations of Arithmetic*, 2d. rev. ed., trans. J. L. Austin (Evanston, 1980).

10 For a recent account of the psychologizing imperative in Nietzsche, see Graham Parkes, *Composing the Soul: Reaches of Nietzsche's Psychology* (Chicago, 1994).

11 Gottlob Frege, "Review of E. G. Husserl, *Philosophie der Arithmetik I*," in *Gottlob Frege: Collected Papers on Mathematics, Logic, and Philosophy*, ed. B. McGuinness (Oxford, 1984). For an assessment of the review and its implications, see Jitendranath N. Mohanty, *Husserl and Frege* (Bloomington, Ind., 1982), chap. 2. He claims that Husserl was already moving beyond psychologism by 1891 and that Frege's attribution of a strong version of it to him was mistaken. See also, Claire Ortiz Hill, *Word and Object in Husserl, Frege, and Russell: The Roots of Twentieth-Century Philosophy* (Athens, Ohio, 1991).

12 See David F. Lindenfeld, *The Transformation of Positivism: Alexius Meinong and European Thought, 1880–1920* (Berkeley, 1980), chap. 5; Thomas E. Willey, *Back to Kant: The Revival of Kantianism in German Social and Historical Thought, 1860–1914* (Detroit, 1978), 108f; Gillian Rose, *Hegel Contra Sociology* (London, 1981), chap. 1. It should be noted that Heidegger's initial critique of psychologism, *Die Lehre vom Urteil im Psychologismus: Ein kritischpositiver Beitrag zur Logik* (Leipzig, 1914), was written when he was a student of the neo-Kantian Heinrich Rickert.

13 "Energeticism" was an attempt to subsume all phenomena under the category of energy, "matter" being merely an anthropomorphic projection onto a world of flux.

14 Although Durkheim's sociology, echoing that of Auguste Comte, was more resolutely hostile to methodological individualism than Weber's, even Weber insisted that a proper sociological explanation of behavior was irreducible to psychological states of mind. Dilthey's attitude toward psychologism was intensified by his reading of Husserl's *Philosophical Investigations*, but he showed signs of skepticism as early as 1860. See the discussion in Michael Ermarth, *Wilhelm Dilthey: The Critique of Historical Reason* (Chicago, 1978), 182f.

15 Kusch, in *Psychologism*, shows how loose and amorphous the debate was, with almost every figure on both sides of the fence, including Husserl himself, being accused of some variety of psychologism. Kusch situates the debate in the context of the institutional challenge to philosophy presented by the rise of experimental psychology, exemplified by Wilhelm Wundt, Hermann Ebbinghaus, Georg Elias Müller, and Carl Stumpf, in the late 1880s.

16 It is important to note, as Dagfinn Føllesdal was perhaps the first to underline ("Hus-

serl's Notion of Noema," Journal of Philosophy 66 [1969]: 680–87), that both the analytical and phenomenological traditions shared a common root in anti-psychologism (although Frege was more important for the analytical tradition and Husserl for the continental). Here the celebrated gap between Anglo-American and continental philosophy yawned far less widely than is normally assumed. This is not to deny, of course, that some later philosophers in these traditions reopened the question of the links between psychology and philosophy, e.g., Maurice Merleau-Ponty, whose debts to Gestalt psychology are evident.

17 Cora Diamond, The Realistic Spirit: Wittgenstein, Philosophy, and the Mind (Cambridge, Mass., 1991). See also Nicholas F. Gier, Wittgenstein and Phenomenology: A Comparative Study of the Later Wittgenstein, Husserl, Heidegger and Merleau-Ponty (Albany, 1981), 2c4–6, for a discussion of Wittgenstein's complicated debt to Frege's anti-psychologism.

18 Lucien Goldmann, to take one example, was hostile to psychologism only when it meant the individual, libidinal psyche. But he supported the idea of a collective, cognitive psyche and derided neo-Kantians for their attempt to deny any human origins to the objects of knowledge. See his Immanuel Kant, trans. Robert Black (London, 1971), 153–56. In general, Marxist critics of psychologism refused the absolutizing of logic evident in Frege, the neo-Kantians, and Husserl, which they saw as the acceptance of reification. Their anti-psychologism only meant a resistance to understanding the subject of knowledge in psychological rather than transindividual, social terms.

19 Frege, "Thoughts," in McGuinness, Collected Papers, 369.

20 For a typical anti-psychologistic elaboration of this distinction, see Ralph Eaton, General Logic: An Introductory Survey (New York, 1959), 16f.

21 For comparisons of Husserl and Frege, see Mohanty, Husserl and Frege, and Robert Hanna, "Logical Cognition: Husserl's Prolegomena and the Truth in Psychologism," Philosophy and Phenomenological Research 53.2 (June 1993).

22 Frege, The Foundations of Arithmetic, vi.

23 See, for example, J. Meiland, "Psychologism in Logic: Husserl's Critique," Inquiry 19 (1976), and John Aach, "Psychologism Reconsidered: A Re-evaluation of the Arguments of Frege and Husserl," Synthese 85.2 (November 1990): 315–38. Aach claims Skinnerian behaviorism can avoid the pitfalls of the associationist psychology that Frege and Husserl mistakenly identified with psychology tout court.

24 Kusch argues that the war itself, at least in Germany, produced a general intellectual consensus that stilled the battle over psychologism, leaving phenomenology the winner. The war also provided a new role for experimental psychology as an applied discipline, which took its practitioners away from philosophical disputes. Those who remained in philosophy departments in a general atmosphere that was anti-scientific and anti-atomistic made their peace with the reigning orthodoxy. See Kusch, Psychologism, chap. 8.

25 Theodor W. Adorno, Aesthetic Theory, ed. Gretel Adorno and Rolf Tiedemann, trans. C. Lenhardt (London, 1984), 12. Adorno, to be sure, goes on to challenge Kant's contrary denial of any interest, any desire in allegedly autotelic works of art. "In contrast to the

Kantian and Freudian views on the matter," he argues, "works of art necessarily evolve in a dialectic of interests and disinterestedness" (17). Earlier, Adorno provided an equally dialectical treatme.it of Husserl's one-sided anti-psychologism. See *Against Epistemology: A Metacritique*, trans. Willis Domingo (Cambridge, Mass., 1983), chap. 1.

26   Peter Bürger's controversial distinction between modernism and the avant-garde in his *Theory of the Avant-Garde* (trans. Michael Shaw [Minneapolis, 1984]), is useful in this context. Those artists who most feared psychologistic pollution conform to his definition of modernist, whereas those who were less anxious, for example, the Surrealists, were members of the avant-garde that sought to reconcile art and life.

27   Renato Poggioli, *The Theory of the Avant-Garde*, trans. Gerald Fitzgerald (Cambridge, Mass., 1968), 201. For another discussion of the modernist fetish of purity, see Frederick R. Karl, *Modern and Modernism: The Sovereignty of the Artist, 1885–1925* (New York, 1985), 162–69. Karl claims that the demand for purification ultimately means that "authority of style was based not on the assimilation of other styles but on the expression of honest feeling which is then transformed into individuality of style" (153). Such an argument underestimates the modernist desire to purify the work of psychological and emotional residues.

28   See, for example, H. Stuart Hughes's classic study, *Consciousness and Society: The Reorientation of European Social Thought 1890–1930* (New York, 1958).

29   Andreas Huyssen, *After the Great Divide: Modernism, Mass Culture, Postmodernism* (Bloomington, Ind., 1986). Huyssen points to the links between certain misogynist theories of psychology during this period, such as Nietzsche's and Freud's, and modernist elitism, but he neglects the opposite connection, which ties anti-psychologism with misogyny. By isolating works from the contexts of their production and reception, anti-psychologism furthered the fiction that they were timeless, universal creations undisturbed by issues of gender.

30   See, for example, Sanford Schwartz, *The Matrix of Modernism: Pound, Eliot, and Early Twentieth-century Thought* (Princeton, 1985), and Michael H. Levenson, *A Genealogy of Modernism: A Study of English Literary Doctrine 1908–1922* (Cambridge, 1984). On the vexed notion of "impersonality," see in particular, Brian Lee, *Theory and Personality: The Significance of T. S. Eliot's Criticism* (London, 1979).

31   For persuasive accounts, see Levenson, *A Genealogy of Modernism*, chap. 6; Richard Shusterman, "Remembering Hulme: A Neglected Philosopher-Critic-Poet," *Journal of the History of Ideas* 46, 4 (October–December 1985): 559–76; and Shusterman, *T. S. Eliot and the Philosophy of Criticism* (London, 1988), 30f. They are directed against the earlier claims by Murray Krieger (*The New Apologists for Poetry* [Minneapolis, 1956]) and Frank Kermode (*Romantic Image* [London, 1961]) that Hulme was actually in the romantic tradition, even Coleridgean, because of his debts to Bergson.

32   For an argument about the importance of analytical philosophy for Hulme and then T. S. Eliot, see Shusterman, *T. S. Eliot and the Philosophy of Criticism*.

33   T. E. Hulme, *Speculations: Essays on Humanism and the Philosophy of Art*, ed. Herbert Read (London, 1924).

34 Among certain German neo-Kantians, most notably the Heidelberg School around Windelband and Rickert, a search for objective values (Werte) rather than mere validity (Geltung) had also been conducted. But Hulme does not seem to have been influenced directly by their work.

35 Wilhelm Worringer, Abstraction and Empathy: A Contribution to the Psychology of Style, trans. Michael Bullock (New York, 1943). As his subtitle indicates, Worringer was actually interested in providing a psychological explanation for the stylistic dispositions of different artists and periods of the kind Hulme disdained. For recent analyses of the complicated reception of Worringer's work, see Neil H Donahue, ed., Invisible Cathedrals: The Expressionist Art History of Wilhelm Worringer (University Park, Pa., 1995).

  Aesthetic empathy, it should be noted, had been most extensively defended by the German philosophy Theodor Lipps. As Levenson notes, "Lipps also appeared in Husserl's Logical Investigations, where he s criticized as a proponent of psychologism. Indeed, Worringer's argument against Lipps and on behalf of abstraction bears notable similarities to Husserl's defense of 'pure logic,' and although I know of no evidence of any contact or influence, the theories of the two figures met in Hulme's enthusiastic embrace" (A Genealogy of Modernism, 95).

36 A similar argument, with a far less positive evaluation, was famously made in 1925 by José Ortega y Gasset, The Dehumanization of Art and Other Essays on Art, Culture, and Literature, trans. Helene Weyl (Princeton, 1963).

37 Hulme, Speculations, 118. Romanticism blundered by trying to realize perfection, which belongs only to the religious sphere, in human affairs. Modern art wisely sought its perfection only in the sphere of art and eschewed the romantics' redemptive hope of transfiguring life as well.

38 For one attempt to underscore his political influence, see John R. Harrison, The Reactionaries (New York, 1967).

39 For a discussion of Woolf, which shows her links to the work of Russell and the technique of "speakerless sentences" pioneered by Flaubert, see Ann Banfield, "Describing the Unobserved: Events Grouped around an Empty Centre," in The Linguistics of Writing: Arguments between Language and Literature, ed. Nigel Fabb et al. (Manchester, 1987). Banfield provides a useful corrective to Judith Ryan's claim in The Vanishing Subject (chap. 15), that Woolf presents another example of the influence of impressionistic psychological empiricism, with a touch of psychoanalysis.

40 See Joseph Frank, "Spatial Form in Modern Literature," in The Avant-garde Tradition in Modern Literature, ed. Richard Kostelanetz (Buffalo, N.Y., 1982), 72–76.

41 T. S. Eliot, "Tradition and the Individual Talent," Selected Essays, 1917–1932 (New York, 1932), 10. It is even cited in Sass's Madness and Modernism as an example of the impersonal aesthetic of early modernism, which replaced the romantic concern with inner experience and the unique self. Sass then goes on to say, however, that in the latter's stead was soon put a fetish for innovation that "placed, if anything, even more emphasis on novelty of perspective" (135).

42 Schwartz, The Matrix of Modernism, 166–67.

43   On Eliot's debt to F. H. Bradley, see, for example, Lewis Freed, T. S. Eliot: The Critic as Philosopher (West Lafayette, Ind., 1979).

44   Schwartz, The Matrix of Modernism, 166.

45   For another analysis of the subjective moment in Eliot's criticism, see Shusterman, T. S. Eliot and the Philosophy of Criticism, chap. 3.

46   Charles Altieri, Painterly Abstraction in Modernist American Poetry: The Contemporaneity of Modernism (University Park, Pa., 1989), 38.

47   According to Hulme, poetry "is not a counter language, but a visual concrete one. . . . It always endeavors to arrest you, and to make you continuously see a physical thing, to prevent you gliding through an abstract process" (Speculations, 134).

48   Jonathan Crary, Techniques of the Observer: On Vision and Modernity in the Nineteenth Century (Cambridge, Mass., 1990).

49   Heinrich Wölfflin, Principles of Art History: The Problem of the Development of Style in Later Art, trans. M. D. Hottinger (New York, 1932), 229. As we have noted, Worringer also sought a psychology of style.

50   Norman Bryson, Vision and Painting: The Logic of the Gaze (London, 1983). Jonathan Crary explores the impact of the new models of visuality on Impressionism, most notably Manet, in "Unbinding Vision," October 68 (Spring 1994).

51   Ryan, The Vanishing Subject, 17f.

52   Maurice Merleau-Ponty, "Cézanne's Doubt," Sense and Non-Sense, trans. Hubert L. Dreyfus and Patricia A. Dreyfus (Evanston, 1964).

53   For a selection of Cézanne's remarks about returning to nature and leaving cultural conventions behind, see the section on him in Herschel B. Chipp, Theories of Modern Art: A Source Book by Artists and Critics (Berkeley, 1975).

54   Merleau-Ponty, "Cézanne's Doubt," 15.

55   Altieri, Painterly Abstraction in Modernist American Poetry, 178f.

56   Thierry de Duve, Pictorial Nominalism: On Marcel Duchamp's Passage from Painting to the Readymade, trans. Dana Polan (Minneapolis, 1991), 77–78.

57   One might see certain Surrealist paintings in this light.

58   As Antoine Compagnon writes, "initially, in the mind of the first abstract painter, abstraction was supposed to make individual psychology extinct, to explore a world of meanings and energies, and to produce images with which we would all be able to commune spiritually" (The Five Paradoxes of Modernity, trans. Franklin Philip [New York, 1994], 67).

59   Another philosophical lineage for the impersonality and universalism of modernist abstraction culminating in Mondrian has been suggested by Donald Kuspit in The Cult of the Avant-garde Artist (Cambridge, 1993), 45f. He sees Spinoza as the great predecessor of this visual flight from the messiness of human emotions.

60   Clement Greenberg, "Modernist Painting," in The New Art: A Critical Anthology, ed. G. Battcock (New York, 1973), 67.

61   See, for example, John McGowan, Postmodernism and Its Critics (Ithaca, 1991), 9.

62   Robert Storr, "No Joy in Mudville: Greenberg's Modernism Then and Now," in Modern

Art and Popular Culture: Readings in High and Low, ed. Kirk Varnadoe and Adam Gopnik (New York, 1990), 169f. Noting Greenberg's Jewish anxiety about assimilation, he compares it with Eliot's Anglo-Catholicism and concludes that "Greenberg's similar insistence on the aesthetic 'extinction of personality,' and his determination to purge from art all traces of mundane existence, for which kitsch became the shorthand term, reflect not so much a political or even art-historical perspective, as they do a fundamentally religious one. Located against the backdrop of Jewish emigration from the shtetl and the ghetto, the opposition of purity and impurity stands as a metaphor for the perilous choices imposed by cultural assimilation in the New World" (175). Situated in the context of the anti-psychologistic tradition as a whole, however, Greenberg's values seem less quirkily reflective of his own personal predicament.

For a comparison between Greenberg and Adorno, see Compagnon, *The Five Paradoxes of Modernity*, 47. Adorno's position was less internalist than Compagnon suggests, although he was a critic of vulgar Marxist reductionism.

63 See Shusterman, *T. S. Eliot and the Philosophy of Criticism* for comparisons with Gadamer and Rorty.

64 De Duve, *Pictorial Nominalism*. See also his recent essay, "Echoes of the Readymade: Critique of Pure Modernism," *October* 70 (Fall 1994): 61–98.

65 Nor was Duchamp attracted to Cézanne's project of revealing a primordial ontology of visuality, prior to the split between subject and object. See Jean-François Lyotard, *Les transformateurs Duchamp* (Paris, 1977), 68.

66 Werner Hofmann, "Marcel Duchamp and Emblematic Realism," in *Marcel Duchamp in Perspective*, ed. Joseph Masheck (Englewood Cliffs, N.J., 1975), 61.

67 An account of Duchamp's lecture in Houston at the conference "The Creative Act," and the discussion that followed is contained in *Marcel Duchamp: Work and Life*, ed. Pontus Hulten (Cambridge, Mass., 1993), under the listing for April 5, 1957; he liberally cites Eliot. The remark was made to Lawrence D. Steefel, Jr., and is cited in his "Dimension and Development in the *The Passage from the Virgin to the Bride*," in Masheck, *Marcel Duchamp in Perspective*, 97.

68 For an analysis of Duchamp's function as the paradoxical (male) master of a tradition that eschews father figures, see Amelia Jones, *Postmodernism and the Engendering of Marcel Duchamp* (Cambridge, 1994).

69 See, for example, Rosalind E. Krauss, *The Optical Unconscious* (Cambridge, Mass., 1993), chap. 3, in which Duchamp is presented as introducing carnal desire rather than cerebral reflexivity into his art. She explicitly contrasts him with the ascetic, contemplative aesthetics of Bloomsbury theorists such as Roger Fry, which she claims was derived from G. E. Moore's anti-psychologistic ethics. A very different account, which nonetheless also stresses the psychological sources of his work, can be found in Jerrold Seigel, *The Private Worlds of Marcel Duchamp* (Berkeley, 1995). According to Seigel, "behind Duchamp's claim to have devoted his career to destabilizing his personality, countering the pull of taste and habit with an aesthetic of indifference and avoiding the trap of fixed identity by his various strategies of self-contradiction, there lurked an uncompromising

exaltation of the self" (206). This self, however, was less a sovereign maker than a chooser, who worked with the "givens" provided by chance or the debris of the culture around him.

70   The German philosopher Odo Marquard has argued that a "second psychologism" can be discerned as early as the dissemination of psychoanalysis almost a century ago. See his *Transcendentaler Idealismus, Romantische Naturphilosophie, Psychoanalyse* (Cologne, 1987).

71   Pierre Bourdieu, *Distinction: A Social Critique of the Judgment of Taste*, trans., Richard Nice (Cambridge, Mass., 1984); John Guillory, *Cultural Capital: The Problem of Literary Canon Formation* (Chicago, 1993).

72   See, for example, the essays in *The Institution of Philosophy: A Discipline in Crisis?* ed. Avner Cohen and Marcelo Dascal (Lasalle, Ill., 1989).

73   See for example Wilhelm Wundt, "Psychologismus und Logizismus," in his *Kleine Schriften*, vol. 1 (Leipzig, 1910), 511–634.

74   Richard Rorty, *Philosophy and the Mirror of Nature* (Princeton, 1979), 168.

75   Shusterman, *T. S. Eliot and the Philosophy of Criticism*, chap. 8. In an earlier essay, "Remembering Hulme: A Neglected Philosopher-Critic-Poet," Shusterman tries to do the same for the figure who has been taken as the quintessential anti-psychologist. His evidence, however, is basically limited to one aphorism in the unfinished collection entitled *Cinders*, which Herbert Read included in *Speculations*, which begins "The truth is that there are no ultimate principles, upon which the whole of knowledge can be built once and for ever as upon a rock . . ." (233–34). On this basis, Shusterman claims Hulme was close to Rorty in his anti-foundationalist stress on the priority of *Weltanschauungen* to absolute truth. Putting aside the performative contradiction entailed in a sentence against absolute truth that begins "the truth is . . . ," Hulme, it seems to me, was attacking the humanist pretension to combine cognitive, ethical, and religious knowledge in one grand system, not the possibility of foundations in separate spheres. His appeal for strict discontinuity between those spheres and belief in the authority of revealed religion in value questions makes him a far cry from Rorty's philosophy of relativist edification.

76   Jacques Derrida, *Speech and Phenomena and Other Essays on Husserl's Theory of Signs*, trans. David B. Allison (Evanston, 1973), 12f.

77   On Paul de Man's reaction to New Criticism in these terms, see Lindsay Waters, intro. to *Paul de Man, Critical Writings, 1953–1978*, ed. Lindsay Waters (Minneapolis, 1989), xl–lii.

78   See, for example, Roman Ingarden's essay "Psychologism and Psychology," *New Literary History* (Winter 1974): 215–23, for an attempt to distinguish between reductionist psychologism and the subtle use of psychological insights, which respect the relative integrity of the work.

79   Mohanty, *Husserl and Frege*, 115.

80   It is for this reason that many commentators see Surrealism in certain of its guises as an anticipation of many postmodernist positions. See, for example, Hal Foster, *Compulsive Beauty* (Cambridge, Mass., 1993).

81   For example, Mohanty, *Husserl and Frege*.

82   See, for example, Alasdair MacIntyre, *After Virtue: A Study in Moral Theory* (Notre Dame, Ind., 1981).

83   For Derrida on Marx, see Derrida, *Specters of Marx: The State of the Debt, the Work of Mourning, and the New International*, trans. Peggy Kamuf (New York, 1994).

16   Modern and Postmodern Paganism

1   For one consideration of this dynamic, which focuses on nineteenth-century France, see Eugen Weber, "Religion or Superstition?" *My France: Politics, Culture, Myth* (Cambridge, Mass., 1991).

2   For a recent account, see Prudence Jones and Nigel Pennick, *A History of Pagan Europe* (London, 1995), 1. For an account that traces the origin of the concept, if not the word, to Moses and his Egyptian predecessor Akhenaton, see Jan Assmann, "The Mosaic Distinction: Israel, Egypt, and the Invention of Paganism," *Representations* 56 (Fall 1996). He argues that Moses and Akhenaton were the first to distinguish between true and false, or genuine and counterreligions.

3   The claim that early modern witchcraft was a survival of pre-Christian pagan customs was made most insistently by the Egyptologist Margaret Murray in such works as *The Witch Cult in Western Europe* (Oxford, 1921). It has been successfully challenged by Norman Cohn, *Europe's Inner Demons* (London, 1975).

4   Jones and Pennick, *A History of Pagan Europe*, 197f.

5   It might be noted that one of those "others" was secular rationalism, which has often been contrasted with pagan myth. For a powerful attempt to undermine this distinction, see Hans Blumenberg, *Work on Myth*, trans. Robert M. Wallace (Cambridge, Mass., 1985).

6   For a discussion, see Jean Seznec, *The Survival of the Pagan Gods: The Mythological Tradition and Its Place in Renaissance Humanism and the Arts* (Princeton, 1995); see also his excellent article, "Myth in the Middle Ages and the Renaissance," in the *Dictionary of the History of Ideas* (New York, 1973), vol. 3.

7   The persistence of the iconoclastic fear is demonstrated in such recent works as Jacques Ellul, *The Humiliation of the Word*, trans. Joyce Main Hanks (Grand Rapids, Mich., 1985).

8   For a wide variety of such texts, including Bayle's "Jupiter" in *The Dictionary Historical and Critical* and Toland's "Origin of Idolatry" from his *Letters to Serena*, see Burton Feldman and Robert B. Richardson, eds., *The Rise of Modern Mythology, 1680–1860* (Bloomington, Ind., 1972), part 1.

9   Robert Weiss, *The Renaissance Discovery of Classical Antiquity* (Oxford, 1969).

10   Peter Gay, *The Enlightenment: An Interpretation*, vol. 1, *The Rise of Modern Paganism* (New York, 1966), chap. 5.

11   There were, to be sure, nineteenth-century attempts to reconcile classical and Christian values, especially in Britain. But as Richard Jenkyns notes, "some of the greatest Victorians experienced, not always consciously, a conflict between their passion for ancient Greece and their Christianity" *The Victorians and Ancient Greece* (Cambridge, Mass., 1980), 68.

12   Arnold, to be sure, often tried to integrate and balance the "Hellenic" and the "Hebraic." For an account of his efforts, see Joseph Carroll *The Cultural Theory of Matthew Arnold* (Berkeley, 1982), 69f.

13 Keith Thomas, *Man and the Natural World: A History of the Modern Sensibility* (New York, 1983). Thomas notes that "since the Anglo-Saxon times the Christian church in England had stood out against the worship of wells and rivers. The pagan divinities of grove, stream and mountain had been expelled, leaving behind them a disenchanted world, to be shaped, moulded and dominated" (22). He points to many reasons why this attitude was modified, if not reversed, but one was the rediscovery of the classical arcadian pastoral tradition. For the slightly later development of the same sensibility in France, see D. G. Charlton, *New Images of the Natural in France* (Cambridge, 1984), chap. 2.

14 E. M. Butler, *The Tyranny of Greece over Germany* (Boston, 1958); Henry Hatfield, *Aesthetic Paganism in German Literature* (Cambridge, Mass., 1964) and *Clashing Myths in German Literature: From Heine to Rilke* (Cambridge, Mass., 1974); Josef Chytry, *The Aesthetic State: A Quest in Modern German Thought* (Berkeley, 1989); and Suzanne L. Marchand, *Down from Olympus: Archaeology and Philhellenism in Germany, 1750–1970* (Princeton, 1996).

15 On Vico and classical rhetoric, see John D. Schaeffer, *Sensus Communis: Vico, Rhetoric, and the Limits of Relativism* (Durham, N.C., 1990).

16 Robert Darnton, "History of Reading," in *New Perspectives on Historical Writing*, ed. Peter Burke (University Park, Pa.: 1991), 144.

17 Prys Morgan, "From a Death to a View: The Hunt for the Welsh Past in the Romantic Period," in *The Invention of Tradition*, ed. Eric Hobsbawm and Terence Ranger (Cambridge, 1983).

18 For an account of the still potent adoption of Gallic ancestry as a symbol of French identity, see Eugen Weber, "Nos ancêtres les gaulois," *My France*. It should be noted that aristocratic dynasties themselves often evoked an alleged ancestor in the pagan world to establish their pedigree. Here they could draw on the euhemerist reading of the ancient gods, which interpreted them as actual historical figures, who had been transformed over time into deities.

19 Hugh Honour, *Romanticism* (New York, 1979), 206f.

20 Jenkyns, *The Victorians and Ancient Greece*, 8.

21 Freud esteemed Schliemann passionately, collected antiquities, and often compared psychoanalysis to the discovery of Troy. He was, however, ambivalent about the classical legacy, which meant at times he upheld a traditional model of sublimated culture as an alternative to fruitless rebellion. For a reading that argues his "choice was for Winckelmann and the classical balance of ancient Greece rather than the continued political antagonism and strife symbolized by Rome and medieval Europe," see William J. McGrath, *Freud's Discovery of Psychoanalysis: The Politics of Hysteria* (Ithaca, 1986), 228.

22 For one account of the power and variety of this matriarchal ideology in pre–World War I Vienna, see Jacques Le Rider, *Modernity and the Crises of Identity*, trans. Rosemary Morris (New York, 1993), chaps. 6, 7, and 8.

23 For Semper's role in the debate over polychromy on Greek buildings, see Harry Francis Mallgrave, *Gottfried Semper: Architect of the Nineteenth Century* (New Haven, 1996).

24 For an account, see Steven E. Aschheim, *The Nietzsche Legacy in Germany, 1890–1990* (Berkeley, 1992), 223–29.

25   Aschheim, *The Nietzsche Legacy* in *Germany*, shows that the so-called *Glaubensbewegung*, which tried to revive a new Nordic religion, was easily assimilated into Nazism (226). But according to John Yeowell, *Odinism and Christianity under the Third Reich* (London, 1993), worshippers of Odin were persecuted by the Nazis. Amos Funkenstein, moreover, notes the discontinuities between pagan anti-Judaism in the classical world and its more virulent Christian successors and claims that because of its general tolerance of different religions, "whatever 'paganism' may mean, in its historical manifestations it was certainly not less humane than Christianity—or Judaism" *Perceptions of Jewish History* (Berkeley, 1993), 328. For a general assessment of the relations between paganism and *völkisch* thought, see Stefanie V. Schnurbein, *Religion als Kulturkritik: Neugermanisches Heidentum im 20. Jahrhundert* (Heidelberg, 1992).

26   Martin Bernal, *Black Athena: The Afro-Asian Roots of Classical Civilization* (London, 1987).

27   For an account of Jaeger's compromised role in the 1930s before his emigration, see Marchand, *Down from Olympus*, chap. 9.

28   Paul Delany, *The Neo-Pagans: Friendship and Love in the Rupert Brooke Circle* (London, 1987).

29   Jenkyns, *The Victorians and Ancient Greece*, chap. 13.

30   Camille Paglia, *Sexual Personae: Art and Decadence from Nefertiti to Emily Dickinson* (New York, 1991), 25.

31   John Casey, *Pagan Virtue: An Essay in Ethics* (Oxford, 1990).

32   Bernard Williams, *Moral Luck* (Cambridge, 1981) is cited positively by Casey, *Pagan Virtue*, 201.

33   Odo Marquard, "In Praise of Polytheism (On Monomythic and Polymythic Thinking)," *Farewell to Matters of Principle: Philosophical Studies*, trans. Robert M. Wallace (New York, 1989), 104. See Habermas's response in his "The Unity of Reason in the Diversity of Its Voices," in *Postmetaphysical Thinking: Philosophical Essays*, trans. William Mark Hohengarten (Cambridge, 1992), 147–48.

34   Jacques Merlaud, *Le renouveau païen dans la pensée français* (Paris, 1986).

35   Carl L. Becker, *The Heavenly City of the Eighteenth-Century Philosophers* (New Haven, 1932). See Gay's polemic in *The Party of Humanity: Essays in the French Enlightenment* (New York, 1964).

36   Gay, *The Party of Humanity*, 46. Not all of the members of "the party of humanity" were, of course, equally indebted to the classical legacy. In his review of Gay's book in the *American Historical Review* 73.3 (February 1968), Franklin L. Ford claimed that neither Lessing nor Rousseau really qualify.

37   Gay, *The Enlightenment*, 9, 8, 126.

38   Cited in ibid., 70.

39   It is not difficult to discern the continuities between Gay's reading of the Enlightenment and his later defense of Freud as a scientific researcher, more indebted to cosmopolitan traditions of enlightened inquiry and cultivated *Bildung* than to the peculiarities of his Viennese Jewish milieu. Psychoanalysis, Gay wrote in *Freud, Jews and Other Germans: Masters and Victims in Modernist Culture* (Oxford, 1978), "demonstrated that it was more than possible, it was necessary, to be rational about irrationality" (71). Already in his imag-

ined dialogue between Lucian, Erasmus, and Voltaire, *The Bridge of Criticism* (New York, 1970), Gay had Voltaire call Freud "our most distinguished representative in the twentieth century" (91).

40   Peter Gay, *The Enlightenment: An Interpretation*, vol. 2, *The Science of Freedom* (New York, 1969), 125. Lyotard often pits local narratives against the denotative language game of universalizing science, but he is not above drawing on the lessons of computerization for postmodernism, when it suits his purposes. Gay, for his part, acknowledges the importance of historical narrative during the Enlightenment, which, for all its faults, was more than merely Bolingbroke's "philosophy teaching by example."

41   Ernst Cassirer, *The Philosophy of the Enlightenment*, trans. Fritz C. A. Koelln and James P. Pettegrove (Boston, 1951).

42   Gay, *The Enlightenment*, 1:419. In *Weimar Culture: The Outsider as Insider* (New York, 1968), Gay would echo this sentiment in noting that "what Gropius taught, and what most Germans did not want to learn, was the lesson of Bacon and Descartes and the Enlightenment: that one must confront the world and dominate it, that the cure for the ills of modernity is more, and the right kind of modernity" (101).

43   Ibid., 225.

44   Peter Hanns Reill, *The German Enlightenment and the Rise of Historicism* (Berkeley, 1975), 174f. See also, David Sorkin, *Moses Mendelssohn and the Religious Enlightenment* (Berkeley, 1996). Sorkin's current work extends to other examples of religious enlighteners, such as the Anglican William Warburton, the Lutheran Siegmund Jacob Baumgarten, and the Catholic Anselm Desing.

45   Hans Kohn, "The Multidimensional Enlightenment," *Journal of the History of Ideas* 31.3 (July–September 1970): 469.

46   Amos Funkenstein, *Theology and the Scientific Imagination: From the Middle Ages to the Seventeenth Century* (Princeton, 1986), 357.

47   A more recent student of the subject, Margaret C. Jacob has a less critical reading of the implications of the Masons for Gay's thesis. In *Living the Enlightenment: Freemasonry and Politics in Eighteenth-Century Europe* (New York, 1991), she notes the frequent Masonic evocation of a pagan pedigree for their rituals and beliefs, and concludes that "perhaps we can better understand why some historians have seen in the Enlightenment the rise of modern paganism" (153). It should be noted, however, that the paganism in question was more Egyptian than Greek, a pedigree that was ignored by Gay. See the discussion in Assmann, "The Mosaic Distinction."

48   Paglia, *Sexual Personae*, 681.

49   See Peter Gay, *Style in History* (New York, 1974).

50   Lyotard, however, has grown more skeptical over the years about the emancipatory potential in primary process. Such later essays as "Figure Foreclosed" of 1984 (*The Lyotard Reader*, ed. Andrew Benjamin [Oxford, 1989]) signify a more austere reading of the legacy of psychoanalysis.

51   Gay has a short discussion of Burke's *Philosophical Enquiry into the Origin of Our Ideas of the Sublime and the Beautiful* in the second volume of *The Enlightenment: An Interpretation*, but

calls it a "young man's book, energetic, facile, a little irresponsible, and sometimes embarrassing" (305).

52 Lyotard, *Dérive à partir de Marx et Freud* (Paris, 1973). For his account of the change, see "A Memorial of Marxism: For Pierre Souyri," in Lyotard, *Peregrinations: Law, Form, Event* (New York, 1988). He was a member of the group, led by Cornelius Castoriadis and Claude Lefort, from 1954 to 1966 (the last two years as a member of the faction around the journal *Pouvoir Ouvrier*).

53 For his writings during this period, see Lyotard, *Political Writings*, trans. Bill Readings and Kevin Paul Geiman (Minneapolis, 1993).

54 Lyotard, *Rudiments païens: genre dissertatif* (Paris, 1977); several essays of which are translated in Lyotard, *Toward the Postmodern*, ed. Robert Harvey and Mark S. Roberts (Atlantic Highlands, N.J., 1993); *Instructions païennes* (Paris, 1977), translated in Benjamin, ed., *The Lyotard Reader. Au Juste*, with Jean-Loup Thébaud (Paris, 1979), in English as *Just Gaming*, trans. Wlad Godzich (Minneapolis, 1985). For discussions of his paganism, see Bill Readings, *Introducing Lyotard: Art and Politics* (London, 1991), and "Pseudoethica Epidemica: How Pagans Talk to the Gods," *Philosophy Today* 36 (Winter 1992); and Steven Best and Douglas Kellner, *Postmodern Theory* (New York, 1991), 160f.

55 Lyotard, *Just Gaming*, 31.

56 Lyotard, "Lessons in Paganism," 123.

57 Lyotard, "The Grip (Mainmise)," *Political Writings*, 156. This text, from 1990, shows the continuing importance of the pagan ideal in Lyotard's later work, even if it is not as frequently emphasized.

58 Lyotard, *The Postmodern Condition: A Report on Knowledge*, trans. Geoff Bennington and Brian Massumi (Minneapolis, 1984). The original appeared in 1979. It can, however, be argued that polytheism was a form of what Jan Assmann has called "cosmotheism," which means that different religious figures were assumed to be variants of a single God, e.g., the sun. See his "The Mosaic Distinction," 40. If so, paganism did not valorize incommensurability as much as Lyotard claims, but rather intercultural translatability.

59 Lyotard, *Just Gaming*, 16.

60 Lyotard, *The Inhuman: Reflections on Time*, trans. Geoffrey Bennington and Rachel Bowlby (Stanford, 1991). On the general climate of anti-humanism that nurtured his thought, see Richard Wolin, "Antihumanism in the Discourse of Postwar French Theory," in *Labyrinths: Explorations in the Critical History of Ideas* (Amherst, Mass., 1995).

61 Gay, *The Enlightenment: An Interpretation*, 1:178. Lyotard, *Instructions païennes*, 84. The English translation in *The Lyotard Reader* mistranslates "réalisme" as "reason," which makes Lyotard say that "reason is pagan" (152).

62 Lyotard, "Lessons in Paganism," 133. There is now a substantial literature on the political implications of this reading of Kant. See, most recently, Kimberly Hutchings, *Kant, Critique and Politics* (New York, 1996).

63 This accusation is leveled against paganism, for example, by such defenders of Judeo-Christian transcendence as Thomas Molnar in *The Pagan Temptation* (Grand Rapids, Mich., 1987) and "Paganism and Its Renewal," *The Intercollegiate Review* 31.1 (Fall 1995).

64 Lyotard, *Just Gaming*, 42.

65 Lyotard, "Futility in Revolution" in *Toward the Postmodern*, 99.

66 Ibid., 113.

67 Lyotard, *The Differend: Phrases in Dispute*, trans. Georges Van Den Abbeele (Minneapolis, 1988), 151. Readings speculates that the term paganism is "largely dropped by the time of *The Differend*, perhaps because it tends to romanticize the problem of political judgment (it's hard to stop paganism from becoming another religion)" (*Introducing Lyotard*, xxxiii).

68 Lyotard, *Just Gaming*, 38. He also discussed the Cashinahua Indians of Brazil as comparable critics of absolute autonomy.

69 Ibid., 39.

70 Lyotard, however, argued that "in primitive Judaism, the theme of 'nature created' is quite absent; God is not the author of a visible world. It is only later that the Book of Genesis is adopted, and it is full of borrowings from the cult of Baal" ("Figure Foreclosed," *The Lyotard Reader*, 94). It may also be noted that Jewish thought developed a respect for a plurality of textual meanings, if not of gods. As Susan A. Handelman notes, "Rabbinic thought developed the doctrine of polysemy as opposed to polytheism: the multiple meanings that may be heard or read within the Word, rather than the many gods which may be seen" (*The Slayers of Moses: The Emergence of Rabbinic Interpretation in Modern Literary Theory* [Albany, 1982], 34).

71 See Lyotard's essay "Levinas's Logic," in *The Lyotard Reader*. For a discussion of his debt to Levinas on the issue of the primacy of vision, which has links to our general theme through the idolatry that is often associated with paganism, see my *Downcast Eyes: The Denigration of Vision in Twentieth-Century French Thought* (Berkeley, 1993), chap. 10.

72 In his essay "Figure Foreclosed" of 1984, reprinted in *The Lyotard Reader*, he stressed the importance of Judaism for psychoanalysis, especially its refusal of sublation, mediation, and reconciliation. Calling the moment of equilibrium between Apollonian and Dionysian impulses praised by Nietzsche only a fleeting instant in Greek culture, he claimed that "in the nocturnal, figurative and plastic current, we can recognize the old religiosity of reconciliation, which will transmit to Christianity its remnants of mediation and which will give Catholicism its pagan allure" (75). A more attractive paganism, Lyotard suggests, will be pluralist, nontotalized, and agonistic.

73 Lyotard, *Heidegger and "the jews,"* trans. Andreas Michel and Mark Roberts (Minneapolis, 1990), 22–23.

74 In *The Enlightenment*, Gay is at pains to say that a dualist view of history, involving an alteration between Hellenic and Hebraic moments, "rather than the celebrated theory of progress, characterizes the Enlightenment" (1:33).

75 Lyotard, *Just Gaming*, 16.

76 See, for example, ibid., 11 and "Tomb of the Intellectual," in Lyotard, *Political Writings*.

77 See, for example, Richard Rorty, "Habermas and Lyotard on Postmodernity," in *Habermas and Modernity*, ed. Richard J. Bernstein (Cambridge, Mass., 1985); and Peter Dews, introduction to Habermas, *Autonomy and Solidarity: Interviews*, ed. Peter Dews (London, 1986).

It might be noted in passing that there is no rhetoric of secularized paganism in Habermas's defense of the Enlightenment. In *The Philosophical Discourse of Modernity: Twelve Lectures*, trans. Frederick Lawrence (Cambridge, Mass., 1987), he writes, "In the mysticism of the New Paganism, the unbounded charisma of what is outside the everyday does not issue in something liberating, as it does with the aesthetic; nor in something renewing, as with the religious—it has at most the stimulus of charlatanry" (184). This statement is made in the context of a discussion of Derrida, whose escape from pagan mysticism Habermas credits to his roots in Jewish monotheism.

78   More radical students of deconstruction, such as Samuel Weber, in fact chide Lyotard for resisting the complete dedifferentiation of language games. See his afterword to *Just Gaming*, 103. The result of such a dedifferentiation would be what I have called elsewhere a "night in which all cows are piebald," a formulation which Bill Readings justly resists with reference to Lyotard. See his remarks in "Pseudoethica Epidemica," 381.

79   Lyotard, *Le Postmoderne expliqué aux enfants: correspondance, 1982–1985* (Paris, 1986).

80   A number of commentators remark on Lyotard's covert reliance on totalizing claims, e.g., William Righter, *The Myth of Theory* (Cambridge, 1994), chap. 9; Kerwin Lee Klein, "In Search of Narrative Mastery: Postmodernism and the People without History," *History and Theory*, 34 (1995). Indeed, the conversation in *Just Gaming* ends in (embarrassed?) laughter as Lyotard's interlocutor notes "Here you are talking like the great prescriber himself . . ." (100).

81   Robert Harvey and Mark S. Roberts, introduction to Lyotard, *Toward the Postmodern*, xiv.

17   The Manacles of Gavrilo Princip

1   Alain Finkielkraut, *The Imaginary Jew*, trans. Kevin O'Neill and David Suchoff (Lincoln, Neb., 1994), 12.

2   Henryk M. Broder, "Das Shoah-Business," *Der Spiegel*, no. 16 (1993): 249.

3   Amos Funkenstein, "The Incomprehensible Catastrophe: Memory and Narrative," in *The Narrative Study of Lives*, ed. Ruthellen Josselson and Amia Lieblich (Newbury Park, Calif., 1993). Funkenstein argues that the pictures of the Theresienstadt artists imply their ability to sustain a certain narrative control over their lives, which was denied to other Holocaust victims.

Mehlman, Jeffrey, 159, 162, 234, 235
Meiffert, Torsten, 48, 211
Meiland, J., 237
Mendes-Flohr, Paul, 216
Menninghaus, Winfried, 51, 212
Merlaud, Jacques, 245
Merleau-Ponty, Maurice, 4, 93, 174, 206, 237, 240
Michaels, Walter Benn, 17, 19, 218
middle voice, 7, 56–61, 214
    Barthes on, 57–58
    Benveniste on, 56–57
    Derrida on, 57
    representing the Holocaust, 58–59
    See also indirect speech
Miller, Andrew H., 234
Miller, D. A., 139, 231
Miller, J. Hillis, 16, 207, 209
Miller, James, 67–69, 74, 75, 78, 218
Miller, John, 152
Miller, Nancy K., 140
mimesis, 120–37, 225, 226, 228–29
    Adorno on, 10, 121–37, 226, 227
    and allegory, 229
    Aristotelian, 128, 129
    Barthes on, 120, 137
    Benjamin on, 121, 133
    Critical Theory on, 121
    Deleuze and Guattari on, 120, 137
    de Man on, 120
    Derrida on, 120–21, 123, 136, 228–29, 230
    economimesis, 136
    Greek notion of, 123
    Habermas on, 226
    Lacoue-Labarthe on, 10–11, 128–37, 229
    Lyotard on, 120, 137
    Nancy on, 131, 132
    Plato on, 129

and sociability, 227
    See also aesthetic
Mitchell, W. J. T., 208
modernism, 13, 53, 169–80, 238, 239, 240
    Adorno and, 126, 169, 176
    Barthes on, 53, 58
    deconstruction and, 178–80
    as distinct from postmodernism, 180
    Kant and, 175
    literature, 170–73
    and the novel, 53
    and psychologism, 166, 169–77
    and Surrealism, 164
    visual arts, 173–77
    See also Eliot; Greenberg; Hulme; Kandinsky; middle voice; Wölfflin
Mohanty, Jitendranath N., 236, 237, 242
Molnar, Thomas, 247
Mondrian, Piet, 240
Moore, G. E., 171, 241
Morgan, Prys, 244
Mouffe, Chantal, 63, 74, 223
multiculturalism, 6, 31
Münch, Richard, 207
Murray, Margaret, 243
Mussolini, Benito, 96

Nadeau, Maurice, 225
Nägele, Rainer, 213
Nancy, Jean-Luc, 75–77, 114, 131, 132, 221, 225, 229, 230
    on Bataille, 75–77
    on experience, 76, 77
    on mimesis, 131, 132
narrative, 25
Neaman, Elliot, 9, 206
Nehamas, Alexander, 67, 218
Nelson, David, 224